Good Mentoring

JB JOSSEY-BASS

Good Mentoring

Fostering Excellent Practice in Higher Education

Jeanne Nakamura
David J. Shernoff
with Charles H. Hooker

Foreword by
Mihaly Csikszentmihalyi

WILEY

John Wiley & Sons, Inc.

Published by Jossey-Bass
A Wiley Imprint
989 Market Street, San Francisco, CA 94103-1741—www.josseybass.com

Readers should be aware that Internet Web sites offered as citations and/or sources for further information may have changed or disappeared between the time this was written and when it is read.

Limit of Liability/Disclaimer of Warranty: While the publisher and author have used their best efforts in preparing this book, they make no representations or warranties with respect to the accuracy or completeness of the contents of this book and specifically disclaim any implied warranties of merchantability or fitness for a particular purpose. No warranty may be created or extended by sales representatives or written sales materials. The advice and strategies contained herein may not be suitable for your situation. You should consult with a professional where appropriate. Neither the publisher nor author shall be liable for any loss of profit or any other commercial damages, including but not limited to special, incidental, consequential, or other damages.

Jossey-Bass books and products are available through most bookstores. To contact Jossey-Bass directly call our Customer Care Department within the U.S. at 800-956-7739, outside the U.S. at 317-572-3986, or fax 317-572-4002.

Jossey-Bass also publishes its books in a variety of electronic formats. Some content that appears in print may not be available in electronic books.

Library of Congress Cataloging-in-Publication Data

Nakamura, Jeanne.
    Good mentoring: fostering excellent practice in higher education / Jeanne Nakamura, David J. Shernoff, with Charles H. Hooker.
       p. cm.
    Includes bibliographical references and index.
    ISBN 978-0-470-18963-4 (cloth)
      1 Mentoring in science. 2. Science—Study and teaching (Higher) I. Shernoff, David J., 1967-II. Hooker, Charles H. III. Title.
    Q181.N148   2009
    507.1'1—dc22

                                                       2009001144

Printed in the United States of America
FIRST EDITION
HB Printing   10 9 8 7 6 5 4 3 2 1

The Jossey-Bass Higher and Adult
Education Series

CONTENTS

The Authors

Jeanne Nakamura is assistant professor, codirector of the positive psychology concentration, and codirector of the Quality of Life Research Center in the School of Behavioral and Organizational Sciences at Claremont Graduate University. She received her B.A. and Ph.D. from the University of Chicago. She helped direct the GoodWork Project, a series of studies of excellence and social responsibility in professional life that included the Transmission of Excellence Study on which this book is based. She has investigated positive psychology in a developmental context, including engagement and creativity, mentoring and good work, and aging well.

David J. Shernoff is an associate professor in the Department of Leadership, Educational Psychology, and Foundations at Northern Illinois University. He completed his B.S. in human development at Cornell University, Ed.M. at the Harvard Graduate School of Education, and Ph.D. in education at the University of Chicago. From 2000 to 2003, he served as a post-doctoral fellow at the University of Wisconsin-Madison. He teaches courses on adolescent development, motivation, and theories of educational psychology, and his research interests include mentoring, early career development, positive youth development, and contexts fostering student engagement. His earlier book, *The Individual-Maker: A Master Teacher and His Transformational Curriculum*, was a life portrait of an exemplary high school teacher who was a personal mentor.

Charles H. Hooker is a doctoral student in religion at Emory University and an intellectual property attorney at Kilpatrick Stockton LLP in Atlanta, Georgia. He completed his B.A. in psychology at Rhodes College, his M.A. in religion at the University of Chicago, and his J.D. at Emory University School of Law, where he was the editor in chief of the *Emory International Law Review* and codirector of Legal Services. From 2000 to 2001, he worked at the Quality of Life Research Center in the School of Behavioral and Organizational Sciences at Claremont Graduate University.

Foreword

Our lives depend on having access to the knowledge our ances-
tors have accumulated and passed down from one generation to
the next. Yet like the fish is oblivious of water while swimming
in it, we also tend to ignore the fact that most of the things we
care about, from the ability to speak to the ability to cook meals
and to fly planes, are supported by an intricate network of practices for preserving what humanity has learned through the ages.

Talcott Parsons, the most influential sociologist of the previous century, summarized what a society needed in a simple model.
He argued that any group of people had to solve four fundamental problems if they were to continue to exist: the first being how
to produce material necessities, the second how to get along
together, the third how to divide resources and regulate behavior, and the fourth—which is the topic of this book—how to
keep what has been learned from being forgotten. Parsons called
this fourth prerequisite for social survival *Pattern Maintenance*,
because it involves preserving the knowledge, the beliefs, the
ways of living that give shape to the identity of a group—what
anthropologist call the *culture*. There are many ways people
solve the problem of how to preserve and pass on what they have
found useful: through the informal learning that takes place in
families, formal schooling, and the various repositories of information such as books, churches, museums, and computers.

One of the oldest ways Pattern Maintenance is achieved is
through the face-to-face interaction of older and younger members of a community. When this takes place in an occupational

setting, we call it *mentoring*—it is how young men learned to be hunters and young women weavers; how farmers, builders, and healers learned their craft. Mentoring is still an essential link in the chain of maintaining the pattern of culture, yet one that is still not that well understood, even in this age of sophisticated media for storing and distributing information.

Nakamura and Shernoff's study reported in this book is an original and insightful contribution to our understanding of how the practices of a profession—what is known, how it is done, and why—get passed down from masters to apprentices through three successive "generations" of practitioners. The profession in question here—genetics—is state of the art, but the issues geneticists face are shared by every group responsible for a specialized knowledge, from plumbers to poets, from physicists to priests: How do we train new cohorts so that they will carry on what they are supposed to do, without losing what is good about the past, yet adding fresh knowledge as they go along?

To deal with this question, in-depth interviews were conducted with some of the most distinguished scientists in the area of genetics. Given that this is still a relatively small field, it was possible for them to identify three separate "lineages," each with its own traditions and lab environments, comprising scientists who had worked together as mentors or apprentices. This allows the authors to deal with some of the central issues in the maintenance of cultural patterns through mentoring. What are the common memes—or units of information—present in all lineages, and which ones are unique? What are the practices that make mentors effective? What kind of relationships support good mentoring?

In three early chapters, the authors present the heads of the three lineages, their particular approach to the science, and the effect that they had on young scientists who worked in their labs; and then on which memes the students of these "second-generation" lab heads absorbed in their turn, which ones were rejected, and for what reasons. These case studies, written with elegance and precision, unveil three very different ways of approaching science, motivated by different goals, and emphasizing different procedures and outcomes. These vivid case studies provide unique glimpses into the relation between personal experiences, values, ideologies, and the practice of what to all intents and purposes is an abstract, objective science.

Yet as later chapters reveal, beneath the almost idiosyncratic diversity of skills and values absorbed in various laboratories, there is also a common core of memes that keeps the science of genetics from disintegrating into divergent subfields. The centrifugal trends are kept in check by a commitment to certain basic values and accepted knowledge. Of course, science advances by rejecting previous paradigms, but it is difficult to imagine how genetics, for instance, could continue to exist for long as a vital form of knowledge if its young practitioners did not learn that honesty and precision in their work are essential, or that they have to know what their predecessors thought before they can add to that knowledge, and so on.

Given the design of their study, Nakamura and Shernoff are able to add to their qualitative analyses some highly interesting quantitative data that show which memes are shared by all lineages and which ones are "signature memes" of a particular lineage; which ones endure for at least three generations, and which do not. These analyses clearly confirm some of the earlier arguments, as well as providing a model for how to measure the sharing and the transmission of complex units of culture in a way that will be useful to any researcher who embarks on similar pursuits.

What follows are more qualitative chapters that focus on best practice traits of these outstanding laboratories: what the mentors do right and the (many fewer) things they do wrong. The quality of the relationships that develop, the ways the work in the labs is organized, and the kind of resources—material and psychological—that facilitate the absorption and retention of memes are discussed in lucid detail. Several counterintuitive patterns emerge in these chapters, adding a great deal of fresh knowledge to our understanding of how mentoring works in the context of science labs.

Many of the findings of this book will be new to readers. Mentoring will never again appear to be a simple, automatic process after one reads its pages. I could report what I found to be the most intriguing new ideas I learned from the book, but that would be unfair to the authors, who have taken great pains to weave their argument in a deliberate progression. And it would be unfair to the readers, whose enjoyment of the book depends in large part from their ability to discover the treasures buried in its pages on their own.

Throughout the book, the authors avoid some obvious pitfalls that their approach would present to the unwary scholar. For example, they do not claim that mentoring is a one-way process; the impact of apprentices on their own development is never ignored. And the authors recognize also that the history of science—or memes more generally—can never be simply an account of the transmission of existing values or knowledge. If it were, the domain would soon shrivel into a historical relic. Instead, all cultural domains must be open to growth and transformation brought about by the new generation of practitioners. It is this delicate balance between respect for tradition and openness to change that good mentors in science must practice and transmit to their apprentices. On a larger scale, the same balance has to be achieved by education at all levels, from preschool to graduate training.

It is for this reason that a book written about a rather esoteric branch of science can illuminate much broader cultural issues, addressing these questions: What is worth remembering? And how do we make sure that it will be remembered? Educators, leaders of organizations, masters and apprentices ranging from businesses to laboratories, from religious seminaries to athletic programs, will learn and benefit from its pages. In essence, this carefully researched and extremely well-written book is an example of interdisciplinary scholarship at its best. One could almost say that the book can be read ignoring the content, just to savor the intricacy of the design, the clarity of the prose, and the ideas that shimmer below it. But it would not be right. Form and content are here united seamlessly in a work that is a benchmark for our understanding of how knowledge is generated and transmitted, and then reshaped, from one generation to the next.

Mihaly Csikszentmihalyi
Cofounder of the GoodWork Project
Distinguished Professor of Psychology
Claremont Graduate University

Preface

This is at once a book about good mentoring and how it takes place at the outset of careers; a book about successful graduate education, particularly in fields such as science, where it occurs through an extended apprenticeship; a book about good work, as embodied by three remarkable professionals who together illuminate both its common and variable features; and a book about mentor-protégé lineages, and their role in the preservation and evolution of good work across generations in one far-reaching domain, genetic research. In multiple respects, it thus is also a work about positive psychology or human flourishing and its conditions.

Origins and Contribution

We view this book foremost as contributing to current theory, research, and practice in mentoring and graduate education. Interest in mentoring has grown steadily for over two decades, as seen in the popular press (Albom, 1997; Cuomo, 2002) and the academic literature (Allen & Eby, 2007; Ragins & Kram, 2007; Rhodes, 2002). When researchers began to trace the course of human development across the adult years, several of them drew attention to the significance of mentoring relationships for both the young adults constructing a vision of themselves in the world and the middle-aged adults who, by mentoring them, gained from contributing to something beyond themselves (Erikson, 1959/1980; Levinson, 1978; Vaillant, 1977). In the large body of subsequent research and practice, what has not been foregrounded is the role of mentoring in the transmission of values, practices, and goals from one generation to the next within a profession, encompassing what protégés absorb through mentoring relationships, and the pathways by which they do so.

By framing the outcomes of mentoring relationships primarily in terms of protégés' career development and personal growth, the field has had limited attention left over for examining how mentors help students develop professional excellence and ethics. Yet it could be argued that when mentoring encourages novices to strive for excellence and care for the ethical commitments and basic purpose of their profession—that is, to do "good work" (Gardner, Csikszentmihalyi, & Damon, 2001)—the experience contributes in an essential way to their subsequent pursuit of work that engages them personally, strengthens the profession, and furthers the welfare of the communities they serve. This book is a call to those studying, overseeing, and doing the work of mentoring, as well as those who receive it, to think about mentoring in this expanded sense.

Whereas the mentoring literature has not focused on the formation of the values, practices, and goals associated with good work, other work has. Developmental psychology has shown that early experiences in the family and community play a major role in the formation of values and beliefs; however, much research on adulthood makes clear that change continues to occur across the postadolescent years (Alexander & Langer, 1990; Baltes, 1987; Kegan, 1982; Neugarten, 1969). Of special relevance is one study that concluded that the values, beliefs, and goals of "moral exemplars" remained open to transformation throughout adulthood (Colby & Damon, 1992). The observation of adult malleability undergirds work on education in professional ethics (Davis, 2002; Rest & Narvaez, 1994). However, previous treatments of the transmission of professional ethics primarily have concerned the rationale for formal ethics courses and designs for their delivery. This book investigates how values and conduct as a professional are influenced organically through the extended mentoring relationships that emerge and evolve as novices enter a new profession.

While this book speaks to the theory and practice of mentoring, as well as graduate education and professional training more generally, its original roots lie elsewhere. The questions the book addresses grew out of an earlier study that the first author conducted with Mihaly Csikszentmihalyi and In-Soo Choe as part of the groundwork for Gardner, Csikszentmihalyi, and Damon's GoodWork Project. Concern about the popular view of a disconnection between creativity and social responsibility was Gardner and colleagues' initial impetus for establishing the GoodWork Project, the large-scale investigation of which this book is one part. Creative work often is presumed to be the province of selfish iconoclasts and thus to exist in a profoundly uneasy relationship to what Gardner, Csikszentmihalyi, and Damon called "good work." Rather than accept the popular stereotype, a preliminary study turned to interviews with scientists, artists, scholars, and others who had been working for years at the leading edge of their respective domains, and it asked: When describing their work, did these individuals position their lifelong undertakings outside of—or even in opposition to—the claims of enduring cultural values and ethics? If not, what commitments guided their activity?

Far from rejecting responsibility or endorsing only values such as originality, risk taking, openness, and independence, the interviews with these creative women and men proved rich in statements of commitment to integrity and truth, and references to concern for the common good and care for the welfare of future generations. Among these individuals were several physicists whose experiences during World War II had brought home to them the global impact of their work as scientists.

The interviews thus provided some evidence that creativity and responsibility, professional success and good work, can coexist. Interestingly, the cadre of senior physicists interviewed in that study recalled being deeply influenced as younger men in their approaches to both science and life by their relationships with one exceptional mentor, Niels Bohr. Their shared experience inspired us, all associated with the GoodWork Project, to address the question: Can one generation's "good workers" nurture similar commitments in members of the next generation, even as changing sociocultural conditions pose new challenges to the pursuit of excellence and ethics in a field? Through what means might such "good mentoring" occur? These were the precursors of our book.

Exploring the role of mentoring in the transmission of values and practices across generations required studying the values and practices of multiple generations, eliciting a mentor's and multiple students' accounts of the mentor's practices. We studied three "lineages" of scientists—the lines of descent from three exceptional scientists. Past scholars have examined similar cultural lines of descent or influence, on the analogy with biological ones, but most of their work has focused on the evolution of ideas (for example, Collins, 1998; Pledge, 1966) or the transmission of practices that support creative achievement (Zuckerman, 1978) as distinct from the propagation of good work. Relevant scholarship in psychology has examined how ideas, practices, and other units of culture, which Richard Dawkins (1976) dubbed "memes," are transmitted over time, including interpersonally (Csikszentmihalyi & Massimini, 1985; Heath, 1996; Inghilleri, 1999); however, this work has not focused on the role that mentors play in intergenerational processes. Within the field of mentoring itself, the possibility of a multigenerational or lineage approach to mentoring has gone almost entirely unnoted (for two exceptions of which we are aware, see Hardcastle, 1988; Kealy & Mullen, 1996).

Although mentoring is here conceptualized in terms of its mediating role in a process of cultural evolution, the actual interpersonal and psychological processes that mentors and protégés described comport with contemporary images of the learner as active and constructive, and current theories of how successful learning takes place in a social context. Indeed, as the book details, in these complex, real-life settings of significant adult learning, multiple psychosocial processes of learning and development coexist. The book describes how the processes of modeling, active observation and selective absorption, peer interaction, working in a community of practice, and building supportive relationships can reinforce each other. Within the mentoring literature, much of which continues to attribute mentoring outcomes to a dyadic process between one novice and one experienced professional, the book thus contributes to the body of work that addresses the importance of peer relationships and developmental networks (Higgins & Kram, 2001; Kram, 1985; Kram & Isabella, 1985).

Finally, this book is part of a growing body of research on admirable human qualities and institutions, much of it conducted under the broad umbrella of positive psychology (Dutton & Ragins, 2007; Keyes & Haidt, 2002; Peterson & Seligman, 2004; Seligman, 2002; Seligman & Csikszentmihalyi, 2000; Snyder & Lopez, 2001). Positive psychology investigates what have long been comparatively neglected aspects of human functioning: positive personality qualities, experiences, and social contexts (Seligman & Csikszentmihalyi, 2000). In investigating good work, good mentoring, and good learning environments, we contribute to this growing literature, particularly the emerging study of personal strengths, positive relationships, and positive institutions.

Audience

For the reasons we have suggested, this book should be relevant to a wide spectrum of people in the fields of education, psychology, professional ethics, and professional training. Researchers, scholars, and educators, as well as sophisticated general readers, will find here a new conceptual framework and empirical basis for theory, research, and practice in the areas of mentoring, graduate advising, and ethics education in adulthood. Teachers and students in a variety of fields will find a discussion of the social processes of learning during professional education. Graduate students preparing for careers in research, particularly in the sciences, will gain a fuller view of training processes and their formative impact on professional identity. This book may be used in university courses in any of these or related fields. It might be appropriately assigned to participants in the growing number of programs for graduate students such as Preparing Future Faculty and Entering Mentoring. Nearly anyone interested in higher education and the professions may benefit from a new perspective on time-tested ways of transmitting an area of specialized practice from one generation to the next: mentoring and apprenticeship.

For researchers, practitioners, and general readers familiar with the GoodWork Project, this book provides an empirically grounded illustration of one significant means by which good work is successfully promoted. The notion of good work has been taken up by those building positive psychology (Peterson, 2006); for such readers, the book additionally offers new ideas, methods, and findings concerning positive relationships and the signature strengths that groups (in this case, lineages) can share. Finally, the book develops a concrete example of the social context of cultural evolution; students of cultural evolution and scholars in the sociology of science thus may find it of interest.

Overview of Contents

Chapter One introduces the book's underlying issues and guiding questions. It discusses some of the pressures that make it difficult for professionals to do good work and presents "good mentoring," or the fostering of good work by mentors, as one possible counterforce to the influence these pressures can exert on young practitioners' approach to working life. Both the contributions of good mentoring to the evolution of professions and society at large and the more familiar role of mentoring in individual development are discussed. The chapter also provides a brief overview of the study's distinctive methodology.

What happens during an extended period of graduate education that would enable students to absorb not only technical expertise but also a mentor's unique approach to working life? The case exemplar approach provided an indispensable point of entry for meaningfully understanding the complex social-psychological processes involved. Part One, consisting of Chapters Two through Four, presents portraits of three exemplary scientists and their lineages. Each chapter describes a different "lineage head" and the mentoring that he provided, drawing on his own account and multiple students' recollections of their experiences in his laboratory. Then, the lineage that flowed from him is characterized through a third generation's recollections of life in one of his students' labs. These lineage portraits should give readers a window on how good mentors work, and an understanding of how students were influenced by, then later came to practice and teach, the values and practices that their mentors modeled.

A second valuable approach was analytical, adopted to complement the rich detail of the portraits. Part Two lays out what was learned about the key memes that scientists passed on to their students during graduate training and how they did so. Chapter Five identifies values and practices that distinctively characterize each lineage, providing quantitative analyses of which memes were handed down through three successive generations. Chapters Six and Seven summarize common ingredients of good mentoring. Chapter Six focuses on the highly effective modes of transmitting values and practices employed by the lineage heads. Chapter Seven draws lessons from the sample as a whole about mentoring relationships as a context for the perpetuation of a mentor's memes, highlighting both the challenges of the more difficult mentoring relationships and the supportive aspects of the stronger relationships.

Finally, Part Three summarizes what was learned and what remains to be discovered. Chapter Eight provides an integrative discussion of key conclusions drawn from the investigation. Chapter Nine suggests implications for practice to mentors, mentees, and institutions where graduate and professional education occurs, and future directions for researchers studying these topics.

Learning from good mentors, and learning to what extent their strengths influenced later generations, has been a process of discovery. Much remains to be learned. This book stands as an invitation to scholars and practitioners to use the conceptual and methodological tools provided here in order to move beyond these first steps.

Acknowledgments

The publication of this volume is the culmination of years of work, and its completion would not have been possible without the contributions of a great many people. One recurring lesson of the GoodWork Project has been the formidable time press that professionals face. It is thus a special pleasure to be able to express our appreciation to the busy scientists who graciously set aside time to be interviewed for the study and to review the resulting interview transcripts and book passages. The study and the book exist only because of their generosity. We learned a great deal from each of their interviews and are deeply grateful to all. We wish to thank as well the participants in the study's pilot phase and the distinguished scientists and scholars who nominated interviewees for the study.

We are grateful to many others as well.

The study was made possible by the generous support of the Spencer Foundation. We are grateful for the interest and enthusiasm of the foundation's representatives, especially our program officer, Eleni Makris.

The principal investigators of the GoodWork Project—Howard Gardner, Mihaly Csikszentmihalyi, and William Damon—offered counsel, encouragement, and faith in the book project every step of the way. We owe profound thanks for this and for their compelling example and tenacious commitment to studying and furthering good work. To Mihaly Csikszentmihalyi, we owe a special debt of gratitude, which we hope one day to pay forward, for the opportunity to write this book and the gifts of his insight, experience, and time. We have found inspiration in his ideas and his modeling of research as serious play. He has been a steady source of support, offering first the deft balance of freedom and guidance that characterizes good mentoring, and later the very best of colleagueship as we worked through the ideas presented in the book. Thank you for your trust and generosity. We hope that this book is worthy of an intellectual heritage we treasure.

Groundwork for the study was conducted with In-Soo Choe, a wonderful colleague. Over the course of the study on which the book is based, members of the research team included Lynn Barendsen, Heather Campbell, Dan Dillon, Howard Fero, Mollie Galloway, David Gortner, Anne Gregory, Paula Marshall, Mimi Michaelson, Liza Percer, Kim Sheridan, and Leanne Stahnke. We thank them all for their roles in the study's success. Our particular appreciation is warmly extended to Mimi Michaelson, Liza Percer, and Leanne Stahnke, then at Harvard, Stanford, and the University of Chicago, respectively, each of whom contributed to the study's success on many fronts. Scholars beyond the GoodWork Project who kindly offered insight or encouragement at key junctures include John Creswell, Paolo Inghilleri, Carol Mullen, Chris Peterson, and David Sloan Wilson.

We are thankful for the assistance of Loren Bryant, who played key support roles throughout the writing of the book, as well as Rupanwita Gupta, Purva Rushi, Barbara Simeon, and Anna Strati for spending countless hours managing files and correspondence, locating and summarizing articles, proofreading transcripts and chapters, formatting the manuscript, checking references, and undertaking other time-consuming tasks that are too little celebrated yet essential. We appreciate their enthusiasm for our project and research in general, their attention to detail, and sense of humor.

At Jossey-Bass, we extend a wholehearted thank-you to our editor, David Brightman, who embraced the book and the larger GoodWork Project. He gave us the benefit of his experience, intelligence, judgment, and good humor. The book was significantly improved by his guidance. Aneesa Davenport and Carolyn Dumore, members of the editorial staff at Jossey-Bass, were also unfailingly helpful.

Finally, we are forever indebted to our family and close friends for the sacrifices that they have made, and allowed us to make, in order to see the book project through to fruition. Our spouses, Elisa Shernoff and Angie Fox, who have an intimate awareness of what has gone into this book, were unfailing in their encouragement, patience, and understanding. They were consummate companions, supporters, editors, teachers, and sources of unparalleled inspiration. We owe profound personal thanks to our parents, the late Joseph Nakamura, May Nakamura, William Shernoff, JoAnn Shernoff, Charles Hooker, and Anne Hooker, whose love and support could always be counted on. Spencer Shernoff displayed remarkably mature understanding for a one year old when his father was absent to work on the book. Heartfelt gratitude goes out to our friends and colleagues who were with us in spirit at a variety of scattered institutions, including Jennifer Schmidt, Rustin Wolfe, Jeremy Hunter, John Patton, John Planansky, Barbara Novak, Sami Abuhamdeh, David Creswell, Jeff Solomon, Wendy Fischman, Susan Verducci Sandford, Bruce Novak, Ryan Kettler, Todd Glover, Sean Kelly, M. Cecil Smith, Don Hunt, Marc VanOverbeke, and Stephen Tonks. You never failed to sustain us with your collegiality and good cheer.

Good Mentoring

1

WHY MENTORING?

For better or for worse, mentors encountered early in the career occupy a potent position in one's development as a practitioner. By influencing the next generation of practitioners, mentors can also shape the future of their professions. In his book *Academic Duty* (1997), the president emeritus of Stanford University, Donald Kennedy, asserted the critical importance of mentoring for the survival of the academy:

> It is through [mentor-student] relationships that the academic profession reproduces itself. . . . What the new faculty member knows about the university, he or she learned by absorption—in a library or laboratory, under the guidance (or, perhaps, the indifferent sponsorship) of a graduate or postdoctoral mentor. The faculty member's understanding of his or her academic responsibilities is not prescribed by contract or institutional rule; in this respect it is unlike the understanding of duty one would have as a soldier or as a mid-level executive in a large corporation. It is, rather, part of an inherited culture, and the route of transmission is thus of vital importance. (p. 97)

This is a book about the route of transmission that Kennedy found to be of vital importance, a route in which mentors and graduate advisors play a significant role. We report on a systematic investigation into how graduate mentors can amplify specific values and practices that become part of an inherited culture. We interviewed at length not only mentors but also multiple generations of students to discover the extent to which values and practices are inherited and how such a process occurs.

Historically, the ideal mentor has been conceived as someone who serves as advisor, sponsor, host, exemplar, and guide for a relative novice who is moving from dependence and inexperience toward independence and proficiency. An effective mentor may also facilitate the realization of a young person's aspirations by bestowing responsibility, trust, and opportunities to achieve (Levinson, 1978). However, the experience of mentoring during graduate or professional training appears to be more mixed than one might expect. In one large-scale study on perceptions of mentoring, only 56 percent of nearly one thousand students in a variety of programs were "satisfied" or "very satisfied" with their mentoring relationships (Ortolani, 1998). Smaller studies vary by profession but paint a similar picture. For example, in a qualitative study of doctoral students in counseling psychology, 38 percent reported being unsatisfied (Schlosser, Knox, Moskovitz, & Hill, 2003). Dissatisfied students describe their mentors as unavailable, unsupportive of their academic endeavors, and lacking in competence, interpersonal skills, or both.

More worrisome are known cases of abuse of power, including incompatibility of attitudes, sexual harassment, and exploitation, sometimes culminating in disastrous outcomes. From a mentor's point of view, problems arise if a student's expectations of the mentor are unrealistic. From the student's perspective, a bad relationship may significantly taint the entire educational experience, resulting in feelings of alienation (Tenenbaum, Crosby, & Gliner, 2001). When a Nobel laureate's star graduate student in the Harvard chemistry department committed suicide in the late 1990s, leaving a note declaring "this event could have been avoided . . . professors here have too much power over their students," commentaries that followed made clear that the perceived pressures were familiar to academics in the sciences and beyond (Hall, 1998, p. 120). At one extreme, the intense focus of many graduate advisors on their own work leads them to neglect their students. At the other, advisors may be accessible but place crushing demands on their students.

In one leading lab, a sign dictated: "Don't try. Do" (Hall, 1998, p. 120). More darkly, one commentator in the *Chronicle of Higher Education* observed: "The prof is dependent on your work; he/she must often use guilt trips, harsh yelling, insults, or subtle jabs to get you to work. He/she has to" (Schneider, 1998, p. A12).

Advisors thus have the capacity to do real harm. When they mentor well, however, there can be a multitude of benefits. Effective mentoring at the graduate level has been related to completion (Lovitts, 2001), as well as academic success, scholarly productivity, and subsequent career achievement. Graduate students who indicate that they have a mentor produce significantly more predoctoral publications, including first-authored publications, conference papers, and grant applications, compared with students who are not mentored (Cronan-Hillix, Gensheime, Cronan-Hillix, & Davidson, 1986; Reskin, 1979; Smith & Davidson, 1992). After graduation, they are more likely to obtain a tenure-track position at a university, collaborate more on professional research projects, publish more, and garner more advancements over the course of their careers (Cameron & Blackburn, 1981; Reskin, 1979).

These benefits concern only the impact of mentoring on the academic and career success of the individual student. More broadly, as novices move into a profession, they start to construct an understanding of the profession they are entering—what ends it serves, what it asks of them, what it rewards—and begin to define the kind of professional they want to become. They start internalizing standards, forming a distinctive approach to work, shaping their goals and a sense of purpose, and setting a moral compass for their professional conduct. With respect to these aspects of development, an advisor may demonstrate that success can coexist with responsible, ethical practice—or, instead, model conduct that undermines the highest standards of the profession. We were particularly interested in the transmission of orienting values and principles uniting excellence with responsible practice. This book reports on research that systematically examined whether and how exemplary practitioners might influence their students in these areas.

There is reason to believe that mentors may matter a great deal in these areas of development, as well as in career success. For example, mentoring received during graduate or professional training may provide crucial support for a commitment to the common good. Law students may be lured to the profession by the lucrative prospects of working for a corporate law firm rather than by the prospect of practicing law to serve the public good. However, even the students most strongly committed to pursuing public interest law find their dedication waning during law school unless they are encouraged to pursue it by a subculture that includes mentoring relationships with experienced lawyers and teachers (Stover, 1989).

Few disagree that mentoring can be beneficial, and in a variety of ways. The main difficulty appears to be that there is not enough good mentoring to go around. In some instances, this shortage might be the consequence of inattentiveness or laziness on the part of institutions or would-be mentors. We suspect, however, that more often the shortage results from a collective lack of awareness about what it means to mentor well—lack of an adequate understanding of the pathways that successfully foster excellence and perpetuate responsible professional practice. Mentoring is a lot like parenting: something one is expected to pick up naturally, with little or no formal training. However much organizations from university departments to law firms to large corporations may depend on the process for their survival, professionals are still expected to learn the process almost through osmosis, with little effort or energy. While a plethora of how-to books on mentoring have been published, too many are not based on rigorous social-scientific research. In this book, we ask: What exactly is it that early career professionals learn from good mentors? And how does the transformational process occur?

Spanning the Generations: Mentoring in Elite Scientific Lineages

This book relates what we learned by studying the impact of mentors on new practitioners who are forming their approaches to work and their professional identities, and it explains how we view mentoring as a result of our research. The mentoring processes that we examined occurred in a single field—that of genetic research—and yet the lessons learned relate to principles of effective mentoring in any profession where the role of apprenticeship is (or could be) strong. First, however, what indications did we have that experienced professionals can play a positive role in the development of a practitioner in the respects of central interest to us and that this impact can extend down generations of students?

The first promising sign was the case of the great twentieth-century Danish physicist Niels Bohr. We became familiar with Bohr and his profound impact on younger scientists through interviews with several physicists in their seventies and eighties who had worked with him early in their careers. (Unless otherwise indicated, comments by Bohr's students come from unpublished interviews conducted for a study of creativity in later life described in Csikszentmihalyi, 1996.) In their younger years, these scientists were eager to make a contribution to physics, and they were drawn to Bohr because they wanted to learn how to do groundbreaking work from a master in the field. Each of them went on to achieve excellence, winning prestigious awards, and all named Bohr as a crucial figure in their development as successful scientists. He taught them "how to think" as one put it, and "a new way of looking at the world, of raising questions" according to another (see Riordan, 1998, p. 24). His protégés did more than become skilled scientists, however. Their time with Bohr also left them better members of the scientific community. In contrast to scientists determined to get ahead at all costs, Bohr deeply impressed them as "too great for haste, too high for rivalry" (Taylor, 1972, p. 475). He was concerned with exploring what he still did not understand rather than dwelling on his past accomplishments. He struggled mightily with scientific problems yet was always willing to admit if his conclusions were wrong. In short, he was a model of scientific integrity (Pais, 1991).

In addition, Bohr was attentive to his younger colleagues, encouraged them, and made them more sensitive to the scientist's responsibility to society. They recounted influential conversations with Bohr about both the domain of physics and important matters beyond the scope of science. They recalled times when they had shared meals, taken walks, and engaged in other social activities together. They reflected on his concern for them as persons as much as scientists. Bohr had a "special way of teaching," distinguished by a holistic perspective and a sense of caring that modeled collegiality, integrity, responsibility, and scientific excellence.

One of Bohr's students explained, "I lived as a member of his family . . . he had a great feel for people, their careers, and their problems." Another said, "He was always living with or among us. . . . Although he was much better than us, he was accessible. . . . He was interested to talk to us not only about physics, but also about philosophy, politics, and art. We went together to the movies." A third added, "As he walked around the table in his office talking about some of the great questions, you would have the feeling that you could understand how people such as Buddha or Confucius really existed. . . . He took his role as citizen and scientist very seriously. . . . He had a great feeling of responsibility and citizenship."

Some of Bohr's protégés also recalled encounters with Albert Einstein, and the contrast with Bohr is instructive. They learned a great deal about science from the celebrated physicist, but they were not influenced in nearly the same way. Einstein worked more independently than Bohr did, and although he thought and wrote on a broad range of topics as a humanist and pacifist, these younger colleagues did not describe being profoundly influenced by his example. One scientist noted that Einstein was a quintessential independent thinker whose deepest need was "to think separately, to be by himself. Bohr, on the other hand, craved togetherness, in life and in thought" (Pais, 1991, p. 227).

Bohr left an indelible imprint on the generation of younger scientists he mentored. Moreover, the impact of his mentoring extended beyond his protégés' lives. His influence was also felt by the scientists whom his protégés in turn influenced. For example, a junior colleague saw in one of Bohr's protégés, John Wheeler, a set of inherited traits "so charming and insidious that I find myself adopting them." He reported, "I never met Niels Bohr, and yet feel I have watched him through John." He concluded, "In a multiplicity of ways: in print, [but also] in characteristic gesture, in mode of thought, in politeness and openness of mind . . . do the lives of great men reverberate in our own" (Taylor, 1972, p. 476). In this sense, Bohr created a *lineage,* or line of descent. Through his protégés' subsequent conduct as leading scientists, he affected the ethos of the nuclear physics community and the role that it played in the wider society during and after World War II (for a discussion of Bohr's influence on the physics community and beyond, see Pais, 1991).

Bohr's example fueled our interest in whether and how mentors can have a positive influence on their protégés' guiding values and attitudes, in addition to affecting the quality of their work and their subsequent professional success. His example makes clear that the stakes are high: through their impact on the next generation, good mentors can also affect the future character of their profession. How unique was Bohr? In the research on which this book draws, we traced the impact of senior professionals on several subsequent generations of practitioners.

Studying Scientific Lineages

The field of genetics experienced a golden age during the final decades of the twentieth century. We chose to study how mentoring takes place in this important field with the expectation that what was learned would apply to mentoring in the sciences at large, in many respects to graduate education generally, and in some respects to mentoring in any profession. The lessons learned are relevant to advisor-guided graduate training normally occurring within universities and to experience-based professional training, as in medical residencies or law clerkships.

Graduate science education's reliance on learning by apprenticeship makes it an ideal setting for examining mentoring in early career development. Not every graduate student has a mentor, but unlike some other forms of professional preparation, the advisor-student relationship at the heart of graduate training ensures that every student has the possibility of having one. In addition, the state of genetics at the turn of the century is well suited for the study of how mentoring relates to "good work," a topic to which we turn shortly. Briefly, toward the end of the twentieth century, the critical influence of genetics on society became very evident; in addition, with the growth of cloning, biotechnology, and gene therapy and growing competitive pressures within the field, genetics began to be the subject of the kinds of concern that inspired the launch of the larger GoodWork Project. For this reason, a study providing us with a base of knowledge of good work in genetics had been conducted earlier (Gardner, Csikszentmihalyi, & Damon, 2001).

Within genetics, we focused on multigenerational "lineages" among the scientific elite (Zuckerman, 1978). It is not uncommon in academia for individuals to refer in conversation to their intellectual fathers or mothers or to compare notes about their intellectual offspring. At elite levels, lineages have been shown to extend across generations of teachers and students for decades, displaying clear lines of descent from mentor to protégé (see Zuckerman, 1977; Kanigel, 1986). We adapt the concept of generations to refer to the reproduction of practitioners within a profession, such that the first generation of offspring comprises a practitioner's students, the second generation comprises the students' students (the original practitioner's "grandchildren"), and so on. Because the most eminent scientists of one generation train a disproportionate number of the succeeding generation's leaders, we wanted to learn what kinds of values, beliefs, and practices might be communicated from teacher to student across three generations of these elite ranks and how this process occurs.

Prior research suggests that eminent scientists transmit to their apprentices both the standards and practices that support creative accomplishment, and the signature ideas and research style that may distinguish one leading scientist from another. In the pages that follow, we simultaneously explore the direct influence of exemplary senior scientists on their individual students and their indirect influence on future generations, with implications for the health of their profession. Specifically, our study centered on (1) the practices, values, and beliefs embodied by three exemplary senior practitioners; (2) the extent to which these mentors were able to successfully pass on an orientation toward "good work" (as explained next) to subsequent generations; (3) the mentoring practices they employed; and (4) characteristics of the relationships they formed with students.

Professional Pressures and Good Work

Mentors have the capacity to be either harmful or beneficial by virtue of what they may model or pass down to subsequent generations. We were particularly interested in the capacity of mentors to model and pass down practices exemplifying professional excellence and ethical responsibility. This combination has been dubbed "good work" by the GoodWork Project, a research program out of which our study grew. The GoodWork Project was begun in 1996 by Howard Gardner, Mihaly Csikszentmihalyi, and William Damon to investigate a perennial challenge that professionals face, and its intensification under contemporary societal conditions. They argued that the challenge for professionals is to do work that is "good" in two respects: of high quality *and* true to the profession's traditional mission and code of ethics. The growing public distrust harbored today toward virtually every profession—business, health care, law, journalism, and others—reflects the compromised ability to meet this challenge because pressures and incentive systems create temptations to sacrifice responsible practice. Since the turn of the twenty-first century, such temptations have increasingly resulted in publicized instances of public fraud, breaches of good faith, and corporate crimes. The book *Good Work* (Gardner et al., 2001) discussed the nature of work that is both excellent by the profession's standards of quality and ethical, responsibly serving the common good. It focused on the professions of genetic research and journalism to explore the current conditions—such as growing self-interest, cutthroat competition, and ubiquitous profit pressures—that can impede excellence and compromise professional ethics. In recent years, we have seen the consequences in almost every profession.

Genetic research is no exception, particularly in biotechnology, which ties research to lucrative industry. A recently publicized example was the case of Hwang Woo Suk, the South Korean scientist who rose to international prominence after reporting a series of remarkable breakthroughs in stem cell research. He was considered one of the pioneers in the field and became a national hero after publishing two articles in the prestigious journal *Science* in 2004 and 2005, reporting that he had cloned embryonic stem cells, a technique that might lead to cures for a range of diseases. But the reports turned out to be fraudulent, containing a large amount of falsified data, and the journal retracted both papers. After initial denials, Hwang admitted to various fabrications and frauds.

The current situation in the field of genetics has deep roots; indeed, it has been argued that cutthroat competition characterizes the origin story of modern genetics. On a February afternoon in 1953, Francis Crick burst into the Eagle Pub in Cambridge,

England, and exuberantly announced to "everyone in hearing distance" that he and his younger colleague, James Watson, "had found the secret of life" (Watson, 1968, p. 197). In some respects, he was right. Earlier that day, Crick and Watson had identified the double-helix structure of deoxyribose nucleic acid, edging out other researchers in England and the United States racing to do the same. Their discovery was monumental, nothing short of unearthing the holy grail of science at the time, and it made possible the rise of modern genetics. Together they had competed vigorously against their transatlantic rival, Linus Pauling. Within weeks, Watson and Crick published their results in the journal *Nature*, revolutionizing biochemistry and establishing themselves as two of the most celebrated scientists of the twentieth century (Watson & Crick, 1953). Finally, they had won.

James Watson's ascendance in science has rarely been paralleled. He was twenty-five years old when he codiscovered the double helix. In his thirties, he joined the Harvard faculty and shared the 1962 Nobel Prize in chemistry for his role in the landmark discovery. When he was forty, he published *The Double Helix*, his wildly popular chronicle of the events surrounding the 1953 discovery, which now ranks seventh among Modern Library's most important nonfiction books of the twentieth century. Twelve years after joining the Harvard faculty, he took the helm of the prestigious Cold Spring Harbor Laboratory, running it with the same brashness, determination, and competitiveness that carried him to eminence as a young man. The lab gained a reputation as a powerhouse in the field, and Watson's prominence grew steadily as well. He was at Cold Spring Harbor for over twenty years, leaving only when the National Institutes of Health launched the Human Genome Project in the late 1980s and named him as its first head. He resigned from the project in 1992 in protest over the U.S. government's plans to patent gene sequences, and he returned to Cold Spring Harbor for another fifteen years.

A former associate was asked about Watson's impact on the field of genetics (comments come from an unpublished research interview that was conducted for the GoodWork Project in 1998). The researcher offered a surprising appraisal: rather than celebrating Watson's important breakthroughs and lauding his contributions to science, this former colleague instead criticized Watson's approach. He described it in terms of an increasingly pervasive set of practices that he believes scientists and educators should regard with skepticism rather than praise. He advised reading *The Double Helix,* but *not* as an inspirational work: "I say read it, because to me it's a very clear picture of how not to do science. I think that book has probably done more damage than any other book in the field. You know, the lesson of the book is, [however you get it], if you get the right answer it's fine. Life is rosy for you. I don't think that's a good message."

This scientist likened the public's eager embrace of Watson's book, and the scientific community's commendation of Watson, to the unreflective manner in which popular movies and television shows are devoured by the public: "It's a good story . . . it's sort of like reading *The Godfather. The Godfather* is an excellent story, and the film is wonderful, but that's perhaps not what I would want to be, not how I would like to run my life."

Watson's approach has been described as pitting the junior scientists against one another "to get as many people as possible working on the same problem so that it would get solved quickly," garnering prestige for the lab. There can be no doubt that this approach produced results, as well as high acclaim for Watson, but at what cost? Competing to "do the same experiment faster," rather than tackling some other problem well, actively discourages the open exchange of information and sharing of knowledge that is a cornerstone of science (on the norms of science, see Merton, 1973).

This behavior certainly does not rise to the level of public fraud or corporate crime, nor did anyone ever imply that Watson's science was dishonest. The danger is that aspiring scientists may embrace *The Double Helix* as their guide, concluding that the path to professional success must be paved with single-minded competitiveness even at the cost of ethical considerations.

Talented young scientists dream of great accomplishments; they want to leave their mark on the field. Many young professionals aspire to behave ethically and responsibly—so long as it does not harm their chances for professional success. According to one recent study, promising students said that they fully intend to behave ethically—once they have "made it" in their careers (Fischman, Solomon, Greenspan, & Gardner, 2004). Until then, however, some regard integrity as a luxury that they may be unable to afford. During the pressure-filled scramble to get ahead, they may cut corners or even lie about their work. This principle was demonstrated in the case of an ambitious high school student competing in the Intel Science Talent Search, who espoused a strong moral code and intended to live by it—just as soon as she was established in the field. To get ahead, however, she deliberately concealed disqualifying information about her experiment from the competition's judges. Justifying her actions, she stated, "Maybe it was lying, in a way. But I didn't think that it was wrong, because I deserved to be rewarded" (Fischman et al., 2004, pp. 88–89). She had, after all, worked very hard. Was it only a coincidence that this student admired *The Double Helix*?

The most widely publicized examples of succumbing to career pressure may represent extreme cases. However, the pressures and temptations that they highlight are felt by ambitious young people, and even not-so-ambitious individuals, in many professions today. Other challenges include time pressures in the seemingly impossible task of balancing work with home and personal life, which are intense for many young career professionals, both female and male (see Hochschild, 1997). In the absence of senior guidance, such pressures can produce temptations to publish work hastily or before a substantial contribution is made, avoid the sharing of scientific information, or in extreme cases like that of Hwang Woo Suk, misrepresent scientific data or results.

Good Mentoring from an Evolutionary, Systems Perspective

In the face of these conditions, what supports ethical and responsible professional conduct? Surely one of the likeliest bulwarks, as Gardner and his colleagues suggested, is education. But what educative forces exist that can best support the conjunction of responsible practice and high-quality work? It is our thesis that books, the Internet, and classroom lessons about professional ethics cannot—or at least do not—fully convey the values and practices promoting responsible practice. Rather, the best chance for their cultivation is likely to lie with teachers who embody these values and practices and the learning environments that the teachers create. Through them, orienting values can be acquired—to use John Dewey's felicitous phrase—in "intimate organic connection" with the associated knowledge and technical skills (Dewey, 1916, p. 360). In this book, we focus on mentoring that encourages good work, which we call *good mentoring*.

A word about terminology is in order. Researchers use the term *mentoring* to refer to a relationship in which "a more experienced . . . individual acts as a guide, role model, teacher, or sponsor for a less experienced . . . protégé" (Clark, Harden, & Johnson, 2000, p. 263). This needs to be distinguished from use of the term in some popular discourse to refer to a more circumscribed, often brief relationship focused only on aiding professional entry, advancement, and access to resources. We consider the latter to be *sponsorship*. Particularly in the sciences, the graduate student's association with an advisor is an organically developing, long-term relationship integral to becoming a professional. It is relationships of this kind that have sparked interest in creating formal mentoring programs, but the same quality of relationships has often proven difficult to reproduce there. Our book addresses mentoring more than *sponsorship*.

At times, we use the term *apprenticeship* as well as *mentorship*, although they are not synonymous. *Mentoring* commonly refers to a dyadic relationship that involves a one-on-one interplay between two individuals—a more experienced practitioner and a student or novice. The term normally specifies very little about the structure of the interactions through which learning takes place. In contrast, *apprenticeship* refers to the experiential learning that takes place in a community of practice where experts conduct the authentic work of a profession. Much of graduate education is structured loosely on the model of a craft apprenticeship, in which the novice is trained and supervised by a more seasoned practitioner. For a period of months or years, the senior practitioner exposes students, close up, to one possible approach to professional life. Analogous training models characterize other professions as well, though specific practices vary. Because this book takes graduate education in the sciences as the lens through which to study the perpetuation of good work, the mentoring relationships we describe take place within the context of apprenticeships.

In this book, then, we address the potentially profound effects of good mentoring on individual professionals, and in doing so, we broaden the context within which the mentor-student relationship is placed by adopting an evolutionary, systems approach. We consider the long-term transgenerational implications of a mentor's actions, and we recognize repercussions of these actions for the broad set of interacting systems to which the individual mentor and individual student belong. The study of lineages makes this broader view possible.

From a systems perspective (see Csikszentmihalyi, 1996), the relationship of novice to experienced practitioner interweaves three trajectories: one individual, one cultural, and one social. The relationship has the potential to play a role not only in the development and future success of the individual student, but also the perpetuation and transformation of the domain of professional knowledge and practice, and the evolution of the social field, or professional community, to which mentor and student belong. In short, it affects both professionals and the profession. The fate of the professions has consequences for us all. Every profession is also part of the larger sociocultural system, with which it interacts in multiple ways, particularly through its impact on those whom it is meant to serve.

Complementing this systems approach, we employ the perspective of cultural evolution, which provides a vocabulary for describing the transmission of lessons from mentor to student. In his book *The Selfish Gene* (1976), Richard Dawkins introduced the term *meme* to denote the building blocks of culture. Analogous to the role of genes in biological evolution, memes carry instructions for action that are transferred from one generation to the next. Dawkins's notion of memes is controversial, but we found it a valuable heuristic in this study, where we were interested in the role of mentors as potential carriers and transmitters of memes such as skills and knowledge, standards of quality, ethics and integrity, and overarching aims. We were especially interested in memes supporting good work.

Each seasoned practitioner has a characteristic approach to professional work. If we compare lineages headed by different practitioners, members of successive generations in one lineage may share a meme—a value, a practice, a belief—while those in the other lineages do not. If so, it would suggest that the distinctive characteristic of the lineage head had been transmitted over generations in that lineage. The genetic analogy would be blue eyes running through one family tree compared to brown eyes running through another. However, whereas the consequences for a community's welfare may be small if blue eyes selectively persist rather than brown eyes, the same is not true of professional conduct. If a spirit of cooperation is selectively perpetuated in a lineage rather than competitiveness, for example, the lineage will contribute to the profession's evolution toward a culture of collaboration.

How We Conducted the Study

In this study, a unique sampling design was critical. Assembling a sample of leading scientists would have been adequate if the goal had been limited to identifying effective practices in the cultivation of success. Because we also sought to understand processes that span successive generations, and the cultivation of ethical as well as successful practice, we needed a more complex sampling strategy. We studied mentors known as both moral exemplars and highly accomplished scientists, and used a multigenerational sampling design in order to examine the dynamics of the immediate teacher-student relationship, as well as the evolution of values and practices across linked generations of professionals.

We compared three lineages, each comprising three generations of scientists. The study's linchpins were three senior scientists. For these three lineage heads, who constituted Generation 1 of our sample, we sought elite scientists who best met three criteria. They needed to have made major scientific contributions, formed a strong reputation for responsible practice, and mentored a younger generation of practitioners.

Through a combination of background research and expert nomination, we created a list of Generation 1 prospects in the field of genetics. We examined biographical profiles, curriculum vitae, published interviews, newspaper articles, laboratory Web pages, disciplinary and institutional histories, scientific reports, and other materials. In addition, we interviewed several highly qualified consultants (for example, historians of genetics) to provide informed opinions about the candidates. Together, the consultations and research yielded a list of more than two dozen Generation 1 candidates, representing various areas within genetics. We selected three senior scientists, who unambiguously met all three criteria and represented three different subdomains within genetics: cyto-genetics (cell biology), medical genetics, and population genetics.

To identify Generation 2 and 3 representatives, we again employed a combination of background research and nomination. Each lineage head graciously prepared a list of former trainees who had pursued scientific careers. Their lists included many more successful midcareer scientists than we could inter-view. For each lineage head, we interviewed four former students, representatives of Generation 2 who were established researchers and had trained students of their own who were active in the field. To represent Generation 3, we solicited lists of laboratory alumni from the Generation 2 scientists and iden-tified former students who were actively working in the domain and had already begun training students themselves. In each lin-eage, we interviewed six to eight G3s. In selecting Generation 2 and 3 candidates, we favored the clearest instances of authentic apprenticeships. That is, most of those interviewed had pursued their graduate training or a multiyear research fellowship with a lineage member. Who, if anyone, a given representative of Generation 2 or 3 actually saw as a primary influence, and how he or she related to the "expected mentor," could not be known prior to the interview, however. The resulting variability in stu-dents' actual experiences allowed us to compare strong mentor-ing relationships to weaker ones and to assess how well the same mentor met the needs of different students.

In all, we interviewed the three lineage heads in Generation 1 (G1s), twelve members of Generation 2 (G2s), and twenty-one members of Generation 3 (G3s). We employ pseudonyms to protect the identities of the G2s and G3s. The representa-tives of Generation 2 worked at research institutions, includ-ing Princeton, University of Chicago, Yale, Stanford, and University of Washington, all of which house leading programs in the geneticists' respective areas. Their G3 students thus com-pleted their training in elite programs. These students had estab-lished their own labs, and many had already made significant scientific contributions; however, at their comparatively early career stage, most were working at less prestigious institutions than their mentors. Figure 1.1 shows the sample, in schematic form, highlighting the lineage structure. There were thirty-six participants: thirteen from the cell biology lineage, eleven from the medical genetics lineage, and twelve from the population genetics lineage—twenty-four men and twelve women.

Concerning gender representation, the lineage heads are all male. This reflects the prevalence of men within the leading ranks of science in the historical cohort from which the lineage heads were drawn. In addition, all of the senior scientists who met the study's third sampling criterion for G1s, the training of a cadre of students who went on to become active scientists with students of their own, were male. This was true even though we solicited nominations from scholars in science and gender studies in an effort to identify both male and female candidates. However, one lineage head mentored many successful female scientists, and women comprise 50 percent of Generation 2.

Data were collected in a single, face-to-face, audiotaped interview, about two and a half hours in length, conducted by one or two researchers. The semistructured interview was designed to establish the participant's current guiding values, goals, and practices; key formative influences on his or her development as a scientist; the impact of the most influential person during the participant's formal training; and any obstacles or pressures encountered during the participant's career that may have caused his or her goals, commitments, and practices to evolve after the relationship with the mentor. We then investigated what the participant sought to convey to the next generation, and how he or she did so—in other words, the interviewee's own practices as a mentor. Finally, we probed for societal concerns and community involvements extending beyond the domain of genetics. Efforts were made to design an interview schedule that did not influence participants to describe their own approach to science in terms of the expected mentor's

Figure 1.1 Sample Structure for the Three Mentoring Lineages

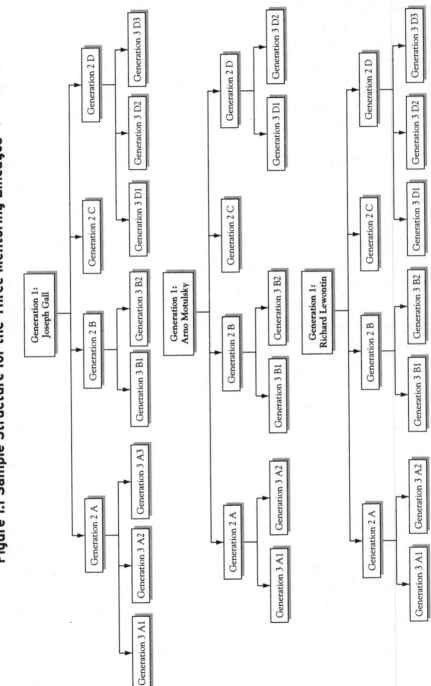

values and practices. Interviewees first described their own approach to science and only afterward were asked about formative influences, including the relationship with the individual who was a member of the lineage.

This research design allowed expanding dramatically the scope of previous studies of mentor-student relationships, by permitting us to compare: the memes possessed and inherited by different generations within a lineage; the memes passed down in one lineage but not another; and for selected labs, the different perceptions of the same training environment held by mentors and students. In addition, we were able to draw on the testimonies of multiple students to inform us about the values, practices, and teachings of a single mentor, enhancing the accuracy of our findings.

This was a purposive sample, focusing on best-case examples of what we call *good workers*, who, in addition, had trained a cadre of students and therefore had the opportunity to pass their memes down. In addition, we selected former students who had significant exposure to the lineage heads. However, we did not know the nature of any given relationship or the extent to which a lineage head's memes would or would not be transmitted to subsequent generations. We speculated that some of their memes would be passed on to their own students, but we did not know which ones, and we had no evidence about the likelihood of transmission to a third generation. We hoped that selecting best-case lineage heads would make it possible to address several key questions about the mentoring process, if observed: How, or by what pathways or means, were memes—especially those encouraging good work—passed down to subsequent generations? What were the characteristics of mentoring relationships that fostered the transmission of memes? Each interview was coded and analyzed with these questions in mind. In the chapters that follow, we report what was learned.

We give a full description of how the study was conducted in the appendixes. We provide a brief overview of the coding and data analysis in Appendix A, the interview protocol in Appendix B, and the coding scheme in Appendix C. Here, we limit ourselves to noting that a meme counted as "transmitted" from one generation to the next if an interviewee explicitly stated or clearly suggested that his or her possession of the meme had been influenced by the mentor within the lineage.

Before proceeding to the book's organization, it would be helpful to clarify two points that may invite misunderstanding. First, do we mean to imply that virtues and values, or other memes, are inherited in the same way as eye or hair color? No. The language of *transmission, memes,* and *inheritance* is not meant to suggest a unidirectional process in which the individual passively receives values, beliefs, and knowledge. The terminology is useful shorthand, making it possible to refer collectively to the diverse kinds of intergenerational inheritance; it also highlights the intimate relationship between the proximal interactions of mentor and student on the one hand, and the broader sweep of sociocultural evolution on the other. In fact, the study's findings are consistent with constructivist perspectives on social learning, such as that of the Russian psychologist Lev Vygotsky (for example, Vygotsky, 1978). Such theories recognize that learning is an inherently social-interactive process, and the learner actively constructs the knowledge and attitudes that he or she acquires.

Second, are we suggesting that an individual's approach to professional life—especially the moral compass that guides conduct in ambiguous or difficult situations—is traceable solely or primarily to the influence of mentors encountered during graduate or professional training? Again, the answer is no. Early experiences within the family and community undoubtedly play an important role, particularly in shaping basic values. Mentors encountered before and after entry into the profession may also be formative, and many practitioners have multiple influential mentors during the course of their training years.

The Organization of the Book

Part One of the book (Chapters Two through Four) presents case studies of each of the three lineages. Part Two (Chapters Five through Seven) summarizes what the interviews revealed about the transmission of knowledge, practices, and values across generations, drawing on all three of the lineages simultaneously. Finally, Part Three (Chapters Eight and Nine) summarizes the key lessons learned and draws out some of the implications for practitioners and researchers. We here briefly describe each chapter.

Part One

Like E. O. Wilson, Stephen J. Gould, and other scientists who have communicated the wonders of nature and the joys of scientific discovery to non-scientists, Joseph Gall is a naturalist—he has been drawn to the natural world as long as he can remember. His career as a biologist grew organically out of this life-long passion, and he continues to conduct his own experiments today, a rarity in a time when most successful scientists leave the bench by midcareer to become lab administrators. He is a model of professional integrity, fairness, and honesty. Facilitated by his mentoring, many of his students, including a remarkable number of women, became professors at elite universities. Moreover, so did many of *their* students. How did the process of intergenerational influence occur? Was Gall's integrity and love of science visible to his students? Did he actively try to kindle a passion for science or a sense of integrity in his students? How did he foster the development of successful female scientists in an era when men dominated the discipline? A description of the Gall lineage is presented in Chapter Two.

Arno Motulsky is an emeritus professor of medical genetics and genome sciences. From his origins in prewar East Prussia, Motulsky spent his youth evading Nazi capture. When he and his family finally reunited in the United States, he pursued a career in medicine with a sense of maturity and mission beyond his years. When he was subsequently offered the opportunity to create a program in medical genetics, Motulsky did not hesitate to embark on a career in the still little-known field. He was attracted by the opportunity to work on cutting-edge scientific problems while at the same time applying scientific insights to the treatment of individual patients. In his work, he has bridged the gap between science and medicine and has taken seriously the ethical charge to use scientific knowledge to benefit the lives of individuals. Motulsky is an exemplary physician-scientist. How did Motulsky's values and practices influence the students and medical fellows who worked with him, as well as a third generation of physician-scientists? What was the impact of his extraordinary life and example on his students? Was he able to pass on the deep concern for humanity that has characterized his approach? Such questions are addressed in the context of a portrait of the Motulsky lineage in Chapter Three. In addition, this case study examines how a former student not only emulates the values and practices of the lineage head, but also modulates and adds to them.

One of the world's leading evolutionary geneticists and professor of zoology at Harvard University is Richard Lewontin, whose brilliance as a scientist has been matched only by his reputation as a social critic with a Marxist outlook and socialist values. While earning his doctorate in the 1950s, Lewontin was mentored by the leading population geneticist of his time, Theodosius Dobzhansky. The Russian-trained Dobzhansky was known as a moralist—someone who "knows what is right" and has strong moral convictions. Lewontin enjoyed a privileged relationship with Dobzhansky and regarded him as a moral exemplar in many respects. Lewontin's socialist politics were tightly linked to a set of distinctive professional practices. How did his political views influence his practices as a mentor? Did he influence his students' political views, their approach to science, or both? Chapter Four provides a portrait of the Lewontin lineage and a vivid illustration of students' selective responsiveness to an admired mentor's characteristics—in this case, political and scientific beliefs.

Part Two

What values and practices characterize the three exemplars of good work, and to what extent have any of these memes survived them, shaping future generations? Each lineage head discussed practices, values, or goals that the other two senior scientists did not. In Chapter Five, we explore whether these memes differentially characterized the lineage that a scientist headed, which would provide evidence that signature variants of good work can be propagated through multiple generations of mentor-student relationships. In addition, we examine whether memes supporting good work that are shared by all three lineage heads have come to characterize all of the lineages. If so, it may be that some principles of good work are more universally supported through mentoring relationships. In this chapter, we also identify which memes were transmitted most often and which least often, and discuss the implications for the perpetuation of professional excellence and ethics.

How are values and practices taught and learned? In Chapter Six, we describe the pathways by which mentors influence their students. The popular image of mentoring is that of an intense, sustained, multifaceted dyadic interaction, as exemplified by Niels Bohr's exchanges with the young scientists who visited his institute. In the apprenticeships we studied, mentors interacted with their students, but to a great extent the Bohr model did not pertain. Through what means, then, did good mentoring occur? Chapter Six describes the key pathways by which values, knowledge, and practices were transmitted from one generation to the next.

Mentoring relationships can be fraught with challenges. What were the most common relationship difficulties that we discovered in our sample? We discuss these in Chapter Seven, before turning to the characteristics of positive relationships. We found that successful mentoring relationships were facilitated by students' initial admiration for their mentors. Beyond this power of attraction, the defining quality of positive mentor-student relationships was support, which proved to be multi-faceted in graduate school. This chapter describes the multiple dimensions of support found in strong mentoring relationships, drawing on the perspectives of both mentors and apprentices.

Part Three

In Chapter Eight, we reflect on some of the book's central findings and discuss questions and issues that they raise. We consider the evidence for whether mentors can have a significant impact on the professional values and practices of their students, and if so, how. Also, each mentor possesses a signature approach to science. Do these values and practices survive across multiple generations? What conclusions can be drawn concerning pathways of influence and the characteristics of mentoring relationships?

We end by suggesting in Chapter Nine how the lessons drawn might be used by prospective mentors, mentees, and their institutions in the sciences and other professions. For example, all successful professionals face extraordinarily heavy demands on their time. How can they make the time to mentor well without burning out? We also identify some of the most promising lines of inquiry that the investigation opens up. The lineage heads are exceptional scientists and mentors. Does this mean that good mentoring is the sole province of paragons? The stakes are high, and the role of mentoring is potentially great for the teacher, the student, and the future of the professions.

Reflecting on Mentoring

We hope this book will inspire those responsible for graduate and professional education to appraise systematically their own practices and examine reflectively the type of mentoring that is worth embracing. Were one's practices consciously chosen and critically examined, or did they develop haphazardly, outside awareness? What conditions and motives drive one's work with students? Are one's practices effective? Our hope is that readers will come to see mentoring as more than an assumed skill and an invisible process, and will instead treat it as a crucial and creative endeavor benefiting from analysis, refinement, and dialogue among practitioners. We also hope this book will help students appreciate, and take into account, how a prospective mentor may lastingly shape the kind of professional they become over and above the knowledge, skills, and resources conferred on them.

Part One

THREE EXAMPLES OF GOOD MENTORING

Together, Chapters Two through Four form a set. Each chapter presents the case study of a different lineage, beginning with the story of an exemplary scientist-mentor and the approach to the practice of science that is associated with him, and then describing how this approach has been continued by later generations. The first half of each chapter profiles the senior scientist—the lineage head. It describes his life and career and his scientific values and practices. Each of the three profiled scientists proved to have a clear vision of what constitutes important scientific research. All three are viewed by former students as models of scientific integrity. Each has demonstrated a concern for social welfare that extends beyond his contribution to scientific knowledge. After briefly describing the lineage head as scientist, each chapter turns to his role as an advisor, considering the training environment established by the scientist, the kind of students he has attracted, and the kind of apprenticeship he has provided.

We conceptualize the lineage head's impact on students in terms of the fate of values and practices defining his particular manifestation of good work. The second half of each chapter describes the transmission of the senior scientist's values and practices across subsequent generations. It suggests the fate of the scientist's positive legacy to date and the pathways by which it was transmitted. For each lineage, we describe the experiences of former students (G2s). Then a case study of one G2, and that student's students (G3s), is summarized to render the intergenerational processes more vivid and clear. A given G2 might hand down to students some or all of the values and practices absorbed from the lineage head. He or she might also transmit memes other than the mentor's—ones possessed prior to the apprenticeship or acquired outside it, for example, in the course of the early career. Each of the G3s in turn might absorb some or all of these memes when exposed to them in the G2's lab.

Case studies allow us to place memes and their means of transmission within the context of the lineage head's biography, and his impact on science as a community or social field, as contrasted with his impact on science as a domain of knowledge. When we conducted this study, we interviewed the senior scientists first. Each unhesitatingly articulated both the distinctive kind of scientist he was, and what he wanted students to absorb in his lab. The divergence of histories and personalities that gave rise to their distinctive approaches to science was quite striking. We then interviewed alumni of each lineage head's lab who had stayed in science. Would they even mention the lineage head as a formative influence on their development as scientists? We wondered if the students would see the lineage heads differently than the G1s saw themselves, and whether alumni of the same lab would tell complementary or conflicting stories.

The case approach makes it possible to unfold what we learned, and convey the distinctive *Rashomon* quality of these interviews. For all three lineages to some extent, and most systematically and explicitly in the initial case study presented in

Chapter Two, the lineage head's intentions are compared to the students' experiences, drawing on all of the G2 interviews; how the lineage head perceived the lab is compared to the narratives of his students; and we consider whether the multiple G2s offered compatible portrayals. In addition, while any one of the lineages alone might tell a good story, only by examining several is it possible to observe a range of distinctive approaches to good work and good mentoring. Together these three cases begin to provide a sense of the commonalities and also the variations in the transmission of excellence that evolve in a profession.

At the most general level, an established scientist has forged three relationships: a way of using and contributing to the domain of scientific knowledge, a way of participating in the scientific community or field, and a way of relating to the broad sociocultural ends that the occupation was meant to serve. Scientists differ not only in how they do each of these, but also in how they divide their attention and energies among these three broad relationships. One general question to consider in Part One is how each of the lineage heads in his work as a scientist relates to the domain, the field, and larger ends, and the relative importance each of these holds for him. A companion question is which aspects of the mentor's way of being a scientist were absorbed by students and, later, by those students' students. Some of the memes that survived into subsequent generations were shared by the three lineages; others differed.

At the same time that the chapters introduce key memes, they jointly describe how memes evolve transgenerationally through the actions of mentor and student. With respect to the mentor's role, a few major means of influencing students become evident in all three chapters. Several other patterns recur across lineages that depended on the student. They include preexisting, shared interests that the student brought to the table, as well as the student's admiration for the mentor, both of which served to catalyze mentoring relationships; selective absorption, or absorption of some of the mentor's memes but not others;

putting their own twist or variation on the mentor's memes in actual practice; and modeling completely new memes for their own students.

Two procedural notes are needed. First, except for the three lineage heads, pseudonyms are employed to protect the identities of the individuals described in the book. Second, our focus is primarily on individuals in these chapters. When we refer to a lineage head's G2s or G3s as a group, we follow existing conventions for qualitative research and employ terms like *some* and *most* to indicate the generality of a pattern. In these cases, *some* indicates that a pattern characterizes half or less of those interviewed, and *most* signifies that the pattern applies to more than half.

In sum, the chapters in Part One describe three exceptional scientists in order to portray with some richness of detail what good work and good mentoring look like; the aim is not to describe three typical senior scientist-advisors. Furthermore, each chapter deliberately singles out a sublineage headed not by a randomly selected interviewee from the senior scientist's lab, but instead by a scientist who told us that the lineage head had played a major formative role and was someone whom he or she has tried to emulate. The aim is to portray concretely what it looks like when memes are transmitted with high fidelity from mentor to student down through multiple generations. In short, our approach was to draw on positive case studies of the processes of interest, not necessarily representative ones. In Part Two, we place the sublineages within a broader context by looking more panoramically at both strong and weak patterns with respect to the transmission of memes and dynamics of mentor-student relationships, though even there our sample necessarily emphasizes positive interactions and examples.

2

THE NATURALIST

One well-recognized type of scientist is the naturalist (Wilson, 1994): the individual whose participation in the scientific enterprise arises out of, and remains grounded in, an intense and enduring love of the natural world. The cytogeneticist Joseph Gall is such a scientist. In an era when technological advances and the rise of big science encourage senior researchers to insert legions of graduate students and postdocs between themselves and the phenomena they study, the naturalist is a vanishing breed. In his seventies when interviewed for this project, Gall continues to be that rarest of creatures: a senior scientist still working daily at the bench and conducting his own experiments. In the process of satisfying his curiosity about nature, he has distinguished himself as an exemplar of what we have called good work, uniting scientific excellence with ethical responsibility.

In terms of creative accomplishment, Gall has been "continually at the forefront of [nuclear biology], asking important questions and finding unexpected answers" (Pardue, 1998, p. 208). He has been a leader in modern cell biology, particularly the study of chromosomes and nucleic acids, codeveloping the method of in situ hybridization that researchers use throughout the world. Elected to the prestigious National Academy of Sciences and American Academy of Arts and Sciences, honored with a special achievement Lasker Award, former president of both the Society for Developmental Biology and the American Society of Cell Biology, Gall has progressed from discovery to discovery across the course of a long research career.

Many of these discoveries were made collaboratively with his graduate students or postdocs, and it is in his role as lab head that Gall's ethically responsible practices are most evident. In 1996, the American Association for the Advancement of Science (AAAS) recognized his exceptional record as a graduate advisor with the Mentor Award for Lifetime Achievement. Gall mentored more than thirty women—in addition to many men—during his career. Moreover, women who trained in his lab went on to thrive professionally. Many of them teach and direct labs at elite research institutions, including Princeton, Brown, Yale, Duke, and MIT. They have made major contributions to their domains, and the alumni of their own labs include at least one Nobel laureate. Three have gone on to join Gall as members of the National Academy of Sciences. What makes this particularly remarkable is the historical period during which it occurred. Gall became a lab head in 1953, a time when the number of women training to be scientists was small and those seeking a career in science encountered discrimination and even sexual harassment.

Gall's equal treatment of women and men in his lab has been the most often noted demonstration of his character, but he is known more generally within the field for his quiet yet consistently principled conduct. In writing about him, former students lauded his scientific achievements but also his "impeccable integrity" (Endow & Gerbi, 2003, p. 3849). In announcing Gall's receipt of the Lasker, a distinguished colleague noted admiringly that Gall's work is carried out with "a sheer joy at the pleasures of discovery" and with "the highest standards of integrity, respect for others, [and] genuine modesty" (Carnegie Institution, 2006).

Development and Formative Influences

This brief sketch invites the question: To what experiences does Gall ascribe formative significance when asked to account for his deep love of the work that he does, his sustained creativity, and his marked commitment to equality and fairness?

Although interpersonal influences played a supporting role, Gall is like many other naturalists in tracing his scientific life to an unmediated relationship with the world of nature itself and only later with the associated domain of formal scientific knowledge. The relationship had early origins, of the kind celebrated by the noted biologist E. O. Wilson in his 1994 autobiography, *Naturalist.* There, Wilson echoed Rachel Carson's (Carson & Pratt, 1965) sentiments, contending that "hands-on experience at the critical time, not systematic knowledge, is what counts in the making of a naturalist. Better to be an untutored savage for a while, not to know the names or anatomical detail. Better to spend long stretches of time just searching and dreaming" (Wilson, 1994, p. 12). As a young child, Wilson explained, the naturalist-to-be greets the world with a sense of wonder and intense curiosity; the initial connection is sensory rather than symbolic. In this vein, Gall reported, "When people ask me how I got interested in biology, I usually say, 'I don't really know.' Because I've never *not* been interested in biology." He explained, "In fact, some of my very first memories are of poking around in ponds and collecting frogs and frog eggs, which I still work on, actually. Insects and almost anything that I could retrieve from outside. So that just has always fascinated me from the very beginning."

One influence was growing up in rural Virginia. Gall's father, an attorney in Washington, D.C., had his roots in the rural South and missed the countryside. He settled the family fifty miles outside Washington on a working farm, which provided Gall with woods and streams to explore at will. A second influence was a supportive family. Gall's interest "could probably have been nipped in the bud." Instead, his parents, especially his mother, smoothed the way through what they chose not to do as well as what they chose to do. His mother never interfered, allowing him to "keep anything in the house or raise anything I wanted to." More affirmatively, she was personally interested and helped him, making nets by hand when he was collecting insects. As his interest in nature grew, he asked his parents to buy him books. He and his older brother built a telescope. When his reading led him to become intrigued by cells, he was able to prevail on his father to buy a research microscope despite a wartime embargo on optical instruments.

Equipped with a microscope, he prepared slides, "looking at everything under the sun." Peering through the microscope was a daily activity. For reasons that he cannot fully explain, he was fascinated with visual patterns: "I couldn't get enough information about how things were put together.... I've always been interested in patterns and how things are organized." The root impulse, it seems, was the basic human desire to make meaning: "fundamentally, it's wanting to see order in the world around you."

Much like his love of nature, Gall also traced his strong moral compass to early roots. However, while his family played a secondary role in the formation of his scientific interests, supporting a passion that seemed to emerge on its own, he saw his parents' example as the key source of his attitudes toward other people. Later experiences were formative only in that they helped him recognize a set of standards that he had tacitly absorbed during childhood. "I think my mother probably treated every single person that she ever met equally," he said. He did not realize that this "isn't the way most people behave" until after he left home; it simply had never occurred to him before. "I think that rubbed off on me a lot," he concluded about his parents' conduct. "That sort of thing to me is extremely important—how you interact with other people." The stance he unconsciously acquired was egalitarian and open-minded: "You still have to fight constantly to treat people individually as equals, but until I find out that there's something particularly distasteful or evil about some person, I give them the benefit of the doubt."

In contrast to the early origins of his interest in science and his attitudes about interpersonal conduct, Gall portrays his formal path into a scientific career in terms of naiveté, external influences, and convenience—even drift. He played little role in selecting the college that he attended (Yale); adults in his life orchestrated his enrollment. He "didn't even know that research biology was a career" until well into college, thinking instead that people interested in science became doctors. He stayed on for graduate work at Yale chiefly because he had not explored other programs. He could not identify any particular individual whose influence on his approach to science rivaled that of his own direct experience or family background.

Gall's graduate school advisor was the developmental biologist Donald Poulson, a Yale professor who had been supportive during Gall's college years. Gall called Poulson's influence "very important," but he traced only one of his own signature characteristics to him: the willingness to grant independence to students. "I think that one of the good things was that he let his students work on anything they wanted to, so I did certainly pick that up as a trait," Gall said. "As far as I'm concerned, my students can work on anything they want to, as long as it's within some broad outline of things that I have some competence in."

The latitude Gall encountered was a good fit. He explained, "I certainly got a lot from him but maybe just one measure of my independence was that my thesis had nothing to do with anything that he'd ever worked on." The inventory of other lessons learned was modest: having patience, being sure to publish one's work (a lesson learned from Poulson's negative example; that is, one "should not *not* publish the way he did"), and examining prior work on a topic before beginning research in the area. And Gall only partially endorsed the latter advice, recognizing that a fresh perspective may be crucial to discoveries and noting that familiarity with prior work sometimes discouraged him from setting out on a topic at all, especially if the prior work had not been fruitful. All in all, Gall concluded that he was influenced by "the sum total, the mix of all the people that I was exposed to in my graduate work, more than my advisor in and of himself."

In stark contrast to the career path of most research scientists today, Gall charted his course after college by taking the freedom to pursue research as his lodestar. He was a professor at the University of Minnesota by age twenty-four, eager to establish his own lab, having completed his Ph.D. in three years. Ten years later, he relocated to Yale, largely because it was more research oriented. At age fifty-five, he left Yale for the Carnegie Institution, partially because administrative responsibilities at Yale increasingly competed with research for his time and energy.

Gall contrasted the good fortune that he has experienced with the challenges faced by colleagues in other countries and of other generations. In this context, his path has been very smooth: "I have never been to war. I have never been in a warring country. I have never been under an oppressive government. I have never not had enough money. I have never not had something to eat." Rather than taking this for granted, however, he ascribed to it an enduring sense of responsibility: "I always feel like I have had things so easy that to have done anything less than I have done would have been not worthy."

Gall as a Mature Scientist

Gall exemplifies the creative research scientist. First and most obvious is his intrinsic motivation as a researcher: love of science is the strong thread of continuity that has run through his life since childhood. Gall summarized that "the thing that drives me ultimately is the awe and the wonder of the whole thing out there" and the curiosity that it inspires: "What makes science, I think, so enjoyable, is to continue to view it as something new every day." The more you study, he said, the more you realize that "the things you take the most for granted are really the most amazing and complicated, and almost impossible to fathom. And it's just that wanting to know how things work, I guess, that's what keeps me going." Gaining knowledge has been the goal for him, not fame or fortune. Nor has he been motivated by the promise of wealth, especially at the expense of science. He never sought a patent for in situ hybridization, though a former student, who admired Gall's attitude that science should be "pure," observed that the patent would have made him a millionaire. Unlike so many of his contemporaries and younger colleagues, Gall cannot envision straddling academia and industry. In his mind, to do so would be to "serve two masters": "If somebody gets a product that they're busily marketing and so forth, and advertising and so forth, it's really hard for them to keep the sort of unencumbered attitude toward their own research."

Of course, gaining knowledge may have been his goal, but at its frontiers, scientific research is an uncertain enterprise. A problem may prove insoluble, or somebody else may solve it first. Gall underlined that, for him, "enjoying the process of doing the science as opposed to being focused only on the goal is very important." It has meant that "I can work on an experiment for three or four months, and if it doesn't work, well, that doesn't matter too much to me because it's been fun doing it." The process itself holds several rewards. One is physical: "I was dissecting insects when I was fifteen, and I'm still dissecting things and still enjoying it…. the manipulation of the material. This is why I have to really have some of the laboratory experience, because these literally physical things are what give me the pleasure." A second reward is aesthetic: "To go into a dark room and look through the microscope and see these glowing objects which may be moving around or may be stationary, and in different colors—it's a video game, if you will. It's just beautiful." Separate from the experiment's outcome, it is "a pleasurable experience" to sit at a microscope, and he can do so for hours at a stretch.

In the language of psychology, research has been a flow activity (Csikszentmihalyi, 1990) for Gall, a pursuit affording experiences of complete immersion, or flow. In it, he discovered a complex set of challenges that called on capacities he deeply enjoyed exercising. He becomes thoroughly absorbed in the challenges and opportunities of research, much as a tennis player becomes caught up in a close match or an avid musician gets lost in an exhilarating jam session. Gall's effectiveness at the bench and capacity to enjoy the process of doing research have been facilitated by a prodigious "ability to concentrate, not to be distracted." He acknowledged, "I can probably be very disconcerting to other people in the degree to which I can concentrate on something and not pay too much attention to what's going on around me." This capacity to control one's own attention, rather than letting it be buffeted by external forces, is a hallmark of people consistently able to enjoy deep absorption, or flow.

Perhaps surprisingly given how much Gall emphasizes the intrinsic rewards of science, he holds strong views about the social context of scientific research. Although he is lyrical about the solitary pleasures of scientific activity, he stressed that the activity is ultimately meaningful only because science is a social enterprise. Science's interpersonal and wider social dimensions have been "extraordinarily important" to him. As he put it, he would not pursue research "on a desert island by myself." Viewing science as a collective effort, he is committed to cooperating and sharing information with other researchers, practices increasingly eschewed by the ambitious.

Colleagues have called Gall a "scientist's scientist" (Endow & Gerbi, 2003, p. 3849). Alongside his love of research, he has exemplified both ethical conduct and excellence in the domain of science: scientific honesty and integrity, on the one hand; rigor and high standards for excellence and originality, on the other. While the other values are held by those doing good work in many vocations, esteeming originality is rarer. Even within science, originality may mean priority, that is, being the first one to solve a problem widely viewed as important. Gall took a different tack. "The more people that are working exactly on a particular project, the more obvious it is. It's not really novel," he asserted. "I'd rather find [a] direction and then pursue it until other people start working in that, and then move on to something else."

To do so, he has drawn on encyclopedic knowledge and a host of uncommon skills. Students recalled with awe how he devised an incisive pilot experiment when entering a new area or constructed a complex instrument himself when he could not procure one. As an early autodidact, he "always had confidence that anything I wanted to do in the field, I could probably do by myself. Obviously, I can't," he hastened to add. "One very quickly learns your limitations. Nevertheless, I think it's always good if you start off with the attitude that there aren't too many limitations."

While valuing expertise, originality, and integrity like many other exemplary scientists, Gall's work has been characterized by a breadth of focus that is unusual today. It stems from his early love of nature, coming to science through his own explorations rather than being initiated by teachers or textbooks. Fascinated by pattern and structure, it is the "union of the cytological, morphological, and molecular that I'm interested in—and always have been," he explained. This focus is far broader and more context sensitive than the dominant molecular biology paradigm, which concentrates on chemical reactions in a solution. "You really don't know about a cell just from knowing what reactions take place in it," he contended. "You have to know where they occur and where they don't occur, and how they interact with other reactions."

Gall learned to identify and use the experimental organism ("model system") that is best suited to a research question rather than automatically adopting the most commonly used system. "Having looked at, or dissected, or been familiar with, or read about virtually every kind of animal and plant there is at an early age," he explained, "when there came a question of which one might be useful for some particular purpose, I would know something about the properties of those animals or plants." As we will see, Gall's signature breadth also underlies the most distinctive features of his approach to training students. In an era of specialization, he has preserved his interest "in all aspects of the natural world. I really don't like to draw sharp lines between fields, or even between really very different fields." In fact, he said, "one thing I really would not like to be thought of is a narrow specialist, with one interest that was just sort of an idée fixe that I had to manage for some reason in my own life." He acknowledged, "There's a tension between having to focus in order to make any contribution in a particular field, and being so broad that you simply master everything that everybody else has already learned." Still, he explained, "I like to keep as broad a scope as possible."

While Gall's interests within science are broad, his energies appear to center on the natural world rather than extending widely beyond it. His favorite avocation, for example, is collecting books on the history of science. In his interview, Gall gave the impression that science has always been at the core of his life.

Training the Next Generation

Running a lab and training students has been an integral part of Gall's scientific life. Still, when he received the AAAS Mentor Award, it "came as a big surprise." It was also "a big pleasure." He told us, "It's nice to get recognized for something that you weren't working for."

One contributor to this unexpected honor was historical circumstance. Gall's lab produced a striking number of successful female scientists during a period when women with professional aspirations faced matter-of-fact gender discrimination and sexual harassment. A mentor can actively do good; he or she can also effect a great deal of good by not inflicting harm. At the time, Gall stood out partly because of what he did not do.

Gall related, "In the case of the women, they've been very frank—particularly afterwards—telling me that they wanted to go to a lab where they were sure they were not going to be sexually harassed. It's that simple." In the past and, he suspects, still today, this has been "much more of a problem than people are willing to admit." Gall was no activist. However, he was an individual of great personal integrity whose preexisting ethic of equality found consistent expression in gender-blind selection, treatment, and placement of students. This fact came to be common knowledge among students in his department. He returned from a sabbatical to find three top female students camped at his office door to petition for admission to his lab. He accepted them all. In another time and place, his even-handed conduct might have been expected or taken for granted. Because of the prevailing culture, however, it was a significant virtue, making female students more likely to seek him out.

Within the scientific elite, mentors and students often select each other through a process of mutual search, as documented in sociologist Harriet Zuckerman's (1977) account of the many mentor-student linkages among Nobel Prize winners in science. She found that both prospective mentors and prospective apprentices engage in an active search for "scientists of talent" with whom to work. In the Gall case, criteria beyond talent entered into the process, on both sides. If Gall's reputation for treating students equally was an important reason that female students sought entry to his lab, he had selection criteria as well. He looked for a set of characteristics that mirrored his own motivations and qualities. As he put it, "I think I really look for the things in my students that I see in myself."

What has mattered most to Gall is a student's motivation for doing science. He has sought, first of all, the same strong intrinsic motivation that has driven him: "I want students who are interested in the subject. I want students who can't put a problem down until they get the answer." He favorably compares the resulting doggedness with sheer brilliance as a foundation for scientific accomplishment. He has also sought students eager to pursue their own independent research—the kind of student he was, exploring an area unrelated to his advisor's research. Finally, he has been reluctant to admit students into his lab who were careerist rather than intrinsically motivated.

Gall's selection criteria overlap with the qualities he has attempted to nurture once students are admitted to his lab. He said: "I guess you always think that the most important things [to pass on] are your own attitudes, obviously." Predictably Gall has most consciously attempted to cultivate the orientation toward enjoyment of the research process itself, or flow, that has been central to his own lifelong experience as a researcher. He explained: "I think that in the long run, if people don't like to do what they're doing, it's going to be a disaster. So I do try to emphasize this issue of process, of enjoying what you're doing because of what you're doing, not because of monetary reward or fame or whatever."

No less important is encouraging scientific honesty and integrity. Indeed, these are so important to Gall that they nearly went unremarked in his inventory of the things he seeks to pass on to students: "I'm assuming intellectual honesty, absolutely no hanky-panky as far as data. Those just go without saying." In the context of scientific research, integrity has specific meanings that must be learned. For example, "There is no shading of data. We're not out there to prove a hypothesis, but rather to find out what the actual best hypothesis is. And if it requires more data, we get more data."

Gall also has hoped his students would adopt his practices of cooperation and collaboration. "I have to keep coming back to competition versus cooperation. My students, I'm sure, would tell you this," he asserted. "I always tell my students that you are far better off to cooperate and collaborate, and get your information out quickly to other people, even just a network of people, rather than being secretive." He has always felt that experimental materials, if not unpublished results, should be shared: "If a student makes an antibody or something, even if we haven't published on it, I insist that we share it with other people who want to use it." He urges both collegiality inside one's lab and openness with researchers outside it. Within his own lab, he deliberately created a cooperative, collaborative social system.

Gall has passed on the memes that he values in three main ways. The first, which he was very conscious of, is modeling, or as he put it, "guiding by example." The pedagogy aligns with a stance toward graduate training that is "a little bit laissez-faire." He elaborated: "I think my major function is to work with [students] enough that they see how I work. I'm sufficiently self-confident to think that the way I work has something right about it." Guiding by example has been more compatible with his introverted nature than browbeating or cheerleading. The use of modeling has been supported by Gall's active presence in the lab, which has made his practices and enactment of values continually visible to his students.

In terms of the lab environment, Gall has also passed on memes by the way that he organizes his lab and the culture that he fosters in it. Dozens of graduate students and postdoctoral fellows have passed through the Gall lab over the years. He has maintained a fairly small lab by current "big science" standards, with a mix of graduate students and postdocs from the United States and beyond. At Yale, students had offices, while the lab itself was a common space. Gall worked alongside the students in the lab; his own focused concentration encouraged a quiet atmosphere. Gall was quite private and rather formal early in his career; for instance, only after their graduation did he invite students to call him by his first name. Still, the lab was not overly solemn. Gall fostered a harmonious climate. Many of the students also joined Gall for lunch each day in the cafeteria. They recalled the lunches as congenial occasions, with talk ranging across many topics.

Selectively admitting intrinsically motivated students appears to have favored a basic alignment of attitude among lab members. Students are permitted—indeed, expected—to select their own dissertation projects, although Gall suggests a topic if necessary. His willingness to let students work on what they want, rather than expecting them to follow his dictates or follow in his footsteps, replicated the practice of his own advisor.

Students are not assigned parts of a larger project of Gall's design, nor do they typically collaborate with each other. They are never pitted against each other to see who can solve a problem first. The process of inquiry is allowed to unfold rather than being rushed or fraught with anxiety due to intra-lab competition. There is thus no structural disincentive to the open sharing of information and results.

Gall's lab might be thought of as a flow-supportive learning context. Specifically, the social organization of the lab has functioned to protect the enjoyment that comes from the individual scientist's absorption in the work itself. Toward this end, the goal has been to minimize disruptive social relations: to avoid or prevent the kind of situation, all too familiar in the sciences, where the lab is very productive but the people in it very unhappy. The organization of the lab lets students experience ownership and independence.

Finally, Gall has communicated his values to students through exchanges elicited by specific occasions. Although he emphasized his use of modeling, he provides commentary on his conduct or gives guidance and direction when the situation calls for it. If ethically ambiguous situations arise or the ethos that he has sought to create in the lab is breached, he takes a forceful stand: "I really come down hard. If some student even implies that they don't have to do the experiment again because nobody's going to care whether it's right or wrong, I say, 'Well, I care. And you don't do that in my lab.'" As noted earlier, he has also "urged" students to enjoy the research process and "insisted" that they share.

These occasional exhortations are tied to Gall's meritocratic, benign view of the field. He argued that "one of the great luxuries of our society . . . is that virtue *is* rewarded. To a certain extent." In addition to his own success, he felt "my most successful students do have that attitude [that enjoyment of the process matters most]." By the same token, despite acknowledging that "things are getting really a lot worse" with respect to the sharing of information, Gall concluded: "I think in the long run, we gain by [sharing]. We've been scooped a couple of times by people who were unscrupulous, but it hasn't been a major problem over the years."

Distinct from the values and practices that Gall has transmitted, he has also provided sponsorship. He stressed that science is social: "There's the rare hermit that makes important contributions, but largely you're talking about a social organization." In his role as advisor, he thus held that bringing students into the social network is very important: "taking them to meetings, introducing them to people, so that these [scientists'] names are not something just that they've seen in print."

When students graduate, he has invested time in placing them, and it has been the exception who did not get a job. "I spend a lot of time on the letters of recommendation," he noted; "it will take me a day or so to write a letter for a student—or more." In addition, he has advocated for his students: "I take a very active role. I call up people and tell them they should interview this or that person."

At the same time, he has striven to place students in positions where they could succeed rather than in the best available position. The practice follows from his trust that doing the right thing will generally work out for the best—in this case, for the student, the employer, and Gall himself. "I try to be both supportive and completely honest," he told us. "I think the worst thing you can do for your own reputation is to send people to the wrong place and then have people dissatisfied with the result." He explained, "I recommend them to the jobs that I think they'll do well in and will satisfy themselves."

The Experience of Later Generations

Joseph Gall provided a clear description of his practices as a scientist and intentions as a mentor. How does this account match what subsequent generations described?

Gall's Students

We first consider the descriptions that four former students gave of Gall's impact on them while they were training in his lab. What do lab alumni believe they absorbed from him, and how do they think it occurred? To a great extent, their accounts complemented one another, merging into a single story about Gall's approach to science and mentoring; they also suggested how Gall affected students with different personalities, capacities, and expectations.

The later generations' stories reveal several additional themes as well. These include the importance of admiration as a foundation for the transmission of values and practices, the amplification of existing affinities between mentor and student, and lineage membership as an aspect of professional identity that supports the survival of orientations formed during graduate training. They tell, in addition, the story of how a host of successful female scientists emerged from the lab of a male scientist whose agenda never explicitly included women's rights.

One global contributor to Gall's influence on students is the fact that the students felt deep admiration for him as both a scientist and a person. Admiration of Gall as a mentor was also widely shared; he received the AAAS mentoring award because numerous former students nominated him. At the extreme, when asked to describe her ideal image of a scientist, one former student enthused, "I think it would be pretty close to what Joe Gall is. . . . Just being around him; to this day it's the closest I have ever come to being high on drugs.... He has just an amazing mind, and he was a very kind and patient mentor."

Although none reported joining the lab because of it, all four students recalled Gall's unmistakable love of research and viewed its intensity as one of his distinguishing and admirable qualities. They mentioned little of what he said to them about the importance of loving what you do. However, they all vividly recalled how his feelings about science were expressed in concrete, visible behavior. They emphasized how unusual it was that he has continued to work at the lab bench throughout his career. One student recalled that Gall worked in the lab on weekends, although, unlike some other advisors, he never chastised students who did not do so themselves. Another laughingly remembered that when the National Academy of Sciences phoned to inform Gall of his election to that elite society, he was loath to leave the bench to take the call. The students' recollections are all very similar: he simply enjoyed thinking about science and doing it; he genuinely loved working in the lab and could not understand that anyone would want to do anything else; he conveyed excitement about science; he participated as actively in the lab as the students did. One student concluded, "He just loved the feel of science. He loved that and he still loves it. That is a great thing to have as an example."

A cautionary note is needed here. One might expect this enthusiasm for science to be an entirely unalloyed virtue, but from these students' standpoint, it was not. Each mentioned the same unintended negative consequence of Gall's love of the work itself, whether they did so lightly or with some lingering disappointment. The perception was that they had to compete with Gall's own research for his attention. For example, some smiled while remembering meetings in which they found themselves caught up in a discussion of the latest development in his work rather than their own; but at least one was made terribly reluctant to interrupt him with questions. Every individual's attention is finite. Regardless of whether a mentor's attention is occupied with getting ahead in the field or gaining a deeper understanding of nature, it is still drawn away from the student.

It appears that the interviewed students joined Gall's lab already enthusiastic about doing science. While training in his lab therefore may not have instilled intrinsic motivation in the first place, apprenticing there encouraged it, removed obstacles to it, discouraged the competing motive of careerism, and surrounded students with like-minded peers. Above all, it allowed students to see, in their midst, a scientific life being pursued out of a pure passion for science rather than desire for glory or wealth. And it demonstrated to them that it was possible to be very successful professionally by following that path. Scientists have traditionally emphasized enjoyment of the research process itself alongside the other potential, extrinsic rewards of the profession. Nevertheless, it is tempting to distinguish Gall's as a flow lineage given the attraction that science's intrinsic rewards held for him and his former students.

Students may have been intrinsically motivated from the start, but they attributed two sets of values and practices to Gall. One concerned ethical conduct as a scientist. Gall's students acquired research ethics, such as scientific honesty and integrity, and high standards of quality. They saw how general values were applied in work life—for example, what it means to treat others fairly in professional relationships. They were exposed to a code of participation in the scientific enterprise, centering on the importance of cooperation. Gall was perceived by those we interviewed as a moral exemplar, and they felt his example influenced their own conduct. As one former student put it, "I think he has great personal integrity. . . . And working in his lab, even if he wasn't explicit about it, you could see that was true." As a scientist in training, she said, "to learn to do [research] with integrity and to learn that there is great joy in doing it well—and he was a very rigorous scientist—those are great gifts to give people."

Gall's signature breadth of focus also influenced his students. This approach to science was mentioned by former students in terms of breadth of knowledge, vision, and interest; or in terms of the accompanying mentoring practice of dispersing students across divergent research areas; or both. As the field of genetics grows ever more specialized, with labs routinely using a single signature technique and studying a single type of organism, maintaining breadth becomes an increasingly distinctive characteristic. Furthermore, for some members of Gall's lineage, breadth of focus continues to be linked to an older "biologist" tradition. Gall's interest in cellular context also makes his approach more and more distinctive as genetics increasingly is dominated by molecular biology, which tends to decontextualize biological processes. Having had little basis for comparison when they started out, several students emulated this aspect of their mentor's approach to science but later discovered that the approach slowed the progress of their work or encountered criticism from other scientists for pursuing insufficiently focused research programs. It may be in the nature of learning through emulation not to consider seriously a practice's potential drawbacks or possible alternatives.

Enjoyment of the research process, integrity, breadth— these were characteristics that Gall consistently embodied and actively endorsed, and this was evident to his students. The memes that students tended not to absorb tended to be matters of personal inclination: aesthetics, or a love of pattern and beauty, for example. Part of good mentoring may be the capacity to discriminate between the values and practices that one will insist on and those that one will not press. Gall did not tolerate sloppiness with data, for example, but he reluctantly resigned himself to students' personal messiness. Neatness at the bench was much more weakly transmitted within the lineage than research rigor.

The students' recollections confirm remarkably well Gall's account of how training occurred in his lab. All of them said that he taught by example. They also saw the organization of the lab as a significant means of influence: the dynamics created by dispersing students across dissimilar projects, the independence required, the positive lab atmosphere, and the help provided by senior students. Finally, all but one also mentioned learning through verbal exchanges, either specific formative talks or more ongoing interactions about their respective projects.

Students, for the most part fondly, referred to what Gall called his "laissez-faire" mentoring style as "benign neglect." It seems Gall was generally disinclined to provide assistance to students he considered capable of solving their own problems, but he was willing to provide considerable assistance if he judged that it was needed. Mentor and student may not agree about the need for support, however. One student sought and received considerable guidance; another felt she needed assistance but did not receive it. She recognized that Gall probably felt she did not need his help, and this was both a compliment and a reason that she developed independence; still, she went on to be more selective than other students in emulating Gall's approach to mentoring.

Gall's modeling worked well for students. By providing a visible daily example, one student felt Gall convincingly conveyed a way of life—something difficult, if not impossible, to do through means other than modeling. She said, "He was obviously having a good time doing what he was doing, and he made it look like a very good life."

All of Gall's students enjoyed and later sought to emulate another aspect of his mentoring: the cultivation of a positive lab culture. Like most other lab groups, Gall's students "lived in the lab." In his lab, they did so happily. They recalled "camaraderie," "warm respect," and being a "lab family." The atmosphere was "nice." They went on to care about the atmosphere in their own labs and to think about it in these same affective terms. Individual students described wanting to replicate the feeling of family they had experienced, or the "low-key," harmonious, non-cutthroat relations within the lab. One former student speculated that the presence of so many women affected the culture of the lab and, therefore, the environment for students of both genders.

For female students, life in the lab had special significance. Gall's equal treatment of male and female students had a direct impact on the women's outlook and careers—separate from any particular values or practices he sought to transmit to them—by providing a protected space in which to train and a sense of professional opportunity. Former students who are now at midcareer or beyond described a time when there were few female faculty and a male professor could get away with physically harassing a female student in the elevator. Within this context, Gall's conduct stood out. The lab environment was a "safe" one: interactions were focused on science, whether the student was female or male. As one former student put it, "When Joe shut the door to talk about your data, you talked about data." Moreover, Gall's students could feel confident that other faculty would not openly harass them: Gall was a powerful figure within the department and would not have tolerated it.

There was no sense in the lab that male students were better or more able than female students. Working within an egalitarian daily environment made it easier for Gall's female students to resist sexist attitudes when they did encounter them outside the lab. One lab alumnus speculated about the impact it would have if a respected and admired mentor communicated a message of gender inequality: a female student might believe the implied message and lose confidence in herself.

In addition to a sense of safety in the lab, belonging to the Gall lineage gave female students a sense of career possibility. A succession of female students had trained in the Gall lab and had gone on to find good positions after graduation. Former students returned to visit their mentor's lab; lab alumni connected at conferences and other professional gatherings. One student spoke for all of the women when she recalled how important and unusual it was to belong to a lab with "a history of successful women." Just as Gall's example made it clear that one could do work with integrity and joy and still succeed, the example of earlier female students made it clear that a woman could succeed in a male-dominated profession.

It is harder to know how the breadth of focus characterizing the lab affected female students' success. Although Gall is proud that his students branched out to work in many different areas, apprenticeship in Gall's lab still trained the women in his style and general area of science, cell biology. Avoiding big science, races for priority, obvious research problems, and extreme specialization could be a risky choice, adding to female scientists' burdens by equipping them with a marginal style. However, it also may have conferred a survival advantage at the time by positioning them in a niche with a less combative ethos, less pressure to be cutthroat, and more room to succeed on merit rather than due to membership in an old boys' network.

Having come into their own in an egalitarian lab when gender equity was not the norm, three of the four students mentioned that they went on to take active roles in advancing gender equity within their field. Women are now well represented in cell biology. In fact, the primary professional association for cell biology includes a group focusing on women in science, and a number of the group's leaders have come from the Gall lab. Lab alumni also have become advocates for women in their universities, in the academy at large, and within the wider society. Finally, G2s and, in turn, G3s have gone on to stimulate their students' awareness of gender-equity issues.

One of Gall's Students: A Case Study

As Gall's students graduated and established their own labs, training and launching students of their own, the resulting sublineages reflected Gall's influence to different degrees and in different ways. We describe a sublineage that perpetuates with great fidelity the values and practices that Gall embodied across two subsequent generations of scientists. One of Gall's students in Generation 2, Carolyn Hammond (a pseudonym, as are the G3s' names), went on to become an eminent scientist at a leading university. In many ways, she is an heir to Gall's approach to science. Like other G2 labs, hers has produced outstanding scientists. Two former students, Thomas Key and Michael Barton, identified her as one of the central positive influences on their development. A third successful scientist who studied with Hammond, Bill Porter, admired her but did not consider his time in her lab very formative. Accordingly, we do not foreground his experience here, as our focus is on tracing how Gall's positive influence reverberated across multiple generations.

Even before a student joins a lab, two factors may favor a positive experience. First, the bases on which mentor and student select one another make a difference. Gall selected students who were intrinsically motivated and self-directed; Hammond possessed both qualities. She thus was receptive to the model of an engaged scientist that he provided and the intellectual freedom to develop as an independent scientist that he granted. For her part, Hammond wanted to train in Joe Gall's lab partly because of his reputation for decency. This was a consideration for her as a female student. In contrast, many graduate students choose advisors based only on the research area in which they hope to work and the expertise they want to acquire, giving little attention to the personal characteristics of the advisor and the resulting attributes of the lab. Yet the latter factors may strongly influence the quality and impact of the apprenticeship.

Affinity matters as well. When Hammond entered Gall's lab, she already shared several important qualities with him. Along with being intrinsically motivated and independent, both loved nature, valued originality, and found careerism distasteful. Table 2.1 illustrates these affinities, drawing on the interviews with Gall and Hammond. Both scientists were also even-tempered. Many leading scientists share these qualities—but many others do not. The affinities prepared Hammond to thrive in the apprenticeship with Gall, and she did. The experience in Gall's lab supported and fostered inclinations she already possessed.

The Hammond sublineage illustrates how a mentor's considerable contribution to a student's development can coexist with the student's strong self-direction. Hammond and her students were notably independent and self-determining. One might conjecture that this would make them insensitive, even resistant, to a mentor's influence. However, as advisors, neither Gall nor Hammond aimed to create "clones" of themselves—students

Table 2.1 Affinities Between Gall (G1) and Hammond (G2)

Love of Nature	Originality	Anticareerism
G1: Protozoa, insect parts . . . for some reason, I couldn't get enough information about how things were put together. . . . I guess I've always been interested in patterns and how things are organized.	G1: I tend to choose problems that other people are not working on. . . . The more people that are working exactly on a particular project, the more obvious it is. . . . Those are the things that don't really interest me at all. I'd much rather do something where I'm not quite sure what direction we should go.	G1: If a student . . . starts talking about how many papers they are going to get and whether they're going to be first author and blah, blah, blah and all of those questions of priority and that kind of thing, I get nervous, and that turns me off a bit.
G2: I've always been interested in how living things work and are put together, and I guess that was the interest that drove me to [this career].	G2: I'm most interested by things that other people haven't thought a lot about. I would rather be the first person to start something in a field than the person who did the definitive experiment if the definitive experiment had been obvious for some time.	G2: I think that the warning signs for me are somebody who is very concerned about how what they're doing is going to get them up the next rung of the ladder.

who would champion their scientific ideas and extend their line of work. In fact, Gall spoke with obvious pride about students who had gone in their own directions and done important research. What both Gall and Hammond did hope to encourage were values and practices supporting a general approach to science that is holistic and broad, motivated by curiosity, and true to essential scientific values. Hammond and these outstanding students developed approaches to research and mentoring that reflected their own personalities, values, and experiences. At the same time, already sharing some of their mentors' basic qualities, they also clearly responded to the examples set by Gall and, in turn, Hammond.

Hammond absorbed some of her basic practices and values as a scientist from Gall. As a mentor, the things she has sought to transmit to students are ones that she traced back to him. She aims to communicate "the same things that Joe conveyed to me: how to find an interesting problem, how to try to work your way through a problem where the answers are not easy to come by, and how to treat other people well." Barton, Key, and to a lesser extent Porter absorbed Hammond's lessons in their turn.

Some of the qualities Hammond absorbed were shared with other Gall sublineages. Like other G2s, Hammond absorbed Joe Gall's breadth of focus. Key, Barton, and Porter all endorsed this hallmark of Gall's approach to science and ascribed it to Hammond. Other qualities, notably the capacity to examine scientific work critically, were stressed more strongly by Hammond than by other Gall students. Table 2.2 illustrates how these three memes survived across successive generations within the Hammond sublineage.

Hammond also emulated Gall's mentoring practices: "I suppose I think of an apprenticeship as the way Joe Gall ran his lab, and that's the way that I would like to run mine." First, Gall taught "by example—very much." She explained, "The things I remember most are watching how he went about doing things." She learned a powerful approach to research by observing him, supplemented by conversation when needed. She in turn has taught "by example, unless [the students] needed to be talked to," recognizing that when to intervene is "different with every student."

Like Gall, Hammond sought to foster a harmonious lab and influenced the lab culture through her own example. Key

Table 2.2 Influential Qualities Ascribed to Gall by Hammond (G2), and to Hammond by a Former Student, Key (G3)

Honesty and Integrity in Science	Breadth of Research Focus	Critical Analysis
G2: I've never known anybody to have any question about Joe's motives or integrity. He's one of the most respected people I know in the field of cell biology, just because he has such a very even-handed approach to everything.	G2: His lab was unusual in that not only did you have your own problem, everybody in the lab had almost their own organism…. He knows a lot about natural history, and if he was interested in studying something in particular, he could identify an organism that would be good to study…. We had a whole zoo of organisms.	G2: His approach to science was really to question everything, and he taught me to really look at other people's data, and try to look at it in a new light. And try to see whether looking at it in a different way… gave you new insights that you hadn't had before.
G3: Science is just like everything else. There are all sorts of occasions on which the right thing is a little bit harder than the not right thing, in terms of honesty, in terms of forthright-ness, in terms of competition, in terms of helping out other people or whatever, and she was a paragon in these respects.	G3: She was working on several organisms in her lab, as was Joe Gall, her advisor. . . . She had that experience in her training, so all of that's getting passed on to us, saying, "You don't have to stick to one thing. You can work on multiple things." And the outcome is obvious in my lab.	G3: Looking at a result and not believing it and knowing how to criticize it, things like that I learned a lot from her. . . . Critical science— she was very good at looking at results and thinking of five different explanations for it that weren't the obvious ones.

observed: "Trying to approach tense situations with some calmness and perspective is something that's hard to do, but it's certainly a goal that everybody, I think, sets—some more than others maybe. So that's an influence of her. That . . . having decent relationships with people is important." Barton concurred that the Hammond lab was "nice" and "fun" during this period, characterized by cooperation and camaraderie: "When experiments worked, people were all happy. They shared the feeling of success. When there was a problem, people all sort of pitched in. . . . So it was a very communal thing, but everyone respecting the particular projects that the individuals were working on."

Finally, Barton's observation hints at another aspect of Gall's pedagogy that Hammond sought to emulate: the propensity, as she put it, "to dole out projects that people can take and run with in any way that they want." She deliberately adopted Gall's strenuous strategy of spreading students across a broad range of topics to avoid conflict rather than obliging them to work on pieces of a single research project; this went hand in hand with providing freedom and cultivating independence, as it did for Gall. Key explained, "She challenged me just by giving me a vaguely defined project and letting me run with it and [try] to figure out what was worth doing, and she put in all sorts of good advice along the way."

The sublineage also illustrates how new values and practices are introduced with each new generation. In her deep devotion to science, Hammond resembles Gall. Unlike Gall, however, Hammond has strong interests outside science. This impressed Key and Porter enough that both mentioned being affected positively by it. Key's natural tendencies were reinforced: "She was interested in many things, and therefore you could come to her with something interesting, music or art or travel or adventures or whatever, and she was very receptive, as opposed to, 'That's nice. Now let's get back to the experiment!' That's something I have no choice of not doing because that's the way I am naturally too. I have lots of interests. That's very easy to emulate, perhaps to the point of irresponsibility." Thus, alongside continuity across generations, there was also evidence of change. Gall's version of a life in science was both perpetuated and transformed by subsequent generations.

Finally, much more than the other Gall sublineages we studied, Hammond and her students illustrate the potential impact of membership in a scientific lineage or tradition that extends beyond the training period. Hammond observed that her former labmates all had a warm relationship with Gall and with each other. The relationship also extends to "the ones who have come into his lab since then. It's sort of a family network, that's us." The lineage—the clan, in contrast to the peers within the training lab—provided Gall's students with an expanded sense of social community and identity.

The same was true for at least some members of the next generation. Key and Barton saw themselves as part of a tradition that prided itself on adhering to certain values and seeks to transmit these values to the next generation. Both were aware of Hammond's lineage. As Barton put it, "In [her] lab, Joe Gall was the ultimate, great scientist. And she made it very clear that a lot of her differences in attitudes and approach to science [that is, ways she differed from other scientists] were just—that was what Joe's lab was like."

While we have seen that some of Hammond's qualities predated rather than resulted from apprenticing with Gall, the two scientists in some respects represented a unified tradition in the third generation's eyes. While Barton constructed his own distinctive approach to science and to mentoring, he nevertheless stated: "Just hearing about *his* lab and experiencing *her* lab and the way it worked there, to me had a big impact." Furthermore, he described how the foundation for a sense of wider belonging was laid during his graduate years: "If you're from somebody's lab [as Hammond was from Gall's lab], other people from that lab tend to stop in." He recalled, "I started meeting a lot of other people who had been in Joe's lab, and they were all like that. They were incredibly nice, incredibly interesting, the kind of people you sort of want to hang around with. And they all knew a lot. They all seemed to be able to tell you some really interesting little tidbit of biology or whatever you happened to be looking at…. It was just a very positive experience to be around people like this."

Conclusion

Most research on transgenerational intellectual influence has focused on the transmission of a mentor's ideas and theories: the perpetuation of intellectual legacies by students or followers. In contrast, Gall's practices as a mentor have perpetuated a variant of good work and good mentoring across generations, as this chapter has detailed. He has cultivated independence, intrinsic motivation, and broad interests, and he has deliberately encouraged students in his lab to pursue very different projects. Students who passed through his lab absorbed these memes, and as a result, their research agendas after leaving the lab tended to diverge from Gall's and from one another's. Former students recognized this. As Hammond put it, "We haven't just gone off and worked with what Joe was doing; we sort of branched off into our own things. Which isn't surprising given the way he set up our thesis research to begin with."

What Gall did transmit was a consistent vision of good work. A variety of pressures challenge the survival of Gall's approach to scientific practice today, making the influence of successful models all the more important. Small science, active presence in the lab, cooperating rather than competing, sharing information rather than jealously guarding it, eschewing the financial rewards that accompany industry involvement: each of these faces strong extinction pressures. Gall's students were not immune to these pressures. At midcareer, most of the G2s were no longer at the bench full time. The sharing of experimental materials and the fostering of cooperative relations within labs continued, but specific instances of being hurt by sharing information had led one or two G2s to be cautious with other labs. Yet the characteristics Gall did pass on include some that are indispensable for the survival of science. Without integrity, love for the process of discovery, a focus on the advancement of knowledge rather than self, the practice of science would slowly erode. Exposure to Gall's example bolstered core values and practices of good science for his students and, in turn, for at least some of his students' students.

3

THE PHYSICIAN-SCIENTIST

Charles H. Hooker

In his book *The Courage to Teach* (1998), Parker Palmer argues that good teaching is not reducible to formulaic techniques. Rather, it stems from two key personal attributes of the teacher: a healthy sense of identity and a natural sense of integrity, both of which enable good teachers to develop a strong connection with students (see Shernoff, 2001). This characterization of good teaching explains why mentoring has come naturally to Arno Motulsky, professor of medicine (medical genetics) and genome sciences at the University of Washington. Motulsky developed a strong sense of identity and unshakable integrity over the course of his career largely as a result of arduous early life experiences.

Motulsky has worked in population, biochemical, and medical genetics for forty-seven years. Now an active emeritus professor, Motulsky is perhaps best known to geneticists as coauthor of a prominent textbook, *Human Genetics: Problems and Approaches* (Vogel & Motulsky, 1979), and a founder of the field of pharmacogenetics, the study of genetic variation in response to drugs. He has received wide recognition within his field, including the prestigious Allan Award of the American Society of Human Genetics, and his contributions to science have been celebrated through induction into the National Academy of Sciences and the American Academy of Arts and Sciences.

Development and Formative Influences

Motulsky's early years were rife with obstacles and uncertainty, the likes of which few have witnessed and even fewer have successfully navigated. Born into a Jewish family in East Prussia in 1923, Motulsky can recall living in the small town of Fischhausen when he was ten years old. It was around that time that the Nazis began their brutal crusade across Europe. "I remember very well the Nazi environment," Motulsky told us, "such as storm troopers marching through the streets, singing how 'it goes better when the Jew's blood comes from the knife.'" When the anti-Semitism in Fischhausen became intolerable, the Motulskys moved to Hamburg, hoping to find respite in more cosmopolitan surroundings. If they found any solace, it was short lived; soon after, Arno's father was forced to leave Germany ahead of the rest of the family. His father voyaged to Cuba, where he remained until he was eventually able to join his brother in Chicago. Arno, along with his mother, brother, and sister, later attempted to join his father in Cuba. They sailed on the *Saint Louis* with 950 other refugees, but when the ship reached Havana, Motulsky's family and the other emigrants were denied entry and forced to recross the Atlantic.

They were spared a return to Germany by being allowed into Belgium, where Arno went to high school until 1940, when the Germans attacked. At age sixteen, he was arrested by the Belgians as an "enemy alien" and sent to internment camps. "The Germans won the war [against Belgium] very rapidly and sent the Nazis and 'real Germans' back to Belgium," Motulsky recalled. "The Jews were kept in Vichy French internment camps under horrible conditions. I really learned what hunger is." Motulsky eventually was sent to a camp near Marseilles, where he was permitted to visit the U.S. consulate and renew an expired visa (Dreifus, 2008). He was able to get out of the internment camp one week before his eighteenth birthday. With the visa, he made it to Spain and then to Portugal and then finally to the United States by boat. "I was very lucky," he told us. "After my eighteenth birthday, Spain would not have given me a visa to transit since they worried about young men joining the British army. Finding the money to pay for the ship's passage to America was very complicated. So I got out of Europe and in retrospect avoided certain death by the skin of my teeth."

When Motulsky spoke of the effect this experience had on his later scientific career, he could only hint at its impact: "I don't know whether that experience affected my scientific career. Maybe it did, maybe it didn't, but all these happenings matured me very rapidly. I became pretty serious about life. I did not experience a normal adolescence. I lived under horrible anti-Semitic conditions in Germany and then in French internment camps, where there were typhoid epidemics. I saw people dying and found out how hunger distorted human behavior. All this must have had some influence. There is no question that these experiences must have affected me emotionally in general." Motulsky's subsequent development as a researcher, teacher, and citizen once he arrived in the United States suggests that his early experiences—his uncommonly difficult adolescence in unthinkable surroundings—affected his professional career as deeply as they did his personal maturation.

Once Motulsky settled in Chicago, he completed his high school equivalency exam and set out to earn admission to medical school. His family had no money, so he took a job feeding monkeys and rabbits and cleaning cages in a virology lab at Michael Reese Hospital. This would expose him to medical research, he thought. Eventually he was promoted to lab assistant, and the lab director began teaching him basics about science. In the evenings and on weekends, Motulsky enrolled at the Central YMCA College to take classes required for admission to medical school.

As soon as he was accepted to the University of Illinois Medical School, the army drafted Motulsky to serve in World War II. Fortunately, the military needed well-trained doctors for a war of unknown duration, so Motulsky was sent to Yale University for further premedical training. From Yale, the army specialized training program sent him to the University of Illinois Medical School, where he finished at the top of his class.

Following a rotating internship at Michael Reese Hospital, Motulsky was accepted for a residency in internal medicine at that institution, but had to defer a year because of the flood of young physicians coming back from the war. In the interim, he conducted research on the genetic bases of disease and pathology in a hematology lab of the Michael Reese Research Institute.

Following this year of research, Motulsky completed his residency in internal medicine. He had been accepted for another hematology fellowship, this time at Harvard, but the army intervened yet again. Because of the Korean War, Motulsky was called back into service in a diagnostic ward at an Indiana army hospital. For six months, he practiced his clinical skills in Indiana before receiving a transfer to a new hematology research unit at Walter Reed Hospital, the army's principal research hospital in Washington, D.C. At Walter Reed, Motulsky continued his work with sickle cell anemia and encountered mentors who taught him research techniques and emphasized the importance of cultivating clinical skills to apply knowledge gleaned from research in treating patients.

In 1956, three years after his transfer to Walter Reed, the chair of the department of medicine at the University of Washington invited Motulsky to establish a division of medical genetics. Motulsky accepted, but in preparation, he first spent a year studying statistics in the genetics department of the University of London. Equipped with this training, he left a promising career in hematology to embark on a much less certain venture. In our interview, Motulsky noted, "When I first got interested in [medical genetics], there was no well-defined career in the field." However, his early life odyssey had prepared him for uncertainty and pioneering new terrain. Because genetics held such vast potential to combine basic science with contributions to human welfare, he went forward despite the risk. In his words,

A combination of being able to work in a scientific area where you might explain how human heredity works, and at the same time apply such insights to medicine, was highly attractive. It gave me the chance to do scientific research and at the same time to work with patients. As a medical geneticist, I continue to see patients affected with genetic disease and for genetic counseling. There are very few areas in medicine where you can combine basic science with clinical work. That is what remains attractive to me. It is a real privilege to be able to do solid scientific research and help people at the same time.

Motulsky as a Mature Scientist

Motulsky's passion for combining medicine and scientific study carried him into the field of genetics, where he became distinguished as a preeminent figure among his peers. Combining research excellence with the humane care of patients has been a central value for Motulsky throughout his career. He is a pioneer of the physician-scientist approach to genetics.

However central this balance has been, it has always been a challenging one to maintain, especially in the early days of his career when genetics operated at the outer margin of acceptability in the medical research community. Motulsky explained, "It took many years before the importance of genetics for medicine caught on. I sometimes felt that I should have spent much more time on the hospital wards and clinics to convince residents and colleagues about the role of genetics in medicine." Motulsky's predecessors were ignored in their efforts to bring genetic research to bear on medical problems. The persistence required was tremendous. In light of this, his commitment to caring for patients was truly remarkable. Motulsky viewed the relation between research and practice not as one between competing interests—caring for patients versus devoting time to research—but rather as symbiotic and mutually beneficial. His research sharpened his medical acumen, and his exposure to patients' problems provided important ideas for research.

The interrelationship of research and application was important to Motulsky not only in his own work; he has also strived to impress it on those he has trained. His message is that "a doctor must be well trained in science and at the same time must be able to understand that there is a strong influence of personality and emotions on a patient's symptoms. An excellent doctor must be both scientific and holistic."

Taking this holistic message beyond the context of medicine, Motulsky has, throughout his career, proselytized the broader scientific community on the scientist's duty to educate the public and participate in social discourse surrounding ethical issues in science. Again influenced by his early experiences of social upheaval, Motulsky has modeled the scientist's unique role in shaping society: "We as scientists should educate people. I have done some of my duty in not just talking to specialist colleagues, but worked on commissions and committees dealing with psychosocial and ethical aspects of genetics. [I worked on] the Presidential Commission on Bioethics in the 1980s.... More recently I chaired a committee of the Institute of Medicine on assessing genetic risks. In this work, I tried to tell the public and others what we know, what we don't know, what we need to worry about, and what we need to guard against." Motulsky expressed concern over the way many scientists today focus exclusively on their own narrow research agenda without giving due attention to its impact on their social surroundings. For this reason, Motulsky has worked diligently to teach young scientists and physicians to take their public roles seriously: "I strongly feel that most decisions about ethical issues should be made by informed citizens. One of our tasks [as scientists] is to help people understand the nature of these issues— what can be done, what can't be done, and what might be done. We are not doing enough of this. Young scientists should be aware of the need for public education."

Motulsky's emphasis on this role of the scientist was not lost on his students whom we interviewed. One of his former students remembered exactly when the critical importance of this value crystallized for him. At the time of his fellowship with Motulsky after medical school, Motulsky was very involved in many of the ethical aspects of human genetics. He was serving on a committee in Israel for the in absentia trial of a former Nazi doctor who had worked at the Auschwitz concentration camp. Motulsky was asked to travel to Israel to participate because the doctor had been a geneticist before being swept into Nazi machinations. For this G2, the crystallizing moment came during a conversation with Motulsky:

> One time I came in to talk to him about lab stuff, and we ended up talking about this [trial], because I think he had been very affected by it. [He said] that the scariest part of the whole trial, or the worst part of the whole trial, wasn't as much the horrible things that this guy did, although he clearly did horrible things, but it was the realization that before the war, this guy had been a regular guy. He wasn't a monster. He was one of us. He could have been the geneticist down the hall. Then something about the war or himself . . . turned him into this person who was capable of doing just awful, terrible things.

What struck Motulsky and what impressed this G2 was that "within each of us, there may be this capacity for evil that you just can't know how you're going to react in a given situation." Motulsky stressed the need for continuous vigilance within the scientific community. Without a community that holds its members accountable, there lies the potential for any individual to wander into malevolence. The Latin adage *sine ecclesia nulla religio* ("without the church, there is no religion") articulates this insight. Active community and communication foster reflection and accountability by preparing individuals to behave conscientiously and in keeping with their professed values, rather than acquiescing under pressure to the lowest common denominators of human nature.

Motulsky has not been naive in encouraging young scientists to embrace social obligations. He was quick to emphasize that these duties cannot be undertaken at the expense of scientific proficiency and expertise. Scientists who become overly involved in public education quickly "lose contact with the nitty-gritty of science [and] . . . begin to make pronouncements along broad and superficial lines." This diminishes the quality of the scientific enterprise while simultaneously performing a disservice to the public.

Like his commitment to caring for patients, Motulsky's dedication to public education and participation in public discourse would seem to erode his chances for success as a researcher. In fact, it has worked the other way around. Not only has Motulsky's constant interaction with patients and the broader public informed and enhanced his sensitivity to the pressing questions that researchers need to pursue, it has also played a vital role in propelling the field of genetics from the status of an esoteric, ancillary discipline, considered distinct from biology and medicine, to a position at the cutting edge of biology and medicine.

Of course, Motulsky's scientific success has not been simply a matter of public action and clinical attentiveness. He has also taken a thoughtful approach to his research. "The most important key to success is to have the right idea and to select a problem that's ready to be worked on," he told us. "Science is the art of the solvable." A scientist ideally ought to select problems that hold the potential for making a large impact and at the same time are realistically solvable by available methods: "Some really important problems are not trivial, but they are also not solvable. You have to pick something that is interesting and will give you new insight, but its solution must be doable. Furthermore, the design of your ideal study should be such that whatever answer you get will be of interest and publishable." With this practical approach, Motulsky has been able to strike a balance between significance and feasibility.

The Experience of Later Generations

Over the course of his career, Motulsky has trained many young scientists and physicians. As a mentor, he has attempted to convey the values and practices most important to him in his own career: the physician-scientist model of research and practice that integrates genetic research with humane care for patients, the duty of the scientist to educate the public, and a pragmatic approach to research that views science as the art of the solvable. Motulsky has also emphasized memes more widely shared within the scientific community, including the values of hard work and persistence, collaboration, and honesty and integrity, which form a baseline expectation for good work in science.

To transmit these memes to students, Motulsky adopted several strategies. First, he selected trainees whose interests and inclinations were compatible with his own. Many of his G2s already held medical degrees and had an interest in becoming physician-scientists. Others were Ph.D.s interested in researching the problems of people suffering the effects of genetic disease.

With trainees, Motulsky used several key means to teach his values and approach. First, he provided a careful balance of supervision and intellectual freedom. Motulsky believed "the ideal scientist needs to be inner directed." Accordingly, he selected students who were capable of working independently and encouraged them to develop the ability to successfully pursue their own research agendas. He urged them to develop an internal sense of the solvable: identifying problems that were interesting to them and to the field, and whose solutions were attainable by currently available means. In order to develop this sense of how to do science, Motulsky had students select their own research problems, design their own analyses, and, to the extent possible, discern the overall significance of their own results. As much as he could, Motulsky aimed to treat his trainees as colleagues rather than subordinates.

While he believed in granting extensive independence and intellectual freedom, Motulsky also realized that trainees need guidance from time to time. During the latter part of his career, he has not had a lab in the traditional sense of a shared work space where he and his students regularly work on problems and experiments together. Even when he did maintain such a space, Motulsky was not extremely active in supervising his lab.

That is, he was not constantly in the lab, working alongside his mentees, always available to answer any question that arose. Instead, he offered a variety of opportunities to further trainees' development, such as regular feedback and guidance that oriented students to developing trends in the field. He also collaborated with his students on small projects or journal articles, and he provided a working environment rich in social capital, or relational resources.

These techniques made it unnecessary for Motulsky to constantly monitor his trainees. He did not even find it necessary to hold regular lab meetings to provide meaningful feedback. One G2 reported that she and her fellow students shared a strong sense of autonomy. Her studies took place during the earlier period of Motulsky's career, when he maintained an integrated lab space. A medical student when she began working with him, she remembered that his lab was such a busy and bustling place during the day that the only way to conduct experiments was to come at night and work largely on her own. This autonomy, however, did not sacrifice guidance. Motulsky "was very generous," meeting with her weekly, so she was able to pore over her ideas and data with him despite not being exposed to him in the lab during the days. Through this arrangement, she learned and internalized critical scientific skills, insights, and values.

Another G2, who completed a fellowship with Motulsky after medical school later in Motulsky's career, remembered, "I didn't have a lot of formal meetings with him." In fact, at the time, he said, Motulsky "hardly had a lab. He was really sort of getting to be a grand old man of science at the time." The G2 reported that the place where he performed his experiments was down the hall, in other people's labs. He recalled the freedom Motulsky gave him: "He rarely, if ever, came into those labs. . . . I don't think he ever saw me doing an experiment. Although he looked at the results and interpreted them, I don't think he ever actually came and actually watched me doing an experiment.

But there was a sense within those labs, because he was the overall person, that they were all his labs in some sense, and they were all kind of working together."

Because Motulsky founded the Division of Medical Genetics at the University of Washington, he was able to maintain a kind of omnipresence while at the same time remaining more aloof than some of the mentors we interviewed. Perhaps an extension of his Germanic personality, he tended to be on the formal side and to deal with affairs at arm's length (one student told us he rarely, if ever, saw Motulsky without a tie). Motulsky's somewhat reserved way of relating should not be mistaken for abnegation of his mentoring role, however. It is crucial to note that although Motulsky was slightly more detached than many other mentors, the students interviewed reported his deep and abiding interest in their ideas, as well as his willingness to give them critical feedback and direction whenever they asked for or needed it. Across the board, Motulsky's students reported a warm sense of support flowing from him. Most characterized him as fatherly (or grandfatherly). Whether concerning their research, a problem in the lab, or a job prospect, Motulsky offered assistance and encouragement, even if it was not effusive. What Motulsky did not do in terms of regularity and frequency of contact with his students, he made up for by the quality of his interactions.

Another important advantage Motulsky offered trainees was his distinctive perspective on the field of genetics. Because he played an instrumental role in pulling the field from the margins of medical relevance to center stage, he was exceptionally attuned to developing trends in genetics, and he helped his students move in these directions to stay ahead of the curve. One G2 recalled, "He was really good at knowing where the field was going and putting you in a position of being able to participate in the process, which is really exciting when you're . . . a junior person." Motulsky used his familiarity with the development of the field both to encourage his students when they were headed in the right direction and to let them know when something was going to lack impact or not work.

In addition to intellectual freedom, guidance, feedback, and support, Motulsky provided his students with a rich network of social and cultural capital. That is, he possessed a set of social relationships and resources that provided his students with opportunities for intellectual and vocational development that would not otherwise be possible. Motulsky supplied students with social and cultural capital in several ways. Most obviously, he provided all of the necessary tools for doing genetic research, such as equipment, materials, and exposure to the pertinent literature in journals and books. In addition to these necessary provisions, Motulsky created an environment that was dense in diverse human resources. When asked how he trained younger scientists and physicians, he repeatedly eschewed the singular *I* for the plural *we*. Because of his reputation and high stature in the field, students came to his department to study with him; however, he insisted that the education of his trainees was a departmental effort that depended enormously on other professors, lab technicians, and the quality of interaction among students.

As the founding father of medical genetics at the University of Washington, Motulsky had been able to structure the department and hire faculty and assistants in a way that ensured a variegated network of capability and expertise—in short, rich social capital. Motulsky intentionally brought on board other physicians and scientists with skills and interests distinct from his own so that students could avail themselves of a broad range of know-how to help approach and solve any research question they might pursue. In this way, Motulsky was a catalyst of memes as much as he was a direct transmitter.

Of course, it would not make sense to have such an abundance of social capital without encouraging students to interact intensely and intimately. For this reason, Motulsky balanced his insistence on autonomy and independence of thought with a strong emphasis on collaboration. To stress the importance of collaboration as a scientific virtue, he modeled teamwork for his trainees. He explained:

> I often work with a biochemist, a molecular biologist who is collaborating closely with me, and so the postdoc fellow works with the two of us. The fellow would get together more frequently with the molecular biologist for the lab aspects. We have conferences where we discuss things together. And again, the fellow can see the interaction between me and the molecular biologist, what he or she has done in the laboratory, and see this kind of collaboration. And get some ideas about the teamwork that I do with someone else, and the care we are taking.

Illustrating the good that has grown out of his collaborative efforts with students, Motulsky mentioned a former student whose work with Motulsky became the basis for Nobel Prize— winning research.

In addition to collaborating with his students for the sake of collaboration, Motulsky took advantage of these interactions as opportunities to convey his social and ethical values by the power of his example. For much of his career, he ran a genetics clinic once a week with postdocs and medical students. A story that one of the G2s related illustrates how Motulsky was able to teach by example not only the value of caring for patients, but also the skills necessary to do so. This G2 remembered watching Motulsky interact with a married couple whose child had Down syndrome. At one point, she recollected the parents saying, "This child is a blessing." Struck by the incongruence of this statement with the devastating nature of their child's condition, the G2 recalled feeling incredulous. But Motulsky was able to reframe the parents' sentiment in a way that was both sensitive and straightforward in helping them come to terms with the realities of their child's condition. He responded, "It is true that this child has changed your family. Your family will never be the same again. But I understand what you're saying in the sense that the challenge your family has experienced with this child has made all of you grow." In this way, Motulsky conveyed his appreciation for the child's profound impact on the family, while maintaining the ability to move on and discuss harsh and difficult realities with the parents. Motulsky's approach was not dismissive or hurried. Rather, he took time to talk with the families he assisted and to understand what they were experiencing. For this G2, the experience of watching him interact with patients shaped her approach. She came to understand what parents of disabled children meant when they said their child was a blessing, and she now uses the same approach in her work: "I've absolutely come to understand that it is a blessing. That every family that is tried by having something horrible to deal with is strengthened. We would not wish it on anybody, but the process makes them grow, makes them test their own values. . . . You can call it a conversion, but it's really true. But it was modeled to me by his talking to a family in a sensitive, thoughtful, responsive way."

Whether one views a genetically disabled child as a blessing or as an opportunity for growth, one can appreciate Motulsky's transmission of a caring approach to interacting with patients. One may also appreciate that the learning that took place did not occur in a classroom and probably would not have occurred if Motulsky had espoused the approach but not embodied and enacted it. As this G2 expressed it, "[How to caringly interact with patients] doesn't get taught. They don't teach that in medical school, for heaven's sake! Somehow, if you're really lucky, you've had a mentor who will talk about it or demonstrate it." When we asked this G2 why this kind of approach was not taught in medical school, she responded:

> I think it's because people don't put it into words well. When you talk in words, it's an intellectual process. And this is an emotional and spiritual process that is part of human interactions and

medicine. It comes out more in genetics because there are more stresses in clinical genetics. There are life-and-death choices and situations. [Learning to respond can] not [be] packaged. It's what this family needed at the given time. And it comes out of a depth of experience. And from very fundamental beliefs in the good of people and their ability to grow. And you believe in them, that they have the capacity to handle this hopeless situation.

Returning to a central theme of this book, the practices and values that distinguish professionals as both ethical and excellent in their field often lose their force when conveyed in the context of a classroom or textbook. There are certainly other personal and societal wellsprings for learning values: a person's upbringing, parents, former teachers, and religious and philosophical orientations are a few such sources. But training with an ethical exemplar can have a profound and perhaps irreplaceable impact on an individual's professional training. Many students of such paragons intentionally and explicitly steer their careers in the ethical directions that their mentors modeled.

Thus, many of Motulsky's commitments and practices were transmitted to subsequent generations. Humanitarianism, for example, was almost universally absorbed and attributed to mentoring. The physician-scientist model of working was also almost universally absorbed and attributed to mentors' influence—the exceptions being the G2 and G3 who were not clinicians and thus unable to incorporate this specific meme. Motulsky also transmitted commitments to educating the public about science; to honesty and integrity in research; to industriousness; to collaboration, which entails the selection of good colleagues; and to affording those around him intellectual freedom and guidance.

In Chapter Five, we present quantitative findings about the patterns of transmission across generations. To explore the richness of these mentoring processes, we examine here one of Motulsky's sublineages—one line of his scientific descendants. The former student who heads the sublineage ascribed many of his guiding values and practices to Motulsky. These include some memes that Motulsky actively tried to transmit to students, as just described, and others that Motulsky did not even mention. The former student, an impressive scientist in his own right, also possesses and transmits some values and practices that he himself introduced to the lineage in the sense that he did not inherit them from Motulsky.

One of Motulsky's Students: A Case Study

Samuel Boyer (a pseudonym), a professor at a midwestern university, studied with Motulsky as a postdoctoral fellow after graduating from medical school. His career resembles his mentor's in some key respects. He has mentored many graduate and postgraduate students over the years, including both M.D.s and Ph.D.s. Boyer has established and directed a number of important research centers. He has received numerous awards in his field, and he speaks regularly around the country about his work, on which he has become a leading authority, and on areas of ethical concern in genetics. In addition, Boyer maintains a clinical practice. Like Motulsky, he is a physician-scientist who both attends to the needs of patients and works to solve the basic science questions underlying their problems.

In keeping with his training under Motulsky, Boyer takes a remarkably humanitarian, compassionate, and committed approach to his work. As he described his various work goals, he quickly moved through those that were at their core basic science. He did not dwell on genetic sequencing techniques, experiment design, or his commitment to precision. Although those things clearly occupy a crucial place in his work, Boyer chose to devote much more of the interview to discussing the immediate, nongenetic strategies he and his colleagues are developing to help a population they study in the developing world.

Boyer has come to realize that even if he discovers a genetically based cure for specific diseases through his research, the people he studies will not benefit from it any time soon because of their country's poverty. Prioritizing the solving of human problems beyond scientific ones is something Boyer traces back to his time with Motulsky; it is also something he tries to teach his own students. In the same way Motulsky taught Boyer and other G2s the vital importance of caring for patients, Boyer embodies and actively professes caring about the people who participate in his research.

Motulsky spent substantial time with Boyer discussing and collaborating on social and ethical issues, especially after inviting him to publish together on social and ethical issues in science. Boyer was also the student with whom Motulsky shared his experience on the war crimes tribunal in Israel. These experiences had a dramatic impact on Boyer's approach to his career. Again and again, he expressed gratitude for the serendipity that had landed him in a lab with such a humanitarian emphasis, and he stressed the ways in which he attempts to impress a similar disposition on his students: "I talk to them a lot about the social and ethical aspects of science. I tell them the stories I've told you about Motulsky." When asked specifically about his conscientiousness and the amount of time he spends on such topics, Boyer had this to say:

> That's a big part of my career, and I spend a lot of my time talking about those issues and have been involved in them in both formal and informal ways. I've been on some committees, and I've written a little bit about it, and I spend a lot of time in my lab with students, especially undergraduate students and graduate students, talking about those aspects of medicine and science. I teach medical students the same thing. I spend a lot of time on this sort of moral and social aspect of science as well as the hardcore aspects. In fact, I think I probably am not as good a basic scientist as I could be because I've spent a lot of energy and time on some of these other issues. I don't regret that. I think those things are at least of equal importance.

In addition to caring for his research subjects and the ethical welfare of the scientific community, Boyer absorbed from Motulsky a commitment to educating the public about science—a value he, like Motulsky, practices and transmits. For example, Boyer writes textbook materials for high school students, hoping, as Motulsky has hoped, to create a more informed citizenry concerning social and political decisions on issues relating to science and genetics. Beyond his writing, Boyer's primary vehicle for educating the public is his public speaking:

> I sort of make fun of myself when I give talks and say that this is going to be a proselytizing session. But in fact, I've been lucky to be able to go to some of these [distant] places and see both how happy people can be [despite poverty], but also how tragic lots of elements of their lives are. And so I try and make other people aware of that so that people who haven't been as lucky as me in getting a chance to go to those places will be able to . . . invest a little bit of time, money, effort in making the planet a little bit better. Because I think it makes you feel better about yourself. And, ultimately, I think we owe it to our children and our grandchildren to make their lives be a little better than ours were. Not just my kids. My kids are going to be fine. But the kids of people in [these impoverished regions].

Ethical vigilance, global social responsibility, and caring for research subjects and patients were some of the most important memes Boyer stressed to his students. But they do not exhaust what he embodied or what he offered students. He encouraged students to become well rounded, cultivate broad interests, and create a healthy balance between work and family. Boyer ascribed much of his emphasis on work-family balance to his own personality and disposition, but he also credited Motulsky with encouraging and reinforcing these practices in the context of a scientific career. At one point during his training, Boyer used Motulsky's family as a DNA control group in an experiment, and thus met his adult children. He was "impressed by how they talked about [Motulsky]. For us, he was kind of our parent too. He was kind of my father in a lot of ways, too. And it was really interesting to see how his kids saw him in different ways." Boyer recalled that each of Motulsky's children was unique, but that it was "cool to see how he loved all of his kids equally. . . . He had a very good relationship with his wife as well, and I remember being impressed by that." Motulsky's commitment to his family reassured Boyer of the feasibility of having a highly successful scientific career while maintaining strong family relationships.

Boyer enjoys and values his own family greatly, and he makes every effort to convince his students to do the same. It has even become a stated policy for his lab:

> I tell them, you can't not do anything at work, but for things that are family oriented it's always okay to make a decision that you're going to choose your family over work, because that's ultimately what's going to matter to you when you're seventy. All these science people aren't going to matter. People make important science discoveries, but those get made by everybody. The things that really matter to you in your life and the legacy that you leave is really through your biological family as much as through your scientific family. . . . I want to still be friends with my kids and have contact with them thirty years from now. Most of the people I'll see next week, I won't even remember those people's names thirty years from now.

Like Motulsky, Boyer believed that it was possible to keep strong family ties and active outside interests while maintaining scientific excellence. Also like Motulsky, he preached the importance of rigorous research standards in terms of both quality and integrity. "Your science has to be rigorous and honest and true," he told students. "You always have to be willing to accept and interpret results of experiments in that kind of way. . . .

The best way to get ahead is to be a nice person and to be honest and fair in your science, and to work with other people who feel the same way that you do."

Consistent with this approach to science, Boyer adopted Motulsky's practice of choosing good colleagues. The collaboration with colleagues and students that Motulsky modeled took root deeply in Boyer, becoming a cornerstone of his career and something he urges his students to adopt. He articulated it this way: "From Motulsky, I think [I learned] the collaborative component of stuff. He knew lots of people and worked with lots of different people on projects. And I think that's something that's continued to be important to me.... I think the collaborative aspects of science are a really important component of it, and I think I got that largely from him."

Boyer's international research is a joint effort with other scientists, including geneticists, nutritionists, and anthropologists. Boyer collaborates extensively on other projects as well with colleagues and students. He shares his philosophy of collaboration with his students:

> I tell people it will be the best part of your life in science [to have] good collaborations. And so you should always give everybody at least one chance to screw you. So if you've got a really good idea and you're a little nervous about sharing it with somebody—you know, you won't survive in science if you have only one good idea your whole life. So you should always give people the first chance to do things with you and share things with them. And then if they do something bad to you, you just don't have to work with them again. In fact, my real philosophy is I usually give people two chances. The first chance I figure maybe it was just sort of a misunderstanding. And I think that usually works, because I think there's way more in science to do than any of us have time to do, and it's much more fun if you have friends.

Training a Third Generation: Boyer and His Students

Just as Motulsky's teamwork approach had a deep impact on Boyer, so too has Boyer's collaborative emphasis had an impact on his students. One of them told us the most important lesson she learned from Boyer was the value of collaboration in science. He always said, "'You have to be very open when you start a collaboration.' I think the way he put it was, 'You have to let them screw you over once.' And he said, 'It's okay if somebody steals one of your ideas, because it's not the only idea you're going to have in your entire career.' So he was really open to discussing things and seeing what happens."

Another G3 also came to embody Boyer's open-arms approach to collaboration. Boyer encouraged him not to feel overly competitive or as though he had to "beat somebody." This scientist told us, "My ideal mechanism for doing research is on a collaborative basis, because I think as a group, especially on this complex disorder, we know that we have to work together. We know that if we don't, we're actually going to take longer." Moreover, "as a group working together, [my colleagues'] strengths are my weaknesses and vice versa, [and we] end up with a better result in the end. It's a lot more fun."

Within his lab, Boyer has made every effort to forge a collaborative environment that, like Motulsky's lab, is rich in social and cultural capital. One G3 described Boyer's lab as large, growing from fifteen to thirty people during his stay, and "bottom-heavy," with lots of technicians in addition to undergraduate, medical, and dental students. It has been a rich social environment for learning. The G3 reported learning a lot from the technicians and other students in the lab. He described the lab culture as "socialistic" and democratic because there was no real hierarchy, and responsibilities and authority were widely dispersed. The atmosphere was loose and relaxed. Boyer was not "Dr. Boyer," but rather "Sam," even though it was clear who had authority when issues or problems developed. In this respect, Boyer differed from Motulsky. All told, it was this G3's experience that Boyer was away a lot and that he had relied on fellow students and others in and around the lab to learn basic skills and perspectives. As he stated, "In terms of him technically training me, I would have to say to some degree he did. But for the most part . . . he was able to bring in postdocs and good people that I really learned [the basic technical aspects] from."

Just as Motulsky trained him, Boyer taught his students to be self-reliant and able to solve their own problems or use lab resources and colleagues to help solve them. He provided them not only tremendous leeway to work outside his gaze, but also freedom to disagree with him when they reached different conclusions. Like Motulsky, however, we would be remiss to portray Boyer as an absentee mentor. Both of Boyer's G3s recalled important times when Boyer provided individual guidance in the form of feedback, criticism, and often effusive praise—a habit Boyer developed in reaction to Motulsky's reticence. One G3 recalled sitting down many times with Boyer to talk about science, discuss the people involved in their work, and digress onto one fascinating tangent or another. He also recalled valuable time observing Boyer work in the lab, learning new techniques, and garnering new ideas from Boyer's example.

Boyer has drilled into the minds of his students several key sayings to guide them in their careers and approaches to problems. One G3 recalled that after he and Boyer had sparred several times over whether poor-quality data really reflected truth, Boyer put a sign, "The Data Is the Data," on his door. The other G3 recalled that Boyer used to make her opt for giving a talk at academic meetings rather than merely presenting a poster: "Giving a talk is very stressful. Most graduate students don't want to do that. It's much easier to give a poster. But [Boyer] wouldn't let me check the 'poster only' thing. It was like, 'If this work is good enough to give a talk, you damn well better give a talk.'" This G3 now employs this practice in training her own graduate students.

In addition to the guidance he has articulated, Boyer has transmitted memes by example. One value Boyer has clearly conveyed through modeling is hard work. One G3 was amazed at Boyer's ability to function at such high levels on a mere five or six hours of sleep per night for years on end. It was almost superhuman, she thought. The other G3 still invokes Boyer's work ethic in his own career: "Unconsciously I think about it periodically. He was at work at six or six-thirty in the morning and would go home around five-thirty or six [and return] on evenings and on weekends. . . . [He was] extremely driven."

In addition to hard work and discipline, Boyer's G3s embraced the work-family balance value, even though they could not fathom achieving it the way Boyer did. Each G3 recollected the attitude Boyer expressed about the importance of family and making time for them. Both agreed that Boyer maintained remarkable relationships with his wife and children, and in so doing set a wonderful example. One G3 told us: "If you watch [Boyer] with his kids, it's true that there's a significant bond there—mutual respect and love for each other. So I think that was very obvious. I remember when my kid was born—my first son. [Boyer] came over to the house and oohed and aahed over the kid like I'd never seen before. So he knew the importance of children and family. That was obvious—patient care, in talking about that, and probably the human side of just about anything."

Boyer's other G3 similarly recalled spending wonderful times with Boyer and his family and observing their closeness. Boyer went home every evening to be with his family and then came back to the lab late in the evenings. It was Boyer's ability to be both scientist and family man in such a driven fashion that neither of the G3s could exactly emulate. Each had to scale back in one area or another to approach the level of commitment Boyer maintained to both. Nonetheless, both G3s, during and since their time with Boyer, have established and maintained successful family relationships—due in part to the example Boyer set, even if not according to his formula.

Beyond lab practices and skills associated directly with conducting science, Boyer has impressed on his students the lineage trait of social and ethical responsibility. He has done so through his own example but also by engaging his students in discussions, lecturing, and encouraging and shaping their inclinations to social-ethical responsibility. One G3 credited Boyer with encouraging his belief that all people deserve adequate health care.

Both G3s labeled Boyer a superb lecturer whose orations inspired them and others to cultivate greater social awareness and engage in compassionate social action. Each also commented on Boyer's remarkable embodiment of what he preached, pointing, for example, to his work in developing countries. Boyer's involvement in humanitarian work as a result of his scientific research, and exhortation to his students to do the same, apparently made a profound impact. One G3 came into Boyer's lab as a clinician and researcher; he had been planning to phase out his clinical involvement to focus exclusively on his research, but he discovered he could not let go of working with patients. Although Boyer advised him strategically to concentrate exclusively on his doctoral research, the physician-scientist in Boyer could understand and supported this G3's decision to continue his clinical practice. The G3 said, "In the end, I knew that I was able to do what I was doing because of his clinical background. If [Boyer] had been a straight Ph.D. person, it might have been different. He wouldn't have had that understanding." Of course, with this understanding came some ribbing from one physician-scientist to another. The G3 recalled, "[Boyer] made fun of us. We always teased each other. He would ask me how many people I had saved today. And I would answer: 'None. But I made them better.'"

The teasing aside, Boyer has provided a haven for physician-scientists like this G3 to pursue serious genetic research without relinquishing their clinical commitments. Because Boyer inhabits both worlds as well, he was in a unique position to sharpen the skills of his students in ways others might not. For instance, the G3 we have been discussing remembered that one of the things

Boyer repeated was to continue reading voraciously throughout his career. He told this G3 he could not "wait for the day when his students start sending him papers and say: 'Look at this. This is a really cool idea. This is really exciting.'" Years later, having taken Boyer's advice to heart, the same G3 came across an article and found that it perfectly described a patient he was treating. With a little further research, he became "convinced that this patient has a mutation and this disorder [he was reading about]. I'm thinking 'Wow! This would be really cool.' I'm not a clinical geneticist. I actually saw the patient yesterday, and sure enough, it fits the description very well." The patient did in fact have the disorder he had been reading about, and he was able to put it all together. "In large part," the G3 continued, "that was a unique way of pulling the basic research that normally would go with my clinical side, put it together, and hopefully it will give the family some information. And a large part, I think, was due to this drive I learned from Sam to continue to keep on reading."

To a notable degree, Boyer's G3s deliberately run their labs in ways similar to, and fashioned after, Boyer and Motulsky. Both G3s collaborate heavily with their students and encourage them to collaborate with others in the same way Boyer and Motulsky had advised their students. As Boyer's first G3 described, she wants her students to write the first drafts of projects they work on together. Similarly, Boyer's later G3 includes his students on all of his studies and provides them writing opportunities. Like Boyer, his G3s intentionally teach and model basic ethical and quality standards, even when it may be costly to their own productivity to do so.

Like Boyer, both G3s seek to provide their students with a balance of independence and guidance in their work. One G3 said of her students, "I just want them to be able to think independently once they get out of here." Her philosophy of graduate training is to prepare students to enter a postdoc and work productively on their own, conceiving, designing, and solving their own research questions. But to do so, she does not take quite the same hands-off approach that Boyer does when she is with them in the lab. Rather, she asks her students hard questions; through such questioning, she hopes her students will internalize the thought processes necessary to conduct successful independent science, and ultimately this creative process will become second nature.

The other G3 has the same goal but a different approach. His is more laissez-faire: "In terms of interacting with students, I'm probably very similar to [Boyer]. I'm quite hands-off to some degree." This has allowed students the freedom to pursue their own direction and interests and ask their own sets of questions. He has reined them in, however, on important details, scientific techniques, and practices: "I'm a detail-oriented person because I know that when you're down in the trenches . . . the details sooner or later—if you pay attention to them—get important. You'll be ahead. If you don't [pay attention to detail], you get crushed. . . . I know in my lab, I am more detail oriented than Boyer in terms of interacting with students and guiding them. But to some degree, I'm also quite hands-off in terms of their direction they want to go in."

Thus, using different approaches with nuances stemming from their own personal styles, both G3s sought to achieve a balance between intellectual independence and guidance similar to that given to them by Boyer.

In addition to such general themes as intellectual freedom and guidance, the G3s enact specific practices in training young scientists that they learned from Boyer. One G3, for example, enacts the same practice of making students give talks about their work rather than taking the easy, and ultimately less rewarding, option of merely checking the "poster-only" box when submitting conference proposals.

Similarly, Boyer's other G3 attempts to model patient care for his students in much the same way Motulsky and Boyer modeled it for their students. Asked what he most hoped to impress on his students, this G3 began by saying, "[I suppose] just like Boyer never thought about what impact he was having on me,

I don't think that much about what impact I have on them. I live by example and let them draw their own conclusions to some degree." He then discussed at length how he attempts to model patient care for students who, like him, are practitioners.

Last but certainly not least, the Motulsky meme of social responsibility has survived to the G3s and is being conveyed to new generations of memetic "offspring." One G3 continues to collaborate with Boyer in research on a genetic condition and carries on his own practice focused on this problem in lower socioeconomic communities. He continues to transmit this value both tacitly and explicitly to new generations of physician-scientists.

Similarly, in her work with Ph.D. students, Boyer's other G3 carries on the practice of educating the public about science and encouraging her students to do the same. Echoing Boyer and Motulsky before him, she told us:

> One thing I think is important is education for people who don't have science backgrounds.... Some of the really important public policy issues have to be decided by, obviously not me, but by the majority of the people who are going to be affected by it. But if they don't understand the science behind it, it's going to be really hard. What I would love to see is high school students being required to take science all four years.

Through discussing this concern and modeling efforts to educate the public, this G3 engenders a sense of social responsibility in her students and furthers transmission of ethical practices combined with scientific excellence.

Conclusion

In this chapter, we documented clear instances of the intergenerational transmission of memes. We traced values and practices taught by the lineage head, Motulsky: collaboration, social responsibility, humanitarianism, the dual physician-scientist role, research integrity, hard work, and mentoring practices (especially the provision of intellectual freedom and guidance). In some cases, such as balancing work and family, Motulsky taught by example. He did not discuss work-family issues, but his G2s were clearly influenced by his example.

Motulsky's memes were modified as they made their way through changing contexts, shifting interpersonal dynamics, and varying interests. For example, the notion that the rewards of collaboration justify giving others "at least one chance to screw you" was a new spin to a specific philosophy originating with Motulsky. We saw additions to the lineage's "meme pool," such as Boyer's emphasis on voracious reading as a support for the physician-scientist approach. And we saw new practices adopted in reaction to unsatisfying aspects of training. For instance, Boyer praised students lavishly in part because Motulsky did not. On the whole, however, there is remarkable continuity from generation to generation in this sublineage. This was true even for the physician-scientist approach, a complex and demanding signature meme. In ways similar to, and distinct from, those in the Gall and Lewontin lineages, the stories and recollections related by Motulsky and his descendants forcefully illustrate the perpetuation of values and practices down multiple generations.

4

THE MORALIST

Richard C. Lewontin is a professor of zoology at Harvard University and one of the world's preeminent evolutionary geneticists. Author of fourteen books and hundreds of articles, his seminal contributions to theoretical and experimental science in the past half-century have earned him a place in the history of science. Lewontin's firsts include his application of game theory to evolutionary problems and his introduction of molecular methods into population genetics (Coyne & Jones, 1995). Lewontin is also known for his critical stance, urging colleagues to reconsider theories that seem too elegant to be true.

His classic works—*The Triple Helix* (2000b), *It Ain't Necessarily So* (2000a), *The Dialectical Biologist* (Levins & Lewontin, 1985), *The Genetic Basis of Evolutionary Change* (1974), and *Not in Our Genes* (Lewontin, Rose, & Kamin, 1984)—are original and provocative, as much the result of his social views and critique of the field as his scientific contributions. In the words of Stephen J. Gould, "He is the most brilliant scientist I know and his work embodies . . . the very best in genetics combined with a powerful political and moral vision of how science, properly interpreted and used to empower all people, might truly help us to be free" (Lewontin, 1991, back cover).

Lewontin's unique perspective springs in part from his Marxist philosophy and outlook. The renowned population geneticist told us that he considers himself "an unreconstructed orthodox Marxist who nevertheless thinks that Marx got a lot of things wrong." What does that mean? According to Lewontin, "I see a tremendous amount through the glass of class struggle—not class struggle in its vulgar sense, but I see that class identification is extremely important. Where Marx got it wrong is in the possibility of capitalism giving a place to socialism, because Marx failed to take into account that such a drastic shift in human relations would require a deep change in human consciousness, which would in turn require a deep change in human relations."

Lewontin's Marxist perspective has provided a framework for his original scientific and social insights. For one, he understands many scientific discoveries, including those of Darwin, as the result of the class identification of the scientist and of the social relations predominant at the time. In his view, much scientific elitism is unfounded and has the effect of silencing the general public. Most important for his contribution to the domain of science, however, is his dialectical and comprehensive viewpoint on natural and material phenomena. For Lewontin, the natural world cannot be adequately understood through reductionism. "Lower" elements, including genes, are related to the entire organism in a complex fashion in which the organism affects its parts and the parts affect the organism. Moreover, any behavioral outcome results from the organism and the environment mutually affecting and changing each other.

In Lewontin's view, what can be gained from the identification of lower-level elements, such as those studied by the U.S. government's Human Genome Project—the multibillion-dollar effort to sequence and map all human genes—is necessarily limited in helping to explain how organisms develop, adapt, and behave. By the same philosophy, scientists hoping to glean insight into the behavior of humans by studying the instincts of ants can never be entirely successful. Very little about the behavior of humans, a vastly more complex organism living in a complex sociocultural environment, can be understood by the most penetrating insight into ant behavior.

When we asked Lewontin when his political consciousness began to coalesce, he acknowledged, "You've asked me a hard question." His father was a liberal from a labor Zionist family. In high school, Lewontin and his future wife were founding members of The World We Want, a socialist organization of like-minded friends. By the time Lewontin entered college, he had read enough Marx that he found himself in arguments at the student union over how Ford Motor Company could sell cars much more cheaply if it was not so greedy.

Lewontin's path was shaped by several teachers and colleagues whom he met over the course of his scientific training. A self-described "upper-middle-class New York Jew," Lewontin attended Harvard as an undergraduate in the late 1940s with ambitions of becoming a geneticist. His "old-fashioned" professors discouraged him because they thought genetics was a gimmick. He was "saved" from such dubious wisdom by a visiting professor from Columbia University, Leslie Dunn. Lewontin considered himself a "calculating and careerist person." When Dunn offered the chance to work in his lab, Lewontin jumped at the opportunity: Given his college grades (as a sophomore, he got D's in his courses), he knew that this represented his best chance to enter graduate school. His hunch turned out to be right. He became friendly with Dunn, and Dunn arranged for Lewontin to get into Columbia after "certifying I had knowledge of courses of which I had no knowledge." Under those auspices, Lewontin sailed into Columbia for graduate school in 1951.

Lewontin had a wife and children by the time he entered Columbia. He recognized himself as scholarly, but felt universities were "small-time operations" in those days, and he fully expected to become a high school teacher. In retrospect, the world appeared to have other plans. Lewontin was mentored by the leading population geneticist of his time, Theodosius Dobzhansky, and was his student from 1951 to 1954. After working in Dunn's lab at Harvard, Lewontin had become friendly with one of Dobzhansky's former students, an instructor at Harvard, and came to realize that his own work was related to Dobzhansky's. With that knowledge, even though Dunn was his main connection to Columbia, Lewontin matriculated hoping to learn mainly from Dobzhansky. Once at Columbia, he began working with Dobzhansky. At one point his interests changed, and he asked a cytology professor if he could conduct an experiment under his supervision. The cytology professor told him, "Well, I think that's a very good experiment. And I think it's worth doing, but if I took you as my student, Dobzhansky would never speak to me again as long as I live. So go back downstairs where you came from." And so Lewontin did.

Development and Formative Influences

Lewontin's experience, values, and perspective were profoundly influenced by Dobzhansky. In fact, Lewontin diverges from Gall and Motulsky in having a single potent mentor. Said Lewontin about Dobzhansky, "He was terribly important. I admired him immensely, for his exuberance, for his abilities as a teacher and leader of graduate students. He was a role model for me in many ways. He taught me some very important lessons." Dobzhansky, who had been trained in Kiev, came to the United States as a Rockefeller fellow in the late 1920s. He was declared an enemy of the Russian state due to his anti-Lysenkoism, and he stood by his beliefs. In this and other respects, Lewontin regarded him as a great moral exemplar.

Lewontin did not completely idealize Dobzhansky, however. He also saw in Dobzhansky several glaring faults. For example, Lewontin believed Dobzhansky was "an intellectual tyrant." Dobzhansky had such a strong personality that "he would simply eat you up." He would tell students what experiments they were to do, having already arranged them in advance. Lewontin called Dobzhansky's strong treatment of others a form of "bulldozing." He even thought that Dobzhansky bulldozed his scientific data as he did students. Although Dobzhansky would never dream of falsifying data, according to Lewontin, the abstracts of his papers were clearly removed from what the data actually showed. Lewontin would sometimes protest to Dobzhansky when he did this, asserting, "Come on, the data don't show that!" Dobzhansky would then grumble and reconsider. In this sense, Lewontin saw Dobzhansky as a "demonstrator" more than the experimentalist he was best known for being. According to Lewontin, Dobzhansky's experiments were never meant to discover anything, but rather to demonstrate what Dobzhansky already knew.

While Dobzhansky may have succeeded in overpowering most of his students and even his own data, Lewontin claimed that Dobzhansky never succeeded in bulldozing him. Lewontin believed that his parents provided him with a robust enough ego to withstand Dobzhansky's dominating personality. Rather than backing down, he argued constantly with Dobzhansky over intellectual matters, and the two were frequently seen shouting at each other. Dobzhansky dragged Lewontin around to colleagues, saying, "This is the fellow who believes this nonsense." Even so, Lewontin believed that the relationship was like that of a rebellious son who is nevertheless pleasing to his father. He was one of Dobzhansky's better students, and Dobzhansky liked that he had the intellectual muscle and spirit to fight back. "We got along extremely well," Lewontin chuckled.

Lewontin's judgment was that his mentor had no quantitative abilities at all. "He could barely add two and two," Lewontin remembered. Instead, Dobzhansky had to get statisticians and graduate students, including Lewontin, to analyze his data for him. Lewontin himself was quite mathematically inclined by the time he attended graduate school.

The force of Dobzhansky's virtues, and the relationship that formed between mentor and student, appeared to counterbalance any impression those faults made on the young Lewontin. All in all, Lewontin admired a quality about Dobzhansky that made him a demonstrator even if he did take this to extremes: "He was a person who knew what was true," Lewontin reflects. The willingness to risk claiming knowledge of the truth before it can be demonstrated is an attribute of elite scientists. For example, Einstein often exhibited the same quality; he was less surprised and excited than others when evidence supported his theories.

Lewontin profoundly appreciated the opportunities Dobzhansky provided. One advantage to being his student was the opportunity to meet leading members of the field when they visited the lab. Dobzhansky would introduce his students and have them "perform" for the visitors. Lewontin thereby became friendly with a number of leaders in the field. He went to symposia with Dobzhansky in the summer and would sit around drinking beer and eating fish with Dobzhansky and other elite scientists. Hobnobbing with bigwigs in the field, he became a "famous graduate student."

Lewontin certainly enjoyed an elevated status as Dobzhansky's student, but it would be an oversimplification to conclude that Dobzhansky's impact on Lewontin lay mainly in privileged opportunities. As Lewontin says, "There are a couple of things that are important in the formation of one's career. Dobzhansky was, as I say, a great moralist." Lewontin was in awe of him and was profoundly influenced by him mainly by force of the moral principles that characterized Dobzhansky's actions, decisions, and identity.

Politically, Dobzhansky was an ardent critic of Lysenko, a social democrat, and an enemy of the Soviet state, convinced that the United States would eventually become involved in war with the Soviet Union. One day, as was his custom, Dobzhansky was sitting at his microscope reading chromosome slides and talking to his students. Lewontin sat down next to him and started a conversation: "If you really believe that the Soviet Union and the United States are going to be engaged in an armed conflict to the death, and you really believe that Lysenko is doing terrible damage to agricultural production in the Soviet Union, why in the hell are you making such a big stink about it? You should shut up and encourage him because they are our enemy." Dobzhansky turned to the audacious Lewontin and calmly responded, "That has nothing to do with it. It is the obligation of a scientist to speak the truth about science as he knows it, irrespective of the consequences. This man is a bad scientist, and I have an intellectual obligation to oppose him." This viewpoint baffled the young Lewontin. Here the United States was to be engaged in war with a fierce enemy, and Dobzhansky wanted to put abstract scientific truth above that? However, Dobzhansky clearly believed and meant what he said. The weight of his moralism pressed down on the famous graduate student, leaving an indelible impression.

Some of Dobzhansky's practices were as unusual as his beliefs. He frequently created experiments that his students performed and wrote up, but Dobzhansky did not put his name on the papers. He was a moralist about not taking credit for the work of others. According to Lewontin, he even took his practice too far because it falsified history. He did the real intellectual work behind an immense literature that was published mainly by other people. In an age when many of the most publicized problems between students and advisors in universities revolve around issues of credit, authorship, and intellectual property, this practice seems even more unusual today than it did to Lewontin then.

Dobzhansky represented a strange mixture of qualities in another sense. Despite his moralism and seemingly excessive generosity in giving students credit, he remained fundamentally careerist. That is, he never lost the need to be recognized as an important person, a leader, and someone who was always right. Lewontin felt that Dobzhansky, along with others he met at Columbia, such as the Nobel Prize winner Herman Muller, were afflicted by what amounted almost to a sickness. They were possessed by the need for more and more recognition, as with an obsession or drug addiction. "If I were a religious person, I would say they were soul-sick," commented Lewontin.

For his part, Lewontin was a self-described careerist when he entered graduate school. But he asked himself why he would want to be like Dobzhansky and Muller since he did not consider them to be extremely happy people. Even more than these thoughts, what ultimately cured Lewontin of his career-ism was experiencing success at an early age: "One day, I was about thirty-two or something, I realized that my ambition had been achieved. I had become a success." He was relieved to dis-cover that he did not need any more of it. Lewontin's success at that point may not have been on the same order of magni-tude as that which Dobzhansky had achieved, but insofar as Lewontin wanted career success, he had it. By the time he was a full professor at the University of Chicago, he felt himself to be cured.

Whereas Lewontin did not seek to emulate Dobzhansky's drive to the extent that it became addictive and led to per-sonal unhappiness, he did consider himself an extremely mor-alistic person. He held a slight disdain for colleagues who had Dobzhansky's drive but lacked his moralism. One day a colleague boasted to Lewontin about earning a major prize, stressing the pres-tige of the award rather than the significance of the achievement. The behavior repelled Lewontin. He explains, "I would be ashamed to admit that I coveted prizes, awards. . . . I find that shameful. I'd just as well run around with no clothes on."

Lewontin as a Mature Scientist

Although his undergraduate years were fraught with difficulty and poor grades, Lewontin's graduate career proceeded smoothly, and he was awarded his Ph.D. after only three years. His aca-demic career included positions at North Carolina State College in Raleigh from 1954 to 1958, the University of Rochester from 1958 to 1964, the University of Chicago from 1964 to 1973, and finally Harvard from 1973 onward.

Lewontin became increasingly well known to general audi-ences for waging public war, frequently alongside his late col-league Stephen J. Gould, against science that they felt was driven by prejudice and untestable speculation. Lewontin and Gould confronted scholars whose work they believed had racist and sexist implications. Their heated debate with sociobiologist E.O. Wilson, which received wide media attention, was one example. Gould and Lewontin, as well as other prominent scientists like John Maynard Smith, attacked the scientific, political, and moral implications of Wilson's book *Sociobiology* (1975), considering it supportive of social Darwinism's racist attitudes and policies (see Segerstrale, 2001). On another front, in their famous 1979 essay, Gould and Lewontin argued that not all aspects of organisms could be explained by natural selection. Rather, they maintained that many features were merely side effects of adaptive ones, much like the triangular spaces called spandrels that appear between arches in church architecture.

Scientifically, Lewontin has always considered himself to be primarily a methodologist and epistemologist. He has never been particularly surprised or overwhelmed when a scientific principle was supported or unsupported due to being somewhat pessimistic about how much can be shown to be true with respect to nature. He has tended to believe instead that most of what is true of any given organism is unique to that organism. His mantra became, "Organisms are the nexus of a large number of weakly determining causes." Perhaps even more than methodology, he had a great interest in epistemology. He wanted to understand the nature of biological knowledge, particularly knowledge of organisms.

His initial career success was based on an experiment with important epistemological implications, addressing how much genetic variation there is in natural populations by examining events at the molecular level. He had several fundamental hypotheses that could not be resolved because no method to test them existed until he met a University of Chicago researcher, Jack Hubby, who had created just such a method. Lewontin moved to Chicago in order to collaborate with Hubby. Their collaboration was especially fruitful. Their experiments made them famous, revolutionizing population genetics and inspiring a flurry of further work in molecular evolution.

Training the Next Generation

In addition to gaining renown as a scientist, Lewontin became known as a great mentor to his students. At Harvard, he has had a mixture of graduate students and postdoctoral fellows, as well as visiting professors who have come to work with him in the lab for six months to a year. Lewontin's goal has been to create an "intellectually exciting" infrastructure in which his students could flourish. In order to achieve this goal, he has filled his lab with as many qualified people as he has been able to find. His door has been kept open in order for him to be accessible to students. This goal is also reflected in the physical layout of the lab. He and his students designed it to be a very open space. They placed a large table with twenty chairs in the middle of the room, specifically for lab members—regardless of status—to sit around and talk. Affectionately dubbed by one student "The Last Supper Table," it was a map table from Harvard's geography department. Students could not reach their offices without passing the table, which was always filled with colleagues sitting, drinking coffee, and talking. When Lewontin came out and sat at the table, many students would come out of their offices and sit down, pretending all the while that his presence was not the impetus.

In keeping with his Marxist principles, Lewontin prides himself on running a nonhierarchical lab. However, he does not naively believe that it is a lab of equals. He understands his superiority of knowledge and power and has no desire to create some sort of "utopian anarchy." It would be counterproductive for his students to adapt to such an environment because "the world just isn't built that way." Nevertheless, the lab members function independently and have frequent seminars around the table with various visitors. When a postdoctoral fellow, visiting professor, or someone spending significant time in the lab arrives, the guest is invited to a Thursday luncheon for an informal presentation of his or her research, where lab members freely interrupt to ask questions. Lewontin teaches his classes in a nonhierarchical manner as well. As an ideological matter, he does not grade the students in his classes. After some years of struggle, he has arrived at a neutral grade of B+ that he gives to everyone in his class who does the work.

Lewontin never puts his name on students' papers, a practice he learned from Dobzhansky. He explicitly teaches his students that they should not put their names on their future students' papers either. However, Lewontin does not carry the practice as far as Dobzhansky. If he contributes substantively to the paper, he puts his name on it. Because the typical practice in the hard sciences is for the lab head to put his or her name on all papers regardless of contribution, however, Lewontin is reduced to "absurd extremes," like using footnotes specifying the contributions of the various authors. He strives to make it clear that he does not subscribe to the common practice of honorary authorship. Lewontin notes that the standard practice is frequently justified on the grounds that lab heads need to have many authorships in order to secure funding, but he never found that claim to be valid.

Lab activity revolves around collaborations among graduate students, postdocs, and visiting professors. Many of his students work together with so little supervision that Lewontin himself is not entirely aware of all of the collaborations in his lab until he is handed a manuscript or research report. Overall, he feels that his responsibility to the lab and his students is "to get the money, provide the space, give the cover, give the legitimacy, write the recommendations, and be available to talk to people if they want to talk." Although his free and nonhierarchical lab structure is not common practice among research labs, he not only feels comfortable with it on moral grounds, but also believes that it has helped him to do his best work. He believes that he does his best intellectual work only if others are doing theirs, because he can interact with their ideas. He finds that it benefits him more to be surrounded by people whom he considers intellectual peers than by followers carrying out his orders.

Like Dobzhansky, when Lewontin has visitors to his lab, they spend time with his students as well as with him.

Because Lewontin treats his students as intellectual peers, he is careful when selecting them. He admitted being influenced by a prospective student's personality: how they talk to him, raise issues, and behave toward him. He is attracted to older, more mature, and more directed students. When interviewing candidates, he asks them what they are interested in working on and pays attention to how well they appear to know the literature and what they say about themselves. Once he accepts a student into the lab, he does not call weekly meetings or regularly ask students to show him their work, the custom in many doctoral labs. He does not supply his doctoral students with thesis projects. Rather, he expects students to be independent and motivated, yet at the same time he stays in touch with their progress and comfort level in their graduate program. If he realizes a student has a problem, Lewontin goes out of his way to do the necessary repair work to fix it.

Although Lewontin's Marxist politics helped to shape his lab dynamics and nonhierarchical leadership style, his students did not appear to emulate his socialist political beliefs. They knew about his political leanings, but those to whom we spoke did not share or discuss them. "I really think my students regard my interest in political issues with an amused tolerance," says Lewontin. In creating his own lab, it is fair to say that he strove to establish an atmosphere inclusive of the positive aspects of what he learned from Dobzhansky and exclusive of the negative aspects. This pattern appears to characterize not only Lewontin; we found that many mentees actively select the attributes they admire while rejecting others. The mentee's active role in the mentoring relationship is discussed in more depth in later chapters.

Lewontin's Students

Many of Lewontin's students have gone on to important careers and had brilliant students of their own. We interviewed four of Lewontin's former students and asked them about their experiences working with him. Most said that they had been profoundly influenced by him. In particular, we were interested in the most important "things" they had learned, or memes that they had absorbed. Many of his students converged on the same core memes, most of which had also been expressed by Lewontin himself: high standards for research ethics, an anticareerist attitude, intellectual brilliance, broad interests, and, related to his mentoring style, encouraging intellectual independence and interaction in his lab, and valuing mentoring itself.

Most of Lewontin's students spoke of his strong ethics as a scientist with high standards for quality of work, honesty, integrity, and openness. His scientific ethics also included a willingness to share information, stand up for values, and live up to ethical obligations. One of his students said, "He's been an icon in population genetics, but also a person of very deep conviction and principle." While honesty and integrity are discussed in more detail in the following chapter as a meme that all three lineages shared, one particularly distinctive feature of Lewontin's ethics was his refusal to put his name on a student paper unless he had made a substantial contribution to it. Several students commented on this distinctive practice. According to one, "He also made a point of not putting his name on students' papers if he didn't actually do any work. And he was very generous about that. . . . Lewontin, in some ways, could get away with a lot, because he had such a wonderful reputation in his field. And he didn't coauthor papers with his students unless he actually contributed. He set a very high standard for that kind of academic honesty."

Other students commented that this practice became part of their own repertoires as professors, stating that seeing academics put their names on papers where it does not belong violates their own ethical standards. Some were keenly aware of the meme's multigenerational history. One student was aware not only that he was taught this principle by Lewontin, who had been taught it by Dobzhansky, but also that Dobzhansky was taught this principle by Thomas Hunt Morgan, one of the original pioneers of the field of genetics. These respondents considered this stance a personal decision, and yet felt a strong enough conviction about it that they sought to apply pressure to fellow scientists who readily accept undue credit.

Many of Lewontin's students were also influenced by his anticareerist attitude. A careerist person might publish many unimportant or insignificant papers for the purpose of padding his or her publication record. A student who had incorporated Lewontin's attitude into his own practice as a scientist put it like this: "I'm not a prolific publisher of papers. I'm not comfortable publishing every little result I get. Nor was Lewontin. Lewontin set a high standard for publishing important work and not counting the number of your publications. Since I have produced a number of what are thought to be landmark studies, I could get away with it."

Other students recognized the complexity and irony of the issue given Lewontin's fame and stature. They observed that some of his students were anticareerists with a secret desire to be famous like Lewontin. In some ways, this observation suggests that a mentor's actions and overall identity may be more formative than the mentor's words. Of course, for Lewontin, recognition came naturally from his immense scientific contributions; he disdained scientists who aspired to fame without a solid basis for it in terms of contribution. Nevertheless, if a mentor does not "walk the talk," a given meme may not be compelling. In that sense, several of Lewontin's students appeared at least somewhat conflicted about the anticareerist message, much as an antireligious message might be received from the pope.

Lewontin's students were also in awe of his intellectual brilliance, which seemed to place him in an elite category of scientists. One student said, "More so than others, he was able to create his own environment and just pursue science the way he thought it should be done. Most people, a lot of people, are just in there slugging away trying to get their next grant. And there are certain realities that one is constantly faced with.

And in some sense, Lewontin escaped some of those realities just because of his reputation and because of his brilliance."

Another student told about a time when he and his colleagues were resisting work on one of Lewontin's projects. Only when a paper was published about it could they comprehend the path-breaking nature of his contribution:

> He was doing a major piece of work at that point, a major project. He was being coy about telling everybody in the lab exactly what he was doing. He and another guy in another lab were working on this. When the paper came out, it revolutionized the study of genetic variation in populations, but the people in his lab at the time didn't know what was going on, and we thought that this was a loony-sounding project; we were glad to let him work on it. We didn't want to be pushed into this project. He didn't really give us the details, but once we saw the paper, we thought, "Oh my God, he's just totally transformed the field!"

Many of Lewontin's students mentioned his broad interests, depth of perspective, and philosophical grounding. One said, "Lewontin's interests were quite broad, and he didn't force his research agenda on anyone. . . . You could just really delight in listening to him talk about very simple problems in evolutionary biology in beautifully integrated perspective. He's one of those people you maybe can hear the same lecture and there's always something new you can gain from it. There's a lot of depth, texture to his thinking." Another student told us, "His interest extended off into history, philosophy, some in statistics. He's really spread over a very wide area." Several testified that Lewontin's broad interests influenced their own approach to science and kept them from becoming too narrowly focused.

Lewontin was known among his students for encouraging intellectual independence and giving them substantial freedom to follow their own interests. His mentoring style was experienced as very hands off, though he checked in with students periodically. Repeatedly his students told us that they could pursue whatever projects they wished because Lewontin gave them complete freedom. According to one student, "That was the way that lab was. All the resources are there, and anyone can use them for whatever purpose, and no one's going to [keep] tabs on how much you're using of what. Just go; do what you think is interesting."

Others commented that Lewontin did not help them find a research problem, insisting that they find their own. Some of his mentees noted that such a mentoring style is rare. In most cases, when students enter the labs of accomplished scientists, intellectual direction proceeds from the top down. Those in Lewontin's lab, however, had to find their own way. Some noted that Lewontin may have carried this style to the point of taking little interest in his students' work. Even those students, however, greatly appreciated being afforded such a high degree of freedom: "The idea of just trying to have a laboratory environment where people can do their own thing and pursue their own interests to the extent possible—that was really what was so brilliant about being in Lewontin's lab."

Lewontin did support his students when they needed it, however. One student commented on Lewontin's accessibility by remembering that he always gave students time when they requested it. Furthermore, they considered it particularly high-quality time because of his uncanny ability to solve almost any problem of a scientific nature. When one of them went to Lewontin with an idea for research, Lewontin might help reframe it, frequently leading students in a more promising direction. In fact, when it came to playing a crucial advising role, we found much evidence that Lewontin's example influenced the subsequent mentoring practices of his students. As one of them said, "I really benefited greatly, being able to do what I wanted to do, and I try to let my own students do that. . . . I've taken much more of a role, especially as I've gotten older, just working hard to make resources available for them to do their work and give them the freedom."

Students considered Lewontin a master at setting up and encouraging interaction and collaboration, providing an intellectually stimulating environment, and attracting diverse people to the lab. One student noted that "the real experience" and "the most valuable experiences" in the lab were interactions with peers. Another of his students said, "He set a very high standard for openness and for letting his own students pursue their own interests, and cultivating interaction." His students also credited Lewontin with a rare ability to bring a great diversity of people to the lab: "There're very few places where someone has the ability to attract the whole range of expertise." Some students also recalled that during their tenure in his lab, it included many minority, international, and female students. His students resonated with this social stance, but not necessarily his politics, which they saw as a "quirk." But they could see that the open and collaborative lab atmosphere he created stemmed from his political morality and social ethics, and they respected that. They particularly appreciated the significance of the Last Supper Table and his open door policy.

Many students went on to emulate his example when becoming professors themselves. Some even tried to imitate the Last Supper Table by creating a common area for lab collaborators to discuss their activities, or they attempted to foster the same high standard for diversity. One former student noted: "Theoreticians don't come to work with me. I'm not a theoretician. But they do go to work with . . . several of my colleagues here. So that creates an environment here where graduate students are interacting with each other. Some of them are interested in theory. I think that's where they learn, more than anything, from one another." Related to collaboration and respect for diversity, many of his students remembered Lewontin's sense of fairness and collegiality in dealing with others, and his habit of treating others equally. Having a nonhierarchical lab, not pulling rank, and not denigrating students made an important impression on his students, and several indicated the desire to emulate him in these areas.

Several of Lewontin's students paid tribute to his fundamental perspective about the nature of the biological world. One said, "Lewontin is more interested in the way things interact. He was interested in a view of the world in which you could break it down into simple elements, but the simple elements had to interact, and you should pay attention to the ways they interacted and try to model that."

In much the same way, Lewontin was interested in how his own students interacted. It is possible that his outlook, in which parts of a system are equal and interacting, was rooted in his Marxist philosophy and politics. Marxist or not, the intellectual perspectives he adopted were highly integrated: his science, his politics, and his mentoring were all viewed through models of complex systems in which smaller or subordinate parts interacted and influenced each other. His students had an appreciation for the complexity and integration of Lewontin's intellectual outlook. His thinking in one domain seemingly influenced his thinking in the others, as was easily observed in his writings and teachings. Lewontin's complexity provided a great deal of depth to his students' training.

The messages Lewontin imparted extended to valuing mentoring itself, a meme that is perhaps as important to him as any other. He wanted to make sure that the things his students learned from him would be passed on to their students. He was especially adamant that his students treat their future students properly and respectfully. For example, he wanted to make sure that when his students became lab heads, they would reject gratuitous authorship in the same way that he had and would also teach this practice to their own students.

In our interviews with Lewontin and his students, we were not only curious about which memes Lewontin transmitted but also how he did so. Several pathways for transmitting memes stood out in the interviews from Lewontin's lineage. Lewontin had a profound influence seemingly by sheer force of his personality and brilliance. As one student said:

> Being around him can't help but influence anyone and, in fact, I'm just one of so many people who have made contact with him at some point in their careers. Other people [did so] as postdocs. Many people you'll meet will say, "Well, Lewontin just came through and gave a seminar and went to lunch with me as a graduate student and my whole career in the last thirty years was shaped by that one hour of interaction.". . . He's just a very brilliant man. As a student, you say, "I'm interested in this." Then Lewontin will just lay out a much grander vision of how to place your interest in a much more interesting, enlightened context. And then he sets you off in a direction, and that's it. . . . He was a great influence in the sense that he's truly a brilliant person. Much more influential in the courses he taught. We all took his courses. Somehow, it was just the aura of his presence and, as I say, this great wisdom and knowledge about evolutionary biology, which you'd get in little glimpses . . . when he would be around the Last Supper Table, or in his lectures.

Another fundamental way that Lewontin influenced students was by providing them with human and physical resources that embodied his memes. For example, he could impart his theoretical views through open discussions in which senior lab members might help to familiarize the other members with Lewontin's ideas. In addition, the independence Lewontin granted students in his well-stocked lab enabled them to grow on their own while still being rooted in Lewontin's intellectual tradition. His style of being hands-off, and then hands-on when needed, proved effective in transmitting his memes. This is not a trivial point: one of the greatest obstacles to quality mentoring mentioned in our sample was the time that it takes—time that busy professors can scarcely afford. Lewontin's example demonstrates that memes can be effectively transmitted by setting up a fertile environment for growth and allowing students to develop on their own with monitoring and guidance as needed.

The way Lewontin challenged students was also an effective pathway for transmitting his memes, particularly those relating to intellectual depth and scientific excellence. He challenged students to think, and yet he never treated them as inferior. He respected them as valued scientific collaborators. Lewontin challenged in one of the best ways that a mentor can: creating a need for mastery of the material so as to keep up with the level of the dialogue. Several students commented on the necessity of keeping up with the literature in order to have a meaningful exchange with him. Lewontin assumed that his students had a firm grasp of the scientific scholarly environment. Some felt the need to spend the first several years in their program learning the history of evolutionary genetics, a background that not only helped them to be intellectually aware when interacting within the context of Lewontin's lab, but also helped them to prosper as scientists. Lewontin was known for giving challenging scientific problems to solve. The main challenge, however, remained his example. His students wanted to be like him. And being like him meant working very hard in order to obtain mastery of a great deal of scientific knowledge, as well as behaving properly and being considerate of others.

That is, Lewontin also influenced students with respect to ethical conduct through his example. The stand that he took on ethical issues allowed students to incorporate similar positions into their own scientific approach and gave them the confidence to take the moral high ground in their subsequent careers. Some testified that their experience with Lewontin freed them from spending a lot of time defining a code of ethics. Ethical behavior became clear to them by seeing their mentor in action.

One of Lewontin's Students: A Case Study

In this section, we present a case study of one of Lewontin's students to illustrate how students were influenced by Lewontin's memes and how they emulated him when teaching students of their own. We refer to the subject of the case study as Kevin Henderson. Like many other interviewees, Henderson also had another influential mentor, but Lewontin's influence was profound. Henderson felt that he learned many things from Lewontin by force of example, as well as by working in the lab environment he created. He spoke at length of Lewontin's strong ethics and practice of fair authorship. He also commented on the high degree of freedom Lewontin allotted. He recognized his mentor's anticareerism and the diverse and collaborative lab environment he established. Like many of Lewontin's other students, he also discussed Lewontin's brilliance and his mentoring style, which encouraged intellectual freedom and independence.

Henderson had a good relationship with Lewontin. He felt that Lewontin cared about his welfare, and was accessible and generous with his time. Henderson was free to call on Lewontin for advice and had a great deal of confidence in his perspective on career obstacles and other issues.

According to Henderson, Lewontin succeeded in producing students who went on to do high-level work on similar problems. As a mentor, Henderson strove to teach his own students everything he learned from Lewontin, and he felt that his former students shared his research ethics, chose important problems, and treated their own students ethically and fairly. Like Lewontin, he encouraged intellectual independence in his students. One strategy he used to achieve this goal was to encourage his students to challenge him, and even prove him wrong. He was gratified to see his students develop intellectual independence and encouraged them to ask any question, no matter how seemingly ignorant or trivial.

Probably to a greater extent than Lewontin, Henderson sought to give students a lot of attention. For example, he attempted to provide support by giving them perspective when they submitted papers to journals. If the paper was not accepted and the student asked for advice, he encouraged the student to rewrite and resubmit it to a good journal, reassuring them of its quality. If a paper was not accepted, he was inclined to believe that the reviewers were not very competent because he rarely allowed his students to submit papers until they were of high quality. He explained that there were a variety of circumstances in which he had to take his students' emotional temperature and provide some perspective, such as when their experiments did not work. He felt his role even approached that of a counselor or clinical psychologist, occasionally calming students down, helping them to think about their personal adversities, listening to them, and trying to be understanding.

Henderson went out of his way to treat his students equally and to create a nonhierarchical lab environment. He strove to create a congenial atmosphere in which everyone used first names. He invited social activity with his students, like going out for a ball game together. Occasionally he took his students out to lunch. He sensed that his students knew they were being treated as colleagues and were not inhibited from speaking their mind and challenging him or each other. In some cases, he was keenly aware that he was emulating Lewontin in dealing with his own students. He aspired to be like Lewontin in terms of generously supporting his students financially—sponsoring them to attend professional conferences, for example. Even when it required a significant amount of grant money, he would still attempt to support students in this way, as doing so was beneficial for both his students and the profession.

Henderson actively attempted to impart his values to students. Some practices he sought to inculcate were so specific to Lewontin that their source could not be mistaken. For example, the first time that his own students drafted a manuscript, they often put his name on it. He then promptly crossed his name out. When the student asked why, Henderson explained that his role was limited to providing suggestions and the physical space to do the work, a role unworthy of authorship. And so the meme played on.

Kevin Henderson's Students

What did Henderson's students tell us about the most meaningful memes they inherited from him? Henderson was one of two strong influences on one G3 interviewee, Peter Oswaldt. Oswaldt believed that he learned two different sets of memes from his two mentors. He learned a great deal about the scientific process from his undergraduate advisor, and then built on that foundation by learning a great deal about the subject of genetics and a career focused on research from Henderson, who was his graduate advisor.

Some of the memes Henderson mentioned appeared to derive from Lewontin, but they took on a distinctive flavor or style that Henderson seemed to add. For example, hard work is a strong meme running throughout the Lewontin lineage. According to Oswaldt, Henderson was a hard worker, particularly with respect to being very thorough and driven to succeed. In terms of specific aptitudes and skills, however, Henderson sharply differed from Lewontin in some areas. For example, Lewontin had a strong mathematical and statistical inclination, whereas Henderson did not. What he lacked in mathematical prowess, however, he made up for by thoroughness and adopting his mentor's rigorous standards for research. Another example of Henderson's high standards, according to Oswaldt, was his insistence on getting experimental work out for publication quickly and efficiently.

Henderson also demonstrated other core lineage memes that seemed unambiguously passed down by Lewontin, particularly those relating to mentoring and teaching practices. For example, Oswaldt emphasized that Henderson gave him a good deal of independence. Like Lewontin, Henderson insisted that students select their own research projects and challenged them to keep up with the literature. Oswaldt was clearly challenged by Henderson in a positive way and was impressed by his work ethic.

It was clear that Oswaldt absorbed a variety of memes from his mentor, mainly through observation and direct interaction or conversations. Some of them appeared to have been core lineage memes originating with Lewontin, and others appeared to have been distinctive of Henderson. In general, the presence of Lewontin's memes was not as strong in the third generation as it was in the second. This may suggest extinction pressure or dilution as memes make their way down a lineage. (We discuss this possibility in greater depth in Chapter Five.)

In contrast, another of Henderson's students, Leon Jenks, discussed most of the core lineage memes and appeared to have absorbed many of them just as Lewontin's own students had. Perhaps the most prominent memes Jenks mentioned were in the area of ethics. Jenks did not imply that Henderson was highly involved with moral and ethical issues in genetics, but rather that his everyday ethical behavior made such an impression that he himself attempted to emulate it as a scientist. According to Jenks, Henderson took stands on daily ethical issues just as Lewontin had. Henderson's ethical principles included a critical view of those who conducted or published work of minimal value for the purpose of advancing their career. This meme appeared to be transmitted at least through three or four generations, starting with Dobzhansky, if not Morgan. That Jenks sought to consciously emulate the meme testifies to its potency.

Like Oswaldt, Jenks also inherited his mentor's intense work ethic. Jenks's understanding was that Lewontin's expectations for work in his lab were perhaps more relaxed than those of Henderson. This view corroborated Lewontin's own perception that his students verged on being workaholics, while he himself encouraged a balance of personal and professional priorities. It is interesting to wonder if those coming after Lewontin demonstrated a more intense work ethic because they were compensating for lack of his perceived brilliance. Regardless, Jenks appeared to greatly appreciate his mentor's work intensity, a meme that he consciously attempted to pass on to his own students.

Jenks was also aware of other practices that had endured as part of his lineage's tradition. Another example was the practice of not holding the weekly lab meetings common to many labs, which replicated Lewontin's custom and attempted to encourage his students' independence. Jenks was not only aware of this practice as a tradition in the lineage, but was also aware of the exact reason that weekly lab meetings had been considered taboo. Although weekly meetings very well may have been fruitful in his own lab, he still eschewed them. It is possible that how one was mentored may hold an extremely powerful default status when training future generations, such that additional energy and conscious thought are necessary to dethrone old traditions. In lieu of weekly lab meetings, Jenks interacted one-on-one with students to a greater extent than his peers did. This was consistent with what he had experienced during his own training.

Jenks also perceived Henderson as someone who allowed him a great deal of intellectual freedom, including the liberty to challenge his mentor's ideas. Jenks observed that the non-authoritarian and nonhierarchical structure of Lewontin's lab was transmitted down through the lineage, and that while Lewontin's Marxist philosophy may have been the basis of that approach, his political orientation itself was not transmitted.

Jenks noted several memes that he felt were part of his own value system and probably originated with his mentor, as opposed to being indirectly inherited from Lewontin. For example, he emphasized a preference for simplicity in scientific work and theories, a notable attribute of Henderson; Lewontin had not transmitted this meme. New practices and values are continually created by successive generations of scientists even as others begin to fade away.

Jenks described being influenced by his mentor through a variety of pathways. One was the feedback his mentor provided. For example, Henderson was prone to giving Jenks positive feedback for clean, simple solutions to problems. Henderson also provided generous written feedback on student papers in order to teach quality of writing. In other instances, Jenks learned from his mentor just by observing him and desiring to emulate his virtues, such as taking ethical stands and not tolerating careerism or a lack of rigor. Jenks may actually have absorbed some memes directly from Lewontin through his books and articles; for example, Lewontin's breadth of thinking may have been transmitted by the writings themselves. Nevertheless, most memes were channeled through Henderson in the process of direct mentoring by means of dialogue and discussion.

There is perhaps no other core lineage meme more distinctly attributable to Lewontin than that of merited authorship, and Jenks was aware of this practice as an important part of his lineage's legacy. He was not only aware of the tradition, but also conscious of his desire to continue transmitting it down the lineage by explicitly teaching the same practice to his own students. The detailed knowledge that Jenks had of the various traditions in his lineage was a surprise. Of course, it was our hypothesis that we would find such patterns of tradition with respect to specific practices, but we did not expect that the scientists themselves would be intimately aware of them as far back as two or three generations. Jenks noted that his mentor and Lewontin had distinct scientific and lab management styles, and yet certain core memes such as the refusal of gratuitous authorship could be traced back through the lineage.

It is important to remember that at the time of the interview, the scientists had no knowledge of what became the specific theme of our study. We asked many questions about their mentors and how they tried to teach the next generation, but we did not frame the interview in terms of cultural evolution and transmission of memes. Nevertheless, Jenks expressed a combination of humor and pride at the habits, stories, and practices that characterize his scientific lineage and the allegiance that its members consciously or subconsciously feel toward the traditions. He was keenly aware that those in his lineage taught the practices and values that had come to define a proud legacy.

Conclusion

The Lewontin lineage demonstrated a pattern of transmission similar to the other two lineages. It begins with a strong role model—in this case, one who personified strong research ethics, brilliance, a disdain for careerism, and broad interests extending beyond science. His students spoke frequently about the influence of these memes, while also noticing a style of mentoring that encouraged both collaboration and independence. Lewontin's students absorbed these memes through a variety of pathways, including observation, his past writings, and direct collaboration or discussion. Once absorbed, these memes became their own to pass on. Through the personalities and mentoring styles of Lewontin's students, additional distinctive memes eventually came to characterize the lineage in subsequent generations, including rigor and an intense work ethic. The Lewontin lineage illustrates that members can become consciously aware of their involvement in a tradition of specific practices reaching back several generations, and it can become a source of professional identity and pride. As the third generation of the lineage demonstrated, such pride can fuel the deliberate teaching of lineage memes to continue the legacy.

Part Two

HOW GOOD MENTORING WORKS

Part Two provides a second window on mentoring, understood as the transmission of values, practices, knowledge, and other memes across generations. The chapters in Part One presented three lineage case studies: separate portraits of three senior scientists and the research traditions or lineages that each headed. In contrast, each chapter in this part brings together voices drawn from all three lineages.

In contrast to the synthetic approach taken to describe each lineage in Part One, Part Two takes an analytical approach to the scientists' accounts. Each chapter examines one central aspect of good mentoring: the lineage heads' memes and the fate of these memes across generations, the means or pathways by which the lineage heads' memes are passed down, and the mentor-protégé relationships that constitute the matrix or context for transmission. The chapters in Part Two summarize the results of abstracting and analyzing what the scientists reported about these topics.

In Chapter Five, the three lineages are juxtaposed in order to reveal through quantitative analysis whether some memes characterize one lineage and not others and whether any memes characterize all three groups of scientists. We raise as well the related questions of whether the impact of a lineage head is diluted over time and how the transformation of the meme pool occurs across generations. By considering the whole data set, the chapter provides our best empirically based answer to one of the book's central questions: Does mentoring play a role in the perpetuation and evolution of good work?

Chapter Six addresses the companion question: If the lineage heads' memes survive from one generation to the next, by what means does this occur? What do mentors and their former students report about the key pathways through which memes are handed down or absorbed? The lineage heads' insights about their mentoring practices, and the corroborating accounts provided by their former students, take the foreground in this chapter, where the goal is to illuminate the process of good mentoring.

Finally, Chapter Seven examines the relationship between the mentor and protégé; the dyadic context in which the process of transmission occurs. To do so, it draws on all of the scientists' accounts of mentor-protégé relationships, both those as student and those as advisor, the many experiences that were positive and the few that were not, distilling out the attributes of weaker and stronger mentoring relationships. In Chapter Seven, the evolutionary, systems understanding of mentoring that informs Chapters Five and Six is brought together with the relational perspective that has characterized most past research on mentoring.

5

VALUES, PRACTICES, AND KNOWLEDGE THROUGH THE GENERATIONS

Chapters Two through Four described three senior scientists, exploring the particular constellation of values, beliefs, and practices—the memes—that each of them exemplified. In each research tradition, or lineage, some memes were transmitted down at least two generations of students. From the perspective of cultural evolution, the carriers of the profession's cultural DNA—Gall, Motulsky, Lewontin, and their successors—were the focus of the preceding chapters. In this chapter, the memes that these scientists embodied, transmitted, and inherited move to the foreground, and the lineage histories become background or context. The change of ground may strike some readers as unusual. However, this is precisely the shift in thinking that is needed to understand the process of cultural evolution. If memes are the instructions or code that will define the prevailing values and practices in each profession, those interested in the health of the professions may find them just as important a topic for study as geneticists do DNA.

To complement the qualitative lineage portraits, we turn to a quantitative analysis of the transmission of memes by comparing the three lineages and then look across the sample as a whole. These analyses address the values, practices, and qualities that scientists have inherited from their mentors. Juxtaposing lineages makes it possible to address a series of questions. First, are there memes that are successfully transmitted down one lineage but not the others? That is, what is the evidence for the existence of distinctive "lineage-signature" memes? Second, are there memes that do not set one lineage apart from the others but rather are handed down in all of them? All mentors manifest, and may transmit to their students, the particular variant of occupational life of which they are a carrier. Adapting to this setting Kluckhohn and Murray's (1953) aphorism about personality, in some respects a scientist is like all other scientists, like some other scientists, and like no other scientist. We are interested in both the ways that each lineage head is distinctive and the ways that all the lineage heads are alike.

Because we are interested in whether mentoring chains are one means of perpetuating good work, we examine the types of memes that are inherited in the lineages of exemplary scientists. Intellectual and artistic traditions may endure, and evolve, through transmission of a specialized body of knowledge directly from master to disciple across successive generations. This process is well documented, and vivid examples spring readily to mind, such as Freud's intellectual lineage, which has been described by both its members and its chroniclers in terms of paternity, succession, and filial loyalty (for example, Roazen, 1975). It is not only specialized bodies of knowledge that are handed down by scientists, however. Skills and practices supporting creative accomplishment are also intergenerationally transmitted from master to apprentice (see Kanigel, 1986; Zuckerman, 1977). For example, students absorb the ability to sense the importance and feasibility of a problem and the elegance of a solution (compare with Cole, 1979), or they acquire the readiness to follow a hunch that may support scientific discovery in general. Our own interest extends to memes whose impact is not specific to science but rather is crucial to the sustained health of any profession. These memes support ethical conduct and social responsibility as well as excellence—the essential components of good work. Because the lineages we studied are headed by scientists who exemplified good work, we conjectured that any common memes might be characteristics integral to the perpetuation of good work within the scientific community, and any distinguishing qualities might represent variants of good work.

Looking across the sample, we also ask if there are some memes that tend to be possessed specifically because they are absorbed from a mentor during graduate training and others that tend not to be. These might provide some insight into the kinds of values and practices that are susceptible to influence by positive mentoring experiences. For better or worse, other values and practices may crystallize long before a student's graduate education begins, and they therefore are less susceptible to influence. Alternatively, they may be formed only later, once the scientist is working independently in the field, and any impact of the apprenticeship on this process will be indirect. Finally, comparing the memes transmitted by the lineage heads with those passed down by their students, we also ask to what extent the survival of memes attenuates in moving from generation to generation and whether new memes emerge.

The Intergenerational Transmission of Memes

In order to trace the evolution of the profession's traditions as embodied and transmitted by these scientists, we focus on a set of twenty-five inductively derived types of memes, organized by the systems perspective. From this perspective (see Csikszentmihalyi, 1988), a profession implicates four dynamically interacting systems: the three subsystems of the profession—the person, the cultural domain, and the social field—and the broader society, or humanity in general. Seasoned practitioners possess many memes relating to each of these systems, and these memes vary from one practitioner to the next as a result of different constitutions and histories. For example, one physician possesses finely honed clinical skills (domain memes) and knows how to get along professionally (a field meme); another has mastered the latest techniques (domain memes), applying this expertise to problems that afflict his community's poor (society/humanity memes); and so on. The twenty-five types of memes discussed in this chapter flesh out, or differentiate, these four broad categories as they apply to the scientists interviewed.

The *person* category contains characteristics of the individual practitioner that are not limited to his or her scientific work: personal motivational orientations and priorities (for example, broad interests extending beyond science) and personal traits and values (for example, intellectualism). The *domain* category contains aspects of genetics as a sphere of cultural knowledge and practice: memes that concern scientific excellence (for example, high standards of quality, as well as mastery of the body of specialized knowledge and skills that defines the domain), scientific ethics (for example, honesty, integrity, and ethics in research), and scientific approach or style (for example, scientific breadth). The *field* category contains values and practices focused on the social organization of genetics—the individual's own lab and the wider scientific community. It encompasses not only memes having to do with the individual's navigation of the field as a practitioner (for example, collaboration) but also values and practices as a mentor or teacher (for example, providing students with intellectual freedom and guidance). Finally, the *society/humanity* category contains values and practices concerned with the welfare of others, extending beyond the field of genetics. It encompasses humanitarianism and social responsibility, for example.

Whereas the four categories constitute broad areas of professional life in which mentoring relationships carry down to the next generation and, through it, the evolving profession, the twenty-five specific types represent the pool of memes that characterized this particular group of scientists. Of course, because many of the memes are complex and the systems interact, some memes straddle categories. For example, the meme "research-practice integration" describes an approach to research in the domain of genetics that implicates societal aims (see Table 5.1).

Table 5.1 The Scientists' Meme Pool

Category of Memes	Systems Implicated
Primarily practitioner-related memes	
Broad interests, nonscience	Practitioner
Independence, resolve, robust ego	Practitioner
High intellectualism	Practitioner
Intrinsic motivations for science (for example, flow, curiosity)	Practitioner, Domain
Creativity, originality, innovation	Practitioner, Domain
Industriousness, hard work	Practitioner, Domain
Neatness and order	Practitioner, Domain
Marxist, socialist politics	Practitioner, Society/ Humanity
Other traits and personal values	Practitioner
Primarily domain-related memes	
Research skills and domain knowledge	Domain
High research standards	Domain
Honesty, integrity, and ethics in research	Domain, Field
Scientific breadth	Domain
Research-practice integration (for example, the physician-scientist model)	Domain, Society/ Humanity
Other approaches to basic science	Domain
Primarily field-related memes	
Collaboration (for example, cooperation, sharing of information)	Field
Providing intellectual freedom and guidance	Field
Creating a facilitative lab structure	Field
Anticareerism	Field, Practitioner
Authorship based on contribution	Field, Domain
Primarily society- and humanity-related memes	
Humanitarianism, social responsibility	Society/Humanity, Practitioner
Political consciousness, advocacy	Society/Humanity

(Continued)

Table 5.1 (*Continued*)

Category of Memes	Systems Implicated
Educating the public about science	Society/Humanity, Domain
Treating people equally, fairly	Society/Humanity, Field
Teaching, generativity	Society/Humanity, Field

Note: Four interacting systems define an occupation: the individual practitioner, cultural domain, social field, and society or humanity broadly. Each of a practitioner's memes concerns one or more of these systems. For example, neatness and order is a personal preference that translates directly into laboratory practice (therefore: Practitioner, Domain).

Transcripts were coded for mentions of memes that were (1) possessed and (2) inherited or absorbed from mentors. An individual might possess a meme but not inherit it from a mentor in the lineage. "Inheriting" indicates a mention, during the interview, of being influenced by the mentor; it does not imply that the mentor's influence is the sole reason that the respondent possesses the meme today. A respondent might discuss the importance she attaches to honesty in her work; she might also mention that her mentor impressed on her the importance of honesty as a researcher. She would be coded as both possessing and inheriting the meme of honesty, integrity, and ethics in science. The reliance on one-time interviews means that the counts represent minima; respondents simply may not mention possessing or inheriting a given meme during the interview, even if they actually do. (For details of the coding process, see Appendix A.)

Perpetuation of Research Traditions: Lineage-Signature Memes

Each of the lineages emanating from Gall, Motulsky, and Lewontin resembles a biological family with a strong, admired ancestral figure. Certain features of the lineage head appeared to be reproduced with some fidelity in the next generation and survived into a third generation as well. However, qualities such as a spirit of adventure and a sharp wit might appear to distinguish one biological family from other families, only to reveal themselves as qualities shared widely in the community to which the family belongs. Similarly, given a portrait of only a single scientific lineage, we cannot tell which of its salient qualities in fact distinguish the lineage from others. If we compare multiple lineages, however, and restrict attention to memes influenced by apprenticeship, it becomes possible to distinguish values and practices that are inherited within a particular tradition from ones that are common in the wider culture. If we find that members of successive generations in one lineage share a meme and those in the other two lineages do not, there is a clear suggestion that the meme has been transmitted in the first lineage. The genetic analogy would be blue eyes running through one family tree compared to brown eyes running through another. For this reason, it made sense to begin by directly comparing the three lineages for evidence of differential inheritance of memes, which would suggest that apprenticeship is functioning as a mechanism of cultural evolution.

It turns out that eight of the twenty-five memes were absorbed by significantly more members of one lineage than of the other two. Just as psychologists speak of personal signature strengths—the positive attributes that distinguish an individual (Seligman, 2002)—we call these memes *lineage signatures*: distinctive characteristics of the lineage head that were widely reproduced in subsequent generations. For the eight lineage-signature memes, Table 5.2 shows the number of lineage members who were coded as absorbing the meme from their mentor within each lineage. The figures in bold show which lineage was statistically different from the other two, as indicated by the results of a chi-square test.

Joe Gall is a scientist's scientist, distinguished by the intensity of his focus on the sphere of nature, its patterns, and their

Table 5.2 Lineage-Signature Memes: Number of Lineage Members Who Inherited Each Meme

Meme	Gall Lineage ($n = 13$)	Motulsky Lineage ($n = 11$)	Lewontin Lineage ($n = 12$)	$X^2(2)$
Intrinsic motivations for science	7	3	1	6.17*
Scientific breadth	7	0	0	15.37***
Neatness and order	4	0	0	7.96*
Humanitarianism, social responsibility	1	7	0	15.93***
Research-practice integration (for example, physician-scientist model)	0	6	0	16.36***
Anticareerism	1	0	4	5.98*
Authorship based on contribution	3	1	6	5.01†
High intellectualism	0	0	3	6.54*

Note: †$p < .10$. *$p < .05$. ***$p < .001$. Lineage-signature memes are shown in bold.

exploration through scientific research. It thus makes sense that all three of the memes that are most strongly inherited within Gall's lineage highlight the scientist's relationship to the domain itself rather than to the field of practitioners or the wider society.

In terms of motivational orientations, the lineage stands out for the transmission of commitment to the intrinsic motivations for doing science. Curiosity, love of nature, and the enjoyment intrinsic to interaction with the domain are certainly prioritized by many scientists. The Gall lineage nevertheless distinguishes itself by the number of its members who felt that their mentor within the lineage had fostered intrinsic reasons for doing science.

One might expect motivational orientations to be in place long before graduate training. In fact, common characteristics shared at the start of the apprenticeship may play a role in mentors' and students' affinity for one another (Zuckerman, 1977). However, we found that common affinity and inheritance are not mutually exclusive; a student may perceive the mentor as a strong formative influence in areas where such affinities exist. A mentor's influence on a student is always the result of a complex interaction in the context of a developing relationship. Where forces of attraction are strong, a mentor's influence may build on the inclinations that students possessed even before the relationship. What the social scientist might describe as a selection bias therefore might be part and parcel of a dynamic and enduring process of mentoring. This was precisely the case with respect to the tendency toward an intrinsic motivational orientation in the Gall lineage. Both the qualitative and the quantitative analyses make clear that Gall consciously sought out students who were already driven by curiosity about the biological world; after they entered the lab, he actively modeled and encouraged intrinsic reasons for doing science throughout their apprenticeship, and they said that this affected them.

More distinctive is the signature practice of pursuing scientific breadth. Gall maintained a formidable breadth of interest and knowledge as a scientist; indeed, he disdained becoming a "narrow specialist." This approach to the conduct of professional life has become increasingly rare as the scope of knowledge in all domains grows to daunting proportions and conventional wisdom dictates finding a niche, however small, that one can master. Yet about half of the members of the Gall lineage—versus no members of the Motulsky and Lewontin lineages—explicitly endorsed scientific breadth and said they had been influenced in this regard by their mentor within the lineage.

Finally, four members of the Gall lineage mentioned absorbing a habit of neatness and order in their work from their mentor within the lineage. Gall's own neatness in the laboratory may derive from the attraction to visual pattern and order that characterizes his deepest scientific motivations. But he professed a grudging toleration of sloppiness, viewing neatness as a matter of personal preference, and this meme was less widely replicated than the first two signature memes within the Gall lineage. Nevertheless, it stands out because its transmission was not mentioned at all in the other lineages.

We turn next to the Motulsky lineage. Rather than a second, contrasting approach to the domain, the two signature memes of the Motulsky lineage underscore the scientist's relationship to the wider community. It is not that Motulsky and the scientists in his lineage ignore the domain of science. Good work in science—and any other profession—requires mastery of, respect for, and attentive involvement with the domain itself. Much more than for the other lineage heads, however, Motulsky's distinctive relationship to science was closely bound up with its usefulness to humanity.

The Motulsky lineage's signature motivational orientation is humanitarianism. Not only is the orientation widely shared among members of the lineage, which might be expected in any sample of medical geneticists, but in addition, the mentor was often credited with encouraging or inspiring this impulse. Motulsky's evident concern for the welfare of other human beings made a lasting impression on his trainees, the G2s, and some of the G2s made a similar impression on their trainees, the G3s. Humanitarianism encompasses not only putting the patient at the center of medical care, an impetus specific to medical genetics, but also social responsibility, treating others well, and altruism— motivational orientations that might equally characterize scientists without clinical duties. Nevertheless, whereas seven members of the Motulsky lineage indicated that they had been influenced by the humanitarianism of their mentor within the lineage, only a single respondent in the rest of the sample did.

The signature approach of the lineage to the practice of science is integration of research and practice, pursuing both activities so that each can inform the other: work in the domain is placed in dialogue with concerns in the world. In medical genetics specifically, Motulsky has promulgated a physician-scientist model: he has embraced both roles and brought them into dialogue with each other. The integration of inquiry and application might be cultivated in most branches of science. However, whereas six members of Motulsky's lineage sought to integrate research and practice, and attributed this to their mentor's influence, no members of the other lineages did so. As with the lineage's signature motivational orientation, this approach also foregrounds the professional's relationship to humanity.

Turning to the Lewontin lineage, three memes distinguish it from the others. Lewontin's signature memes do not focus on the relationship to the domain, as for Gall; nor do they focus on the relationship to the wider community, as for Motulsky, though Lewontin is keenly aware of science's relationship to society. Rather, his signature memes emphasize the relationship to the field: the scientific community and the individual's standing within it.

The motivational orientation that distinguishes Lewontin's lineage is expressed as anticareerism: rejection of a preoccupation with professional recognition and advancement in the field. One-third of the Lewontin lineage, versus only one individual in the rest of the sample, absorbed an attitude of anticareerism from their mentor within the lineage.

The practice that distinguishes Lewontin's lineage is vigilance about authorship based on contribution. Again the distinctively highlighted locus of concern is the relationship to the community of scientists. Fair allocation of authorship credit was transmitted in the other lineages to some degree, but fully half of the Lewontin lineage's members mentioned absorbing this practice from their mentor. Moreover, as detailed in Chapter Four, Lewontin views fairness about authorship, particularly in relation to student collaborators, through a Marxist lens. As a result, the meme carries a distinctive spin when it is described by Lewontin's professional offspring, reflecting greater consciousness of power relations and an intent to critique and transform (versus simply depart from) the field's standard practice of routinely sharing in the credit for students' work. Vigilance about fair credit and anticareerism exemplify what Lewontin labeled his moralism: each meme expresses a principled position about social relations within the scientific community and clearly contains a moral judgment about the field's existing practices: "I am not the kind of scientist who . . ."

Finally, the personal quality that distinguishes Lewontin's lineage is high intellectualism and disdain for its absence. A student might despair of achieving Lewontin's brilliance, but an orientation toward intellectual life (for example, a seriousness about ideas and pleasure in their exchange) was professed by one-fourth of the Lewontin lineage's members, and the mentor within the lineage was identified as a formative influence. The meme was not mentioned by members of the other lineages.

Perpetuation of Good Work in Science: Memes All Lineages Shared

Alongside the memes that distinguished one lineage from the others, several categories of memes were mentioned as having been absorbed at high rates within all three lineages: honesty, integrity, and ethics in science; treating others equally and fairly; and providing intellectual freedom and guidance to students. In addition, both of the lineages that were lab based were characterized by creating a facilitative lab structure for students. (Training in Motulsky's medical genetics lineage was not exclusively lab based, so memes concerning lab structure were not as meaningfully traced in his lineage.) Table 5.3 shows how many members of each tradition were coded as having inherited the "good-work" memes from their mentor within the lineage. We turn next to a description of the expression of these memes in the three lineages.

Honesty, Integrity, and Ethics in Research

Having honesty, integrity, and ethics is fundamental to doing good work in a profession. It is crucial to the progress of the domain and the well-being of the field. Indeed, even beyond the

Table 5.3 Good-Work Memes: Number of Lineage Members Who Inherited Each Meme

Meme	Gall Lineage ($n = 13$)	Motulsky Lineage ($n = 11$)	Lewontin Lineage ($n = 12$)	$X^2(2)$
Honesty, integrity, and ethics in research	8	7	7	0.07
Treating people equally, fairly	5	4	7	1.42
Providing intellectual freedom and guidance	6	5	4	0.52
Creating a facilitative lab structure	8	2	8	6.48*

Note: *$p < .05$.

professions, one might think of honesty and integrity as a core cultural meme. When members of a community can count on the ethical conduct of those around them, harmonious and productive social relations become more likely.

In fact, habits related to honesty and integrity are so critical to social life that one might expect these memes to be absorbed primarily during childhood, especially within the context of the family. As young children, we are taught not to lie or cheat and to play by the rules. As one interviewee put it: "Obviously, you grow up and your parents tell you what's right or wrong. . . . There's that thing that 'everything you need to know when you grow up, you learned in kindergarten.' Well, in a way it's true. You know you're not supposed to lie. You know you're not supposed to hurt somebody's feelings. . . . I think I was brought up in that way."

In terms of the character of her professional conduct, however, the same scientist reflected: "I think a lot of it came from my graduate advisor, the way he thought about things, and what he thought was right or wrong." This scientist's experience was no exception. In fact, one important finding from the study was that basic virtues such as honesty may be learned early—but effective mentors teach their students the meaning of such virtues within the context of their profession. In the case of honesty, mentors in the sciences may draw attention to accuracy and thoroughness in writing up research findings, fair and appropriate allocation of credit for a publication, and the ethical handling of information about a patient's genetic vulnerabilities. The ethical choices in these cases are not obvious to the uninitiated. They do not necessarily follow automatically from one's general disposition to do the right thing, however strong that might be. It is useful to distinguish morality or general ethics from professional ethics (see Davis, 2002). Whereas morality refers to the standards of behavior that a person wants everyone else to follow strongly enough that he or she is willing to abide by them as well, professional ethics are standards of behavior applying to members of an occupational group. An ethical code defines acceptable conduct in each profession. As an example, perhaps the highest ethical principle for engineers is to ensure public safety. A sound understanding of this principle is just as much a part of the training of engineers as a sound technical skill set. Whereas a person drawn to a career in engineering may already have a strong sense of ethics, the person may not know, prior to professional training, how and why to make the detailed decisions when designing a bridge in order to safeguard public safety. Learning this process might be called *ethical translation* (Davis, 2002).

Scientists are expected to respect the truth on which new knowledge is based, making scientific honesty and integrity paramount to the profession. All three lineage heads were seen as models of honesty and integrity by their former students. Gall was lauded for his "great personal integrity." Motulsky was remembered admiringly as "a very honest person [and] a very honest scientist." Lewontin was described as "an absolutely ethical man." Typical of the G2s in all three lineages, one of Lewontin's former students recalled that throughout his graduate school years, he never saw his mentor "commit an act, either personal or scientific, that I would call shoddy or unethical. I cannot say that about anybody else I've ever known in the field."

The scientific integrity of the lineage heads left a mark. Virtually every G2 explicitly mentioned having been influenced in this critical area of professional conduct by his or her mentor. The path of greatest integrity is not necessarily obvious. The field may come to take for granted certain conventions that may not be the most ethical. Key gatekeepers such as funding agents, department chairs, and journal editors may actively, even if unwittingly, exert pressures in directions that are at odds with the highest professional ethics. Adhering to a debased common practice may be the line of least resistance, and it might easily prove compelling to graduate students in the absence of a mentor's influence.

In allocating research credit, for instance, the path of greatest honesty and integrity may not be obvious. A successful scientist described how her mentor routinely concluded presentations by acknowledging her and other students as the ones who had done most of the work. She inherited the practice: "And now that's just ingrained in me. . . . I would feel so bad not having promoted the people who actually did the work. *And I never thought about that before I was in this guy's lab*. It was just something that really impressed me as, 'Gee, that's the right way to do it.'" Indeed, her mentor's ways of working inspired her to reflect deeply about morals, ethics, and how they are defined in the field, and to question accepted practices. She concluded, "I just know that there are certain areas that I've adopted as my own based on the experiences I've had with him. And they've just made me feel like, 'Yeah, this is right. This is clear to me.'"

Fair and Equal Treatment of Others

A second meme that characterizes all three lineages is fair and equal treatment of others. Whereas habits of scientific honesty and integrity most directly influence the domain, supporting the profession's capacity to generate valid knowledge, habits of fair and equal treatment more directly influence the social field, supporting the health of the scientific community. All of the lineage heads were remembered for the even-handedness with which they treated people in general. Prominent among the recipients of their fair and equal treatment were, predictably, the students themselves and their labmates. In this sense, the meme resembles the good mentoring practices discussed in the two sections that follow. To the credit of the lineage heads, the perception of equal treatment coexists with recollections, discussed in Chapter Seven, that the lineage heads sensitively adjusted their mentoring to the needs of different students.

In Gall's case, even-handedness with students was demonstrated in his matter-of-fact mentoring of a generation of successful female scientists during an era when women in science faced routine discrimination and even overt harassment. As one G2 reflected, "In [his] lab, you were a scientist. There was *no* sense that the men were better than the women or vice versa." As a result, the student was able to dismiss others' "irrational opinions about what women could do or couldn't do." In contrast, there were female students in other labs who had been belittled, and as this interviewee noted, "If that's coming from people who are your mentors, the people you respect, then you might believe [it]."

Students' descriptions of Motulsky stand out against the strongly hierarchical culture of the medical setting in which they knew him. Most of his students were medical fellows, who had already spent a number of years immersed in this culture. One former student described being counseled by Motulsky to "listen to everybody" rather than make assumptions on the basis of credentials because anyone on a medical team might provide a "critical insight."

Although Lewontin acknowledged the differences in power and knowledge between himself and his students, he explained that "to the extent that the objective realities make it possible, we run a nonhierarchical organization." For Lewontin, this practice, and his insistence on respect for others, was rooted in Marxist philosophy. Although his students did not emulate the latter, several did admire and emulate his nonhierarchical disposition toward students.

The meme survived into the third generation of each lineage. One young scientist admiringly recalled how her mentor had treated everyone equally in the lab: technicians, postdocs, and graduate students. Following the mentor's lead, the members of the lab treated each other with respect too. Another young scientist recalled that her advisor's lab was careful to respect their outside collaborators and to be sure that their opinions were voiced in discussions. A G3 in the Lewontin lineage related that Lewontin "preached very loudly . . . 'don't pull rank.' Everyone should have an equal say in the argument. You're judged by the soundness of your argument and the depth of your knowledge, not by the abbreviations that come after your name."

Giving Students Freedom and Guidance

Some of the most prominent memes were mentoring principles or techniques, which are simultaneously mechanisms or pathways for transmitting memes. That is, these memes have a special significance in that—like parenting practices—they foster their own perpetuation, as well as that of the other memes that may be passed down. Some of the memes already mentioned were general principles of conduct that encompassed mentoring practices—treating others equally and sharing credit, for example. It was particularly instructive to discover commonalities across the three lineages that specifically concerned mentoring practices that students actively absorbed. The third good-work meme that these lineages shared was the mentors' propensity to grant students freedom in defining their intellectual interests and pursuing their scientific work, while simultaneously providing enough guidance so that the students did not flounder for too long or progress too far along unfruitful paths. Particularly in leading graduate programs, where most students possess significant scientific aptitude, development of the ability to work independently is usually among the most basic aims of professional preparation. The practice of balancing freedom and guidance in interactions with students appears to be a key way that mentors support a student's development as an independent researcher.

The interviews suggest that mentoring practices are shaped in the course of one's training as a student, much as parenting practices are shaped in the family of origin during childhood. Furthermore, often such practices are explicitly taught to the next generation of scientists, just as the practices of one's parents may be taught to one's children. Gall, for example, learned about providing freedom from his graduate advisor, and he adopted this style of advising himself: "He let his students work on anything they wanted to, so I did certainly pick that up as a trait. As far as I'm concerned, my students can work on anything they want to, as long as it's within some broad outline of things that I have some competence in, that I can judge."

Providing freedom and guidance may be the optimal practice from the students' perspective but many scientists feel it is not optimal from the standpoint of the lab head's own productivity. To provide intellectual freedom means that the lab head must refrain from assigning projects that benefit his own research agenda exclusively, and to provide guidance he must give up time. The provision of freedom and guidance modeled by the lineage heads illustrates their divergence from many of their peers' practices. We suspect that it is particularly when the field does not exact the highest levels of professional conduct that the exemplary conduct of a mentor makes the greatest difference in the values and practices with which a student enters the profession.

A distinctive feature of mentoring practices may contribute to their absorption. In contrast to some memes that scientists embody and model (for example, the imperative to share information with colleagues outside the lab), students experience an advisor's mentoring practices directly, in addition to observing or hearing about them. The benefits of virtuous or prosocial conduct on the mentor's part are not just theoretical, nor do they carry potential drawbacks for the student.

Students of each lineage head described their mentors as encouraging intellectual freedom while still providing some much-needed supervision. Most of Motulsky's students, as medical fellows, had less to say about Motulsky's practices in this regard than students of Gall and Lewontin. Nevertheless, one Motulsky G2 described emulating Motulsky's mentoring practices consciously and unconsciously: "I try to give students lots of freedom and responsibility for projects. . . . I try and include them in things." By providing them with both considerable flexibility as well as responsibilities on projects they might not have otherwise pursued, this respondent sought to emulate Motulsky's practice of giving both intellectual independence and guidance to trainees.

The student's dissertation project is perhaps the central arena in which mentors confront the need to encourage intellectual independence while providing a degree of supervision. Gall was perceived by former students as having provided considerable freedom in selecting a thesis project and encouraged tremendous independence in completing it. According to a Gall G2, when students first came into the lab, Gall would give them something trivial to work on while they settled into the lab, but he expected that they would eventually come up with their own thesis topics. Gall would provide a problem if necessary, but he wanted to see them produce their own. The student felt this was a good way to handle students' dissertations and sought to emulate it when she became a thesis advisor.

Lewontin's students encountered a similar attitude. When asked to identify the key thing he had carried away from his apprenticeship with Lewontin, a G2 replied, "One, by far, was the idea that he encouraged people to pursue their own intellectual interests." This student went on to assert that Lewontin's approach was much preferable to treating advisees as extra hands on the lab head's projects, and he reproduced Lewontin's approach in his own lab. Indeed, the degree of guidance that Lewontin provided often depended on what the student needed and requested. Other students recalled that "he would work with you to design a project" that interested you, and his door was open if you went to him with questions.

Like the generation ahead of them, some G3s noted considerable pressure on lab heads to be productive and to invest their time and attention in their own research agendas. Multiple members of the third generation in each lineage nonetheless reported inheriting their mentor's propensity to provide students in the lab with freedom and guidance to reach their professional goals. In many of the labs, the mentor's example countered the pressure to produce without regard for students' development.

Creating a Facilitative Lab Structure

The fourth good-work meme, creation of a facilitative lab structure, characterized only two of the three lineages. This imbalance does not reflect different pedagogical beliefs; all three lineage heads were thoughtful about how their lab was structured and the atmosphere they cultivated in it. Rather, it derives from the fact that unlike Gall and Lewontin, Motulsky did not consistently maintain a lab over the years where all of his students worked and interacted—nor did the most clinically oriented members of the lineage's second and third generations do so. Thus, although he devoted attention to the impact that his lab and the department as a whole had on students, this was not a key meme in the sense of strongly influencing his students' mentoring practices.

This meme entailed the deliberate use of the lab to facilitate students' development. The role of lab structure and culture will be discussed at length in Chapter Six, which focuses on the means by which memes are transmitted in these lineages. Briefly, Gall, Lewontin, and, to a lesser extent, Motulsky describe and were remembered for providing a felicitous and stimulating matrix within which students could develop as scientists. They did so deliberately. As Lewontin put it, "What I have tried to do for graduate students and postdoctoral fellows . . . is to create an infrastructure, an ambience . . . a psychological infrastructure which would be intellectually exciting to them, and in which they could flourish." A significant part of the stimulation was intended to come from fellow members of the lab. Such interaction was effective because each lineage head set a tone of respect, nonhierarchical relations, and openness that became the culture of the lab as it filtered through and influenced the attitudes of the lab members.

Several specific practices concerning lab structure recurred in the interviews. One was the establishment of a policy with respect to whether to hold regular lab meetings. In some labs, regular, formal meetings were eschewed; in others, weekly meetings provided a setting in which students could share results and practice presentation skills. During these meetings, the lab head's commitment to fairness, scientific honesty, or other values and practices might be modeled for all lab members in the course of reacting to students' presentations and the interpersonal dynamics within the lab group.

The organization of the lab is the clearest example of a meme that is inflected differently from one lineage to the next. While Gall and Lewontin in particular made use of the structure and culture of the learning environment to facilitate student development, these environments had distinctive characteristics in each lineage. Gall created a family-style lab, fostering harmony, and he encouraged students to work on projects within his broad expertise that were individualized to the students' specific talents and interests. Gall G2s and some G3s went on to adopt these practices when they became lab heads. His students reported emulating the establishment of a harmonious, family-style lab and also fostering diverse projects. Lewontin's lab environment provided endless opportunities for stimulating interaction. Much of the learning took place with others through rigorous discussions, and individuals with widely varying backgrounds were treated as peers. As in the Gall lineage, the G2s and some G3s adopted their mentors' practices for creating a facilitative lab environment. Although only a few interviewees described replicating the physical layout of the Lewontin lab organized around the Last Supper Table, they did emulate his social organization of the lab.

In sum, the first two widely inherited good-work memes—scientific ethics and treating others equally and fairly—concern the individual's general conduct as a researcher and a member of the field. The latter two—providing freedom and guidance and creating a facilitative lab structure—concern the individual's conduct as a mentor to future scientists. All three lineage heads have passed down values and practices essential to doing good work and, in addition, memes essential to the kind of mentoring that will perpetuate good work into the future.

Inherited Memes

The twelve memes described thus far were in fact inherited memes in two senses. Among the twenty-five memes identified, these were the ones inherited by the largest number of scientists, either within a single lineage or among all those interviewed. In addition, the scientist possessing one of them nearly always attributed its development to what was learned from his or her mentor within the lineage, even if other individuals or experiences were salient influences as well. What percentage of lineage members possessed these memes, and what percentage not only possessed them but also specifically referred to inheriting them from their mentor? For each of the twelve memes we have reviewed, Table 5.4 provides these percentages by lineage.

Table 5.4 Inherited Memes: Percentage of Lineage Members Who Possess Each Meme and the Percentage Who Inherited Each Meme from Their Mentor

Meme	Gall Lineage (n = 13)		Motulsky Lineage (n = 11)		Lewontin Lineage (n = 12)	
	% Possess	% Inherit	% Possess	% Inherit	% Possess	% Inherit
Lineage-signature memes						
Intrinsic motivations for science	**100**	**54**	73	28	58	8
Scientific breadth	**54**	**54**	0	0	8	0
Neatness and order	**31**	**31**	0	0	0	0
Humanitarianism, social responsibility	23	8	**82**	**64**	33	0
Research-practice integration (for example, physician-scientist model)	0	0	**55**	**55**	0	0
Anticareerism	15	8	0	0	**42**	**33**
Authorship based on contribution	23	23	9	9	**58**	**50**
High intellectualism	0	0	0	0	**25**	**25**
Good-work memes						
Honesty, integrity, and ethics in research	**69**	**62**	**64**	**64**	**75**	**58**
Treating people equally, fairly	**46**	**39**	**46**	**36**	**58**	**58**
Providing intellectual freedom and guidance	**62**	**46**	**46**	**46**	**50**	**33**
Creating a facilitative lab structure	**62**	**62**	18	18	**83**	**67**

Note: Lineage-signature and good-work memes are shown in bold.

Within each lineage, the percentage of members who possessed each meme is presented beside the percentage of lineage members who inherited the meme from their mentor. The percentage who inherited each meme from their mentor is necessarily a subset of those who possess the meme, since a meme would never be considered inherited by an individual who did not also possess it.

For example, most scientists who described providing intellectual freedom and guidance to students also said that their mentor within the lineage had influenced this practice. In the Gall lineage, for instance, eight of thirteen scientists (62 percent) possessed the meme; six of those thirteen (46 percent) said they had absorbed it from their mentor within the lineage. This held true for all four of the good-work memes: if a scientist possessed the meme, the mentor was usually credited with a role in this. To take a second example, over half of the interviewees from each lineage (69 percent, 64 percent, and 75 percent for the Gall, Motulsky, and Lewontin lineages, respectively) were coded as stressing honesty, integrity, and ethics in research. Of the twenty-five scientists possessing the meme, twenty-two cited their mentor within the lineage as an influence in this sphere.

For most of the lineage-signature memes, it was also unusual to possess the meme without the mentor being mentioned as an influence. In the case of scientific breadth and neatness in the Gall lineage, the physician-scientist model of practice in the Motulsky lineage, and high intellectualism in the Lewontin lineage, all students possessing the meme claimed they had been influenced in this respect by their lineage mentor. In such cases, the mentor almost certainly played a central formative role, even if there were other influences as well.

In other cases, and more frequently for the good-work memes, it is likely that the student already possessed the value or disposition at least in germinal form prior to professional training. There were no stories (from mentors or students) about a fundamentally cutthroat or dishonest student who entered a lab and was radically transformed. One reason may be that these heads of elite labs had the luxury of turning away students who possessed such qualities, and they chose to do so. The mentor's influence was more likely to take the form of channeling, affirming, or reinforcing a meme—for example, by reassuring a student that honesty or treating others fairly could be compatible with professional success rather than a fatal impediment to it. This may be no small lesson in an era when pressures to succeed at all costs are great, particularly at elite levels within a field. In addition, it is clear that the lineage heads did not tolerate transgressions in the areas of scientific integrity and interpersonal decency. Such limit setting served to create a lab culture reinforcing predispositions to behave ethically, teaching students concrete ways in which to give their ethical dispositions specific and appropriate expression in scientific practice.

Least Inherited Memes

One may wonder which memes were least often inherited from mentors. This question is important: the answer may be suggestive of the type of memes that are not as susceptible to influence during professional training, even in positive mentoring experiences. Two memes that we have been examining are intriguing in this context: intrinsic reasons for doing science, and humanitarianism and social responsibility (see Table 5.4). About half of the Gall lineage members who reported intrinsic motivational orientations attributed an influence to their mentor (54 percent), but the other half did not (46 percent). The same pattern held for the Motulsky and Lewontin lineages for this meme. In the group as a whole, twenty-eight scientists reported intrinsic reasons for doing science, making it an extremely widespread meme in this sample of elite scientists. Of these twenty-eight scientists, eleven attributed an influence to their mentor (primarily members of the Gall lineage). But even more—seventeen scientists—did not. Humanitarianism was an example of a meme that was influenced strongly in one lineage—in this case Motulsky's: 82 percent of the Motulsky lineage possessed the meme, and 64 percent reported absorbing it from their lineage mentor. At the same time, however, almost all of the scientists who reported possessing the meme in the other lineages did not attribute it to their mentor.

Both intrinsic motivation and humanitarianism are basic motivational orientations—one associated with fields involving research and the other with caring professions such as medicine. It makes sense that many students might come into the profession already possessing—or even because they already possess—such orientations, and that at the same time, working with an influential mentor might inspire or deepen them. It is also possible, of course, that a mentor's motivational orientation rubs off on students but is not discussed, occurring outside awareness and thus going unreported.

Like motivational orientations, many of the infrequently absorbed memes are personal qualities. Among the full set of memes mentioned by the scientists (see Table 5.1), personality traits (for example, being contrarian), creativity, and broad interests extending beyond science are often possessed but not primarily as a result of mentoring, according to our interviewees. Personal qualities may be a kind of meme that mentors typically do not attempt to transmit. Furthermore, despite exceptions such as neatness and order (the Gall lineage-signature meme that Gall himself did not strive to transmit but some members of the lineage nevertheless absorbed), personal qualities may be a kind of meme that students typically do not attempt to emulate, considering them difficult to change or viewing them as discretionary, or both.

Extinction and Emergence

Up to this point, we have seen that graduate mentors can be important agents in the perpetuation of good work. However, a given mentor is one formative influence among many to which a student is exposed. One would therefore expect competing memes to dilute or attenuate that mentor's impact, and increasingly so in successive generations. In addition, the environment in which professionals work is always changing, imposing new challenges and presenting new opportunities, and each generation may bring novel values, practices, and qualities to their work and their mentoring. The best practice for one generation may not be the best for all time. We turn here to the limits of the lineage heads' reach down through the generations. A first question is whether the strength of transmission erodes from one generation to the next as one moves further from the lineage head (that is, extinction of memes), and if so, how much. A second question is whether new memes emerge or become more salient in later generations.

Extinction

Even the values, practices, and qualities that show the strongest sign of perpetuation within lineages face the equivalent of extinction pressures. The memes that undergird good work—honesty, integrity, breadth, fairness, compassion—rarely represent the line of least resistance in professional life. It may be tempting to cut corners or to appropriate credit to oneself for student work conducted in one's lab. To address the extent of attenuation or extinction that has occurred, we distinguish between the rate of absorption from the mentor within the lineage by the lineage heads' students (the G2s) and the G2s' students (the G3s).

For each of the three lineages, Table 5.5 presents these rates for the twelve memes that were inherited with the highest frequency: the eight lineage-signature memes and the four good-work memes. Comparing the rates shows whether the effect of the lineage head attenuated between Generations 2 and 3. For example, in the Gall lineage, intrinsic scientific motivations were absorbed by all four G2s (100 percent) but by only two of the eight G3s (25 percent).

The numbers of cases in each of these comparisons are small. However, it is noteworthy that in most cases of strong transmission down a lineage, the proportion absorbing the meme was higher for the lineage heads' students than it was in the next generation. As illustrated in Table 5.5, absorption was higher in Generation 2 than in Generation 3 for fourteen of the nineteen highlighted pairs of figures. The rate was higher in Generation 3 in only three of the cells. The attenuation was generally substantial. It appears that even the most widely inherited memes have a tendency to lose ground from one generation to the next.

However, we should note that in strong lineages in healthy occupations, there tend to be more members in each successive generation (four students in the second generation giving rise to sixteen students in the third generation, and so on); our sample artificially constrains the numbers in each generation. It thus does not necessarily follow that the lineage head's effect on the community of practice diminishes in absolute terms. For example, if a scientist transmits a meme to four students, even if each transmits it to only two of his or her students, the meme will still be carried by twice as many scientists in the third generation as in Generation 2.

Emergence

Understanding the perpetuation of good work has occupied the foreground in this book. From an evolutionary, systems perspective, however, a picture of the role of mentors and lineages in the occupation's evolution needs to encompass the emergence of memes as well. From the perspective of tracing memes down a lineage in genetics, an occupation that enjoyed a golden age in the twentieth century (Gardner, Csikszentmihalyi, & Damon, 2001), change looks like the erosion of positive values and practices. Had we studied accounting in the Enron era instead, we

Table 5.5 Attenuated Inheritance of Memes: Percentage of G2s and G3s Who Inherited Each Meme, by Lineage

Meme	Gall Lineage		Motulsky Lineage		Lewontin Lineage	
	% G2s (n = 4)	% G3s (n = 8)	% G2s (n = 4)	% G3s (n = 6)	% G2s (n = 4)	% G3s (n = 7)
Lineage-signature memes						
Intrinsic motivations for science	100	25	25	33	0	14
Scientific breadth	75	38	0	0	0	0
Neatness and order	25	25	0	0	0	0
Humanitarianism, social responsibility	0	13	75	50	0	0
Research-practice integration (for example, physician-scientist model)	0	0	75	33	0	0
Anticareerism	0	0	0	0	25	29
Authorship based on contribution	25	25	25	0	75	29
High intellectualism	0	0	0	0	25	14
Good-work memes						
Honesty, integrity, and ethics in research	100	38	75	50	100	43
Treating people equally, fairly	50	25	25	50	75	42
Providing intellectual freedom and guidance	50	38	25	50	50	29
Creating a facilitative lab structure	100	38	0	17	75	57

Note: Lineage-signature and good-work memes are in bold.

might have been foregrounding processes of emergence and reemergence in order to understand the mentoring of good work: new memes would be needed to replace destructive ones. Even in eras when good work prevails in an occupation, a tradition will sustain its vitality and relevance only if it maintains the capacity to adapt to changing conditions and initiate transformation in promising new directions.

Given the focus of this book on the fate of the lineage head's values and practices, we sampled too few individuals within any sublineage to confirm the emergence and perpetuation of new memes in the second or third generation. Chapters Two through Four nevertheless provided several examples of the various ways in which new memes emerge. Sometimes the younger scientist inherited the mentor's meme but gave it a new spin, as was the case in the Motulsky lineage with respect to Boyer and his students. Boyer communicated to his students his self-conscious policy of giving other scientists the benefit of the doubt—at least one opportunity to wrong him, often two—before ending a collaborative relationship. His students adopted this rule of thumb as well as the practice of collaborating, and it may have equipped them to maintain open exchanges with others even as the climate in the field has become increasingly competitive.

Sometimes students took their mentor's meme to a new level. For example, Gall treated others in a gender-blind fashion, but he was not an active feminist. Nevertheless, some of his female students became advocates of gender equity. They sensitized their students to issues of equity and showed the G3s that women can succeed in science despite significant obstacles.

A different sort of variation on emergence occurred when students adopted new memes as a corrective to their mentor's practices. For example, some G3s experienced their advisors as too laissez-faire about helping them navigate career and field matters. These G3s went on to provide more career preparation to their students in reaction to experiencing a gap in their own training.

There are thus multiple ways in which memes may emerge, be transformed, or gather strength across successive generations. It is important to realize that the emergence of new memes may mark the rise of new ways of doing good work in response to changing conditions and realities.

Conclusion

Individual professionals ultimately must determine for themselves what lines they will, or will not, cross; they must live up to their own personal moral code even if there are forces in the environment that discourage doing so. To return to the question posed at the outset of this chapter, are scientists in these lineages inheriting the kinds of memes that might provide the moral compass needed to do good work?

Across multiple generations, the lineages in the study were distinguished from one another by signature memes spanning three generations. These memes were absorbed by the members of one lineage significantly more than by the members of the other two. Respondents were very conscious of some of these memes (and, in some cases, very proud of them) as markers of group membership—characteristics that simultaneously integrated the members of the lineage with each other and differentiated them from nonmembers. The recurrence of these memes within one lineage but not in the others, and the attribution of influence to the mentor within the lineage, may be the clearest suggestion in our study of intergenerational transmission and hence of the role of mentoring in the survival of good work. Ours was a small sample; other lineages both within and outside the sciences undoubtedly exhibit different signature memes. However, lineages in all professions may be characterized by the degree to which their distinctive priorities and practices emphasize the practitioner's relationship to the domain itself (as in the Gall lineage), the field or community of practice (as in the Lewontin lineage), or the wider society or indeed humanity as a whole (as in the Motulsky lineage). Some practitioners may be most concerned with the work itself; others with their relationship to colleagues, gatekeepers, and trainees; and still others with the occupation's larger aims.

Then there were memes that were absorbed widely in all three of the lineages studied. The nature of these values, practices, and qualities and their wide distribution suggest that they are fundamental to the perpetuation of good work within genetics and that mentoring may be an important means for transmitting them. Within these lineages, the students were absorbing not only values and practices that would support their own doing of good work as they moved into independent careers, but also their mentoring practices. The latter equipped them to pass on other memes supporting good work to the next generation once they assumed the role of mentors themselves.

Some memes that were possessed with relatively high frequency were not necessarily absorbed from a mentor. For example, personal qualities may be less likely to be inherited. In addition, some memes strongly influenced by mentors appeared to fall off sharply from one generation to the next. A meme could emerge and take on different forms with successive generations; to be sure, there are individuals in every generation with distinctive memes of their own that may become absorbed by their students. The analyses summarized in this chapter provided a window into the processes of cultural evolution and the role of mentoring in that process.

A set of basic values and dispositions appears to be in place already when students enter graduate school. The respondents did not describe conversion experiences. However, at this sensitive period in the formation of an individual's priorities, expectations, and practices as a professional, the mentor plays a crucial role in cultivating an aspiration and a capacity to do good work within the particular domain being entered. The potential importance of such an influence should not be underestimated, especially in an era when prevailing pressures otherwise may lead practitioners to forsake responsible practice. It is clear how badly young people can be mentored, and how well they can be mentored to do wrong. As Edward Tenner (2004) observed in an essay in *Chronicle of Higher Education*, there was a mentoring subplot in the Enron story. Enron's chief financial officer, Andrew Fastow, was one of "Skilling's boys," protégés of CEO Jeffrey Skilling. The group of protégés absorbed a code of professional conduct from Skilling, presumably because it seemed to be serving him so well. And had the Enron debacle not ensued, Skilling's boys might well have become models of the values and practices that they had absorbed from their mentor and might have passed them on to the next generation. In contrast, by being exposed daily to the example of mentors who had achieved great professional success while adhering to high personal standards of integrity, the scientists in this study received the most concrete evidence possible that they could do the right thing and still succeed as scientists.

6

HOW VALUES, PRACTICES, AND KNOWLEDGE ARE TRANSMITTED

In the previous chapter, we saw that scientists view themselves as having absorbed values and beliefs, practices and knowledge, from their graduate school mentors. But what are the means by which desirable memes are reproduced across generations? Aspiring scientists are motivated to acquire some of the memes that their mentors possess. Mastering cutting-edge technical knowledge and practices is perceived as essential to excellence, and thus to both professional advancement and good work in science. Many young people may have mixed feelings, however, about other kinds of memes. This is especially true with respect to honesty, integrity, cooperation, generosity, and one's approach to mentoring itself—practices essential to good work. Ambitious scientists may perceive a tension, particularly at the outset of their career, between what is required to get ahead, or even to get a job, and what is required to do good work. So how do mentors lead young scientists to embrace virtues like honesty and integrity as they move into professional life?

This chapter describes how values, practices, and knowledge have been transmitted by the three lineage heads, all successful mentors as well as outstanding scientists. Our focus is thus on the G1s' primary mentoring practices, although we illustrate some mentoring practices by using the example of a G2 or G3 scientist. Interviewees described how they absorbed knowledge, values, and practices from key mentors, and what means they were currently using to transmit lessons to their own students.

Mentions of fourteen different means of influence were coded (see Appendix A) and analyzed to determine how often each practice was ascribed to the lineage heads. The interviews suggest that the transmission of memes occurs primarily through the medium of shared experience organized around the conduct of science, entailing sustained, face-to-face interaction. The memes that underpin good work may be particularly dependent on transmission through this pathway. Media such as books and courses about professional ethics lack its key features.

Graduate Training as Apprenticeship

Literature and lore perpetuate an image of the effective mentorship as one in which a caring teacher actively imparts wisdom to an eager young person through a close, one-on-one relationship (Daloz, 1999; Levinson, 1978). We found that graduate training in the sciences is better understood as a form of apprenticeship, or "situated learning" (Lave & Wenger, 1991; Rogoff, 1990): it is experiential learning, or learning by doing, that takes place in a lab pursuing real scientific problems. At its center is the young scientist's own increasingly independent work. Students in the sciences complete course work, but the heart of their training is formulating and solving a research problem. The student learns through engaging this problem. One G2 called graduate training "the complete apprenticeship," likening it to the process of learning how to make sushi from a master chef, with its movement from humble duties to eventual mastery of the whole, complex enterprise.

How, specifically, were memes transmitted through apprenticeships with Motulsky, Gall, or Lewontin? Contrary to popular notions of apprenticeship that narrow their focus to the dyadic relationship between master and apprentice, the lineage heads collectively illustrate a way of mentoring that encompasses two intertwined aspects: the mentor's direct impact on the student through verbal exchanges and other means, and the mentor's indirect impact through student participation in the community within the lab. Good mentoring thereby can coexist with the mentors' immersion in their own work. This chapter considers the roles of the mentor, the mentor's lab, and the student in the transgenerational transmission of memes. Because many other fields also rely on learning by apprenticeship, the implications extend well beyond science.

The Mentor's Role

Each of the three lineage heads directly influenced students by modeling, close up and in situ, what it means to do good work. This modeling was supported by informal exchanges—conversations about the mentor's example, the student's work, and other matters. Finally, much of the mentoring was done not by the lineage head personally, but by his structuring of the training environment and lab culture in such a way that students' accumulated laboratory experiences promoted good work. In addition, students learned how to work within a social system governed by high standards of conduct that might not prevail outside the lab.

The means by which the lineage heads transmitted an orientation toward good work were variations on this common repertoire. Each described employing all three means of influence, but Gall focused on the importance of providing a model, Motulsky emphasized the impact of informal exchanges, and Lewontin stressed the role of the environment created in the lab. None claimed to rely heavily on some of the other ways of influencing students that we examined, such as use of extrinsic rewards or prescriptive talk. In each case, accounts from multiple students converged, and their recollections confirmed the lineage head's self-described approach.

These mentoring practices share several qualities. First, by the very nature of scientific apprenticeships, each individual mentoring practice has an impact that is cumulative, reinforced across multiple occasions over an extended period of time. This density of experience contrasts sharply with the many formal mentoring arrangements that depend on periodic, brief conversations, and it supports the transmission of memes such as scientific integrity. In scientific apprenticeships, the mentor is a sustained presence. The lab is a place where students work and practically live together, often for a number of years. Informal exchanges between mentor and student have a chance to be repeated many times. Memorable incidents are consistent with the overall message that is being absorbed; they are emblematic rather than exceptional.

Second, the different modes of influence are mutually reinforcing, either redundant with one another or complementing each other. For example, the lineage heads did not tell their students, "Do what I say, not what I do." As a consequence, the messages they conveyed were strong and clear, their signal strength boosted by replication across multiple channels. One of Gall's students described lasting lessons about cooperation and fairness learned through the example of his conduct as she observed it, through her conversations with him, and in the way he structured students' experiences in the lab—in short, through each of the mentoring practices he himself identified as key.

Third, positive interpersonal feelings play an important catalytic role, encouraging attentiveness and receptiveness on the students' part (compare with Fredrickson, 2001). This is evident in relation to both mentor and lab community. With respect to the mentor, the conduct and character of all three lineage heads elicited feelings of strong admiration, which inspired emulation. Gall's G2s experienced his enthusiasm as infectious; Lewontin's G2s experienced his moralism as uplifting; Motulsky's G2s were moved by his compassion. With respect to the lab community, the culture was influential because lab members spent so much time together. The constant interaction meant that it was hard for daily life in the labs to have a positive impact unless it was enjoyable. In two very different ways, the emotional climate was positive in the Gall and Lewontin labs, and students lived as members of an agreeable community. The experience of Motulsky's students was not as communal; he directed an entire program, and not all of the interviewees trained alongside other students in a lab under his direction. In addition, the clinical component of the training in medical genetics did not take place in a lab.

With these common characteristics in mind, we turn to the pathways favored by the lineage heads in transmitting values, knowledge, and practices. One question addressed is to what extent any of the pathways are particularly suited to the transmission of good-work memes.

Forms of Talk

We had reason to expect the lineage heads to rely heavily on verbal means to transmit values, practices, and knowledge to students and to expect certain forms of talk to play greater roles than others in good mentoring. Old and new models of good mentoring highlight particular kinds of verbal exchange. Danish physicist Niels Bohr, the extraordinary mentor described in Chapter One, was remembered for wide-ranging, informal conversations that unfolded in his office and during long walks in the woods. In the sciences today, weekly lab meetings directed by the lab head, in which one student presents work to the group and receives feedback, have become a staple of graduate education. Regular individual meetings, in which the student reports on the progress of research and is questioned and advised by the mentor, are also increasingly common. In many other fields, formal mentoring programs now provide novice practitioners with periodic opportunities to seek wisdom from a more seasoned professional. In all of these cases, memes are chiefly transmitted through a particular form of talk.

As it turned out, all three lineage heads transmitted practices, values, and knowledge through verbal exchanges to some extent. However, only Motulsky identified talking with students as his primary way of transmitting memes. He described collaborating—the occasion for some of his most consequential conversations with students—as part of training students. Both Lewontin and Gall indicated that their conversations with students tended to be relatively limited.

It did not come as a surprise that certain forms of talk were rarely mentioned. Neither the lineage heads nor their former students mentioned the kind of hectoring that characterizes some advisor-student relationships—the "guilt trips, harsh yelling, insults or subtle jabs" that are part of the necessary arsenal of graduate advisors according to the scientist quoted in Chapter One. We listened for mentions of scolding, exhorting, and prescribing in interviews with G2s, but they were not features of the lineage heads' interactions with students.

More surprising was the lineage heads' infrequently mentioned use of other forms of verbal exchange that pervade most educational settings: instructing, questioning, and providing systematic feedback. Motulsky explained that "some research mentors are very directive and will give detailed, explicit directions for the trainee's work. This can be overdone and stifles independence." The lineage heads also avoided close, regular questioning of students about the progress of their research. Neither the Socratic method nor frequent feedback figured prominently among their mentoring practices. Desiring to encourage independence, none of the lineage heads favored mentoring by micromanaging students' work. Nor did the lineage heads deliberately tell stories or repeat favorite sayings in order to drive home lessons that they hoped their students would absorb. In all these regards, the former students' recollections again accorded closely with the pictures provided by the lineage heads.

What forms of talk did occur? The lineage heads and their former students primarily recalled expressive and instrumental verbal exchanges, informal in nature: wide-ranging discussions that typically took place in a group setting, either in the lab (for example, Lewontin's occasional appearances at the Last Supper Table) or outside it (for example, Gall's daily lunches with the lab group), and task-focused, one-on-one conversations about a student's work, supporting the process of learning by doing.

Group exchanges contributed to the positive affective climate of each lab culture. A G2 remembered Gall's lab group spending as much as an hour together over lunch each day, enjoying "great camaraderie." With the talk ranging over many topics, "sometimes about science and sometimes other things outside of science," the gatherings were also recalled as times when the lineage head's values, attitudes, or ideas might be on display, even if conveying these was not the point of the interaction.

One-on-one exchanges occurred when a problematic situation arose within the natural course of the student's research as an organic part of learning by doing. For most Gall and Lewontin G2s, the meetings were not frequent. The door was open, they said, but one-on-one talks depended to a large extent on student initiative, and we have seen that many students hesitated to disturb the lineage heads. Motulsky more often than the other two initiated one-on-one meetings with students, which were a key means by which he conveyed the research aspect of good work as a physician-scientist.

Such exchanges reinforced the sense that the lineage heads possessed a much larger scientific perspective than students did. One scientist recalled that Gall's advice in an ethically ambiguous situation provided a "mature, broad way of looking at things." Another remembered discussing issues of medicine and human evolution with Motulsky, appreciating that he had "a much more global picture of medical genetics than I." Lewontin was consistently able to "lay out a much grander vision of how to place your [particular research] interest in a more interesting, enlightened context." Students took every opportunity to absorb his "perceived wisdom."

This sharing of wisdom accords well with the notion of the sagacious mentor. Would more such exchanges have been even better? Perhaps not. In general, the lineage heads expected students to exhibit independence. Motulsky asserted that "the ideal research mentor encourages trainees to think independently, to be inner directed." A former student recalled that Gall might turn away students who sought his advice if he judged them capable of managing without help. Likewise, Lewontin "would tell you, 'Just go do what you want. And don't listen to me.' He encouraged people to really think hard and do what they wanted." The relative infrequency of their exchanges, arising from the combination of students' reluctance to initiate interactions and the lineage heads' reluctance to intervene, may have supported students' development as self-directed scientists.

Providing a Model

According to both the lineage heads and their students, providing an example or model (Bandura, 1985) was a more salient means of transmitting memes than any one form of direct guidance. All three lineage heads, and most G2s, discussed the importance of teaching by example. G2s asserted the importance of long-term role models for learning how to behave ethically, do original research well, and care for patients with sensitivity. One G2 avowed the lineage head's formative influence on her standards of quality as a researcher: "I don't know how a person does that *except* by example."

For the lineage heads, modeling did not mean actively "trying to set a good example" and making artificial efforts to be on one's best behavior (or better) in the presence of students. There was no conscious performance. Rather, modeling consisted mainly in being visible while going about one's business and living (as a student put it) by one's convictions. Gall explained, "My major function is to work with them enough that they see how I work." He was present daily in the lab, doing his own research projects. Lewontin said, conveying a more explicitly moral focus, "I try to serve as an example of how one should behave." Although he was a fleeting presence in the lab and eschewed regular meetings with students about their work, students felt that his spirit pervaded the lab. Finally, more than the others, Motulsky made a point of meeting with his students to discuss their work; in part, he saw these meetings as a setting for modeling: students "get to sample and know how a research mentor thinks about a problem." In the clinical context, he modeled compassionate patient care.

Virtually all G2s identified modeling as a means by which they learned from their mentor. Gall considered modeling the foremost way in which he tried to transmit his values and practices to students. Independent of Gall and of one another, all four of his former students indicated that a major means by which he influenced them was by providing a compelling model.

Teaching by example varied in the degree to which it constituted deliberate modeling. At the more self-conscious end of the spectrum, one G3 made a point to take a turn presenting his research in the lab's weekly meetings to model the process of presenting for his students.

By the same token, learning by observing the mentor's example varied in how much it entailed active emulation versus a diffuse process of absorption occurring outside awareness. In terms of active emulation, students deliberately watch admired mentors in order to learn from their example. It should be underscored that students play an essential role in their own education, and learning through observation is a primary means by which this occurs. Many G2s recalled attentively and closely observing the lineage heads at work and emulating what they saw. One G2 contended that learning to do science depends on this process: "It's not easy to put it into ten sentences: that you do this, this, and this. It's watching somebody do it day by day, and see what they do when confronted with the problem and the options."

Deep admiration for the lineage heads, as both people and scientists, motivated the process, a topic we return to in Chapter Seven. It encouraged students to focus their attention on the lineage heads and actively emulate the models that they provided. As another G2 explained, "We wanted to be like him. In order to be like him, you had to work really hard. You had to have a certain copious [amount] of information. You had to behave properly, be considerate." Similarly, a researcher recalled watching her mentor continually pushing herself to learn new things; the mentor's determination inspired the student to rise to the challenges that she encountered. A G3 observed, about graduate students in general, "I think students want to be honest, but they don't really know how you do science, and they're susceptible to following the lead of people who they admire who are further along in the process than they are."

The scientists interviewed also noted the tacit learning that occurs in long apprenticeships: learning that takes place without this conscious effort, unremarked yet powerful. A G2 described absorbing the lineage head's respectful treatment of younger, less experienced, and less eminent others, explaining that this process "was happening subliminally all the time." Another G2 emulated Motulsky "both consciously and unconsciously." One of Gall's students reflected that she had learned in his lab that "there's a right way to do science and there's a wrong way to do science. . . . You need to do it right, do it well, and do it with integrity." In attempting to account for how she and all her fellow students had absorbed this message, she explained that the means of communication must have been indirect. They all "got it," and yet they agreed that this was not because it was being repeated "like a mantra" in the lab. Instead, she concluded that it must have been "ingrained in the lab in ways that were hard for us to see."

Memes Transmitted by Observation

An important question is whether modeling plays a special role in the cultivation of good work. The lineage heads saw themselves as modeling—and students saw themselves as absorbing by observation—a wide spectrum of practices and values. However, two types of memes in particular may be conveyed better by modeling than by other means. The first are memes that are intrinsically difficult to capture or effectively convey in words: forms of tacit knowledge (Polanyi, 1958). The second are memes that might be less compelling or just plain unconvincing if they were verbalized but not enacted.

First, we have seen that some memes are difficult to express verbally and absorb through verbal description, and these may lend themselves to modeling. This is true of whole domains that are kinesthetic (sport, dance) or interpersonal (psychotherapy, clinical medicine), along with aspects of many other domains (for example, lab technique or "a feeling for the organism," in science). In graduate education as in other contexts, modeling and observation may be among the most effective ways of transmitting tacit knowledge.

An illustration of this dynamic can be seen in the process of acquiring a clinical style or manner of interacting with patients. An eminent medical geneticist was deeply and constructively influenced by observing her mentors on clinical rounds. She was eloquent about her view that modeling is an irreplaceable means of transmitting the situated, emergent, socioemotional, embodied form of expertise required in medical genetics. As she put it, describing Motulsky:

> You tag along on rounds, watch this person function, watch whether it works with that patient or not. I think it's absorbed stuff. So when you start off, you think, "Oh, this is going to be this terrible tragedy situation." You read about the case. "Oh, this is awful." Then you watch this person walk into the room of the [patient] and uplift them by talking about what the options are, by helping them deal with [the fact] that they're going to die. By helping them think about the preparations for dying. By talking about [the fact] that this life is special, you just have a different way you measure it. So there are a lot of words that I use I know

I absorbed from [mentors], about how to deal with a situation. And I've never seen any of this written up.

The lineage heads saw themselves as possessing a valid approach to science or way of being a scientist, and transmitting it to students. Something so global and diffuse perhaps can be absorbed only through extended observation across many situations. Again, the G2s' accounts converged with their mentors'. For instance, one of Gall's former students described learning "how to be a biologist" from his example.

With respect to the second role of modeling in the perpetuation of good work, scientists today face pressures and incentives that challenge some of the values, practices, and motivations traditionally undergirding good work, such as interest in science for its own sake, the practice of cooperating and sharing information, and willingness to put student welfare before their own success. In these cases, actions speak louder than words. If there is a discrepancy between words and deeds, we tend to trust people's habitual actions over what they profess to believe. The example presented by a mentor's actual conduct would seem a distinctively effective pathway for transmitting memes of this kind.

For instance, Gall reported that he talked to students about the importance of pursuing scientific research because of love for the activity itself. However, none of the former students reported conversations with him about this. What they did recall was seeing him demonstrate his own intense passion for science, day in and day out, in a whole variety of ways. In contrast, another scientist avowed a passion for science and maintained that it was the only reason to be a scientist, but at midcareer was spending little time in the lab because of major roles in the wider professional community. Former students attributed other positive qualities to this mentor but not a passion for science—nor did they credit this scientist with feeding their own love of research for its own sake.

Like motivations, ethical and scientific principles of conduct are cases where it is imperative to walk the talk in order to be a convincing advocate. It is hard to imagine students being moved by a mentor's exhortations to exhibit rigor or integrity if the mentor is observed cutting corners or undercutting colleagues. Hard work, courage, generosity, honesty—urgings about any of these ring hollow when they are not matched by action. In contrast, we have seen that students were deeply impressed when they saw a mentor enacting these virtues. One student watched a female mentor stand up for herself even when doing so was risky and hard, and watched her take the high road when another lab behaved unscrupulously toward them. The mentor's example gave the student the strength to show the same courage and integrity later. Could words unmatched by action ever have such an impact?

It is evident in G2s' and some G3s' recollections that it is inspiring to be in the presence of virtue. Students, at least the ones admitted to these labs, were uplifted by the example of mentors who modeled good work—although some scientists attributed only limited impact to mentors who modeled ethical conduct (say, interpersonal decency) but not excellence (for example, scientific rigor or originality). It thus may be that at high levels, excellence is a necessary precondition if a mentor's overall approach to science is to be found attractive and emulated. Today's novice scientists may be unambivalent in their pursuit of professional excellence but uncertain about its compatibility with ethical conduct. Through daily example, the lineage heads provided proof that the highest professional accomplishments can coexist with ethical conduct and the transcendence of narrow self-interest.

Creating a Learning Environment

In apprenticeships, learning by observing is joined to learning by doing. In the research sciences, "doing" means participating in laboratory life. The lab, and the student's role within it, was a central mechanism by which the lineage heads' values and practices were transmitted. For the mentor, this means of influence is markedly different from talking or modeling because it is indirect, mediated by others and an environment. Each lineage head has acted through the community that he established in the lab—in Motulsky's case, in the training program he created. The process has multiple aspects: (1) selecting members of the community; (2) providing cultural and social resources; (3) creating a physical space and social organization that foster certain kinds of interaction and discourage others; and (4) cultivating a culture, climate, or ethos. At the same time, the lab becomes a complex sociocultural system in its own right that is not entirely subject to the lab head's control.

Many lab environments evolve spontaneously, even haphazardly. Some lab heads may not fully appreciate how much the environment affects the work that takes place in labs. Some may recognize the importance of the lab environment, but design theirs with goals other than students' welfare in mind. In such instances, the memes transmitted may not be "good-work" memes. In contrast to these scenarios, the lineage heads were keenly aware of the contribution made by the lab environment or training program to the student's education as a scientist. Lewontin, in particular, saw this as his primary means of formative influence. The lineage heads illustrate how training in certain kinds of environments initiates a novice into the practice of doing good work in a given profession.

How, specifically, did the lineage heads establish lab environments that functioned as an effective mechanism for the transmission of their memes? One important contributor is care in selecting students. The lineage heads favored applicants who appeared likely to become constructive, engaging members of the community. All three sought the capacity for independence, realizing that its absence would ill equip a student for life in their labs. Lewontin favored students who were mature and interesting; Gall favored students who were intrinsically interested in science and dogged. All three distinguished scientists attracted students of great promise, but were willing to turn away very bright students who they suspected might be at odds with the culture of the lab.

The same care in selecting students was mentioned by some G2s and G3s. For example, a Lewontin G2 always paid attention to whether a prospective lab member would be compatible, and avoided individuals who were strident or arrogant even if they were otherwise promising. Applicants were interviewed by the rest of the lab; as a result, he noted, "everybody gets along pretty well, because they choose each other." One Gall G3 described deferring to his lab's judgment about an applicant when it conflicted with his own. Doing so made sense not only because in this case the group proved to be superior judges but also because it is "very important . . . to try to have a group of people who will work together well."

Second, the lineage heads created environments stocked with cultural and social capital. Bourdieu (1985) introduced the concept of *social capital* decades ago, in research addressing how social status and power affect educational outcomes. He found that children born into families with strong social networks achieved greater educational success than children born into more isolated families or families of lower social standing. Bourdieu employed the term *cultural capital* to refer to resources in the form of books or other cultural artifacts (Hooker, Nakamura, & Csikszentmihalyi, 2003). The lineage heads provided both kinds of resources—social networks and sources of cultural information—establishing rich matrices for the transmission of knowledge, skills, and values. They also supplied abundant material resources for the process of learning by doing, including funding, equipment, and space.

Lewontin consciously sought to create an invigorating intellectual environment for students in which they would learn from and with other members of the community and be stimulated by them. That is, he wanted a lab in which interacting with peers was a key means of facilitating intellectual and moral development. He filled the lab with outstanding minds; the group was characterized by great diversity in terms of background, experience, and interests. It was remembered as a vibrant community, and this may have contributed to strong identification with the lineage.

In contrast, Gall stressed the more individual, focused enjoyment of grappling with a self-defined scientific problem at the bench. He sought to create a respectful, supportive, harmonious environment in which individuals could give full attention to the challenges of their work, learning by doing their research as independently as possible. The lab was characterized by students and postdocs who were friendly, bright, and engaged.

Third, the lineage heads used the organization of the physical space to make the lab environment an effective mediator of their transmission of memes. Lewontin deliberately designed the physical layout of his lab to foster interaction. Students' offices were arrayed around a central space filled with a table so large that it seated twenty. In order to reach their offices, students had to pass by this table, where coffee and conversation were almost always brewing. The tone of the interactions was lively, idealistic, and muscular. Whereas Lewontin engineered his lab's physical space to encourage conversation, Gall created a focused, almost silent work environment through his own quiet presence at the bench.

Finally, the lineage heads set the tone in the lab, moral and otherwise; they cultivated an ethos. One G2 recalled that their lab contained some "edgy personalities," but the lineage head was able to overcome this by virtue of his "decency"; he established the lab's emotional climate. A second lineage head was described as creating an environment where people behaved well toward one another because not doing so was "frowned on." A student of the third lineage head referred to "the aura of his presence," which students were keenly aware of, even though the lineage head himself was often absent. Some G2s were described as setting a tone in their own labs that enabled students to flourish. Recalling her mentor's lab, an admiring G3 came to believe that all lab heads should do what hers did so effectively: establish a code of behavior by which all members of the lab abide.

In sum, the lineage heads worked to establish and maintain a training environment cultivating good work. How, then, does a lab function to transmit the lab head's memes? The next section shifts from the lineage heads' efforts to shape the lab environment to an examination of how the lab environment shapes the values and practices of the student.

The Role of the Lab

We next draw primarily on the Lewontin and Gall lineages to describe how the lab acted on the students who entered it: how the lab, and its members, transmitted the mentor's memes. The Motulsky lineage is not highlighted, for the reasons discussed earlier. Both qualitative and quantitative data suggest that the lab played an important role. For example, we analyzed the memes inherited from the expected mentor and rated the importance and quality of the overall apprenticeship experience (see Appendix A). For the sample as a whole, the sheer number of memes that a former student ascribed to his or her expected mentor was significantly related to the quality of the lab culture as conveyed by the student ($r = .36$, $p < .05$, $N = 36$).

Peers as Teachers

Studying modern dance, Keinänen and Gardner (2004) distinguished between lineages in which development is dominated by traditional vertical mentoring of student by teacher, and others characterized by peer, or horizontal, mentoring. In the sciences, vertical and horizontal mentoring coexist; within these exemplars' labs, they were effectively integrated. Fellow graduate students, postdocs, technicians, and other lab members—as individuals and collectively as a community—both complemented and amplified the mentor's influence on new students, facilitating the absorption of multiple kinds of memes.

First, labmates complemented the mentor's role in the transmission of technical knowledge and practices. Senior lab members and peers played different roles. Senior, more expert members of a lab rounded out the mentor's role by modeling practices and skills that the mentor rarely employed, and responding when a need for procedural knowledge arose in the course of a student's work. They often did much of the work of transmitting a lab's cultural capital to its new members in this organic fashion, especially basic research skills (for example, how to design a good experimental control) and the technical knowledge undergirding the lab's distinctive expertise. One respondent echoed Vygotsky's notion of the "slightly more able peer" (Vygotsky, 1978), recalling that procedural knowledge was typically passed on by "people that were pretty close to me from my peer group but just a few steps ahead." Labmates may also transmit the lab's philosophy or intellectual approach. A former student explained that Lewontin was his generation's torch bearer of the philosophy that genetics provides an independent means of studying evolutionary processes. Many students came into his lab knowing and understanding his philosophy. However, "If you didn't, you did very quickly and not through Lewontin's preaching, but through all the other students—peer interactions. It was very much the philosophy of that whole lab environment."

The presence of more advanced students makes it possible for learning to take place in the zone of proximal development (Vygotsky, 1978). A G2 explained that Gall was so adept at anticipating and heading off difficulties as he worked that a novice might never learn how to overcome those problems by observing him. His skill level was too great. This type of skill was learned by observing more senior students. In addition, an eminent scientist can seem beyond emulation in his breadth or depth of knowledge. The expertise of senior students in the lab presents a goal within the younger student's reach. As one scientist recalled, "I couldn't imagine myself being [the lab head], but I could imagine myself being [the more senior protégé]." Another scientist explained:

> Most of the techniques and stuff I did at the bench I learned from other students and postdocs. That's really how the transmission of techniques is done. . . . You find out how to solve problems, and you find out how to design controls for experiments, which is the most important thing you learn as a graduate student. . . . You learn a lot of that from seeing somebody really good at the bench seeing a problem, facing it, confronting it, then solving it, over and over. That's how you learn it, and so that's where great, more senior students or postdocs are terrific—just to see them in action. So in our group meetings, the younger students watch postdocs run head-on into brick walls, and then they see how they climb over them. And that's fantastic education. But you also see it just at the bench, as well as learning all these little tricks for being methodical and keeping good notebooks and all these things like that.

A student's peers within the lab complemented the mentor's and senior students' roles by collaborating in formal and informal education. Members of each lineage learned by exchanging knowledge and exploring new subjects with labmates. A typical recollection, from one Motulsky G2, was that "all of us had different sets of expertise. I think I taught those people some things, and I think I learned things from them." Members of Lewontin's lab stood out, describing a large, fluid, energetic community of learners. One recalled his cohort of graduate students. Day in and day out, they arrived at the lab early in the morning, went out for dinner together, and returned to the lab, working until late in the evening. They studied for courses and discussed what they were learning together. They read and critiqued one another's papers and the latest journal articles. They were constantly forming study groups of two or three to read a book or learn a technique together. A study group might continue for a full year.

Labmates also served to amplify and reinforce the mentor's role with respect to the transmission of a scientific ethos, as contrasted with technical knowledge and practices. To the extent that other students in the lab possessed and embodied the mentor's values, orientations, and standards, new students were exposed to the memes even when the mentor was absent. One G2 recalled the ethos of Lewontin's lab and the fact that "there were some people . . . who drove that more so than others." One such peer was remembered admiringly as "very moralistic" (the term that lineage members so often applied to Lewontin himself) with a "very strong sense of how he should conduct himself in the world." He believed passionately that "this business of science was serious business, and anything people did should withstand the harshest criticism. To him, that was the whole pleasure of science. . . . It taught me to be more critical." The same G2 said that another student embodied "a scientific purism that I really admire." The G2 conveyed the same sense of being elevated by the nobility and purity of peers' conduct that he and others experienced with Lewontin. The main difference was that interaction with peers was far more frequent.

The cliché about graduate school—that one learns the most from fellow students—has decided merit in describing these labs. The atmosphere in the lab must be recognized as a factor in the successful transmission of knowledge, practices, and values. Phenomena like student study groups are self-organizing, growing organically out of students' shared intellectual needs and interests. Their formation and success depend on the quality of relationships among students in the lab. In labs with regular group meetings, the sense of community undoubtedly affects the tenor of these meetings in much the same way. In short, when the lab head establishes a cooperative ethos, it has multiple important effects: it facilitates peer learning, spares students the burden of in-lab competition, and perpetuates the spirit of cooperation itself.

Labs as Microcosms

The interviews made clear that the lab community established by the mentor, and the body of knowledge, practices, and beliefs transmitted in it, introduce the student to the field and domain of science in microcosm. The lab is a small world unto itself, a community in which students spend several years. They learn how to interact with a social field and a domain of knowledge largely as these are instantiated within the lab.

With respect to the domain, any lab is characterized by a focus on certain kinds of scientific problems and not others—a particular vision of what constitutes good scientific work. Students are exposed to the broader domain of scientific knowledge and practice through courses, journals, and conferences. However, Gall's students internalized the version of cytogenetics that they encountered in Gall's lab; the same is true of the version of population genetics internalized by Lewontin's students and the version of medical genetics internalized by Motulsky's.

With respect to the field, a lab is characterized by the kind of scientific community created within it and the relations between this microcosm and the larger field of practitioners. In leading programs, students interact with other researchers and the field's gatekeepers by attending conferences, communicating with labs working on the same scientific problems, and submitting manuscripts and grant proposals. These activities directly expose students to the social dynamics and standards of evaluation that prevail in the wider scientific community. However, it is in the advisor's lab that they gain most of their experience as they interact with others and see the quality of their own and others' work judged, day by day. A microcosm can stand in any of several relationships to the larger social system in terms of their respective social relations (for example, hierarchic versus nonhierarchic, competitive versus cooperative, formal versus informal) and incentive conditions (the prevailing set of rewards and disincentives for different actions). In these exemplary training environments, the lineage head created a social system that expressed his beliefs about the nature of scientific communities engaged in good work, the individual's place within them, and the relationship between the training lab and the larger field.

Before considering types of training labs, it is important to underline that senior scientists establish the relations between lab and field based on their own motives and goals. To the extent that a lab head's goals include successfully preparing students for later professional life, the lab is conceived, at least in part, as a setting for this preparation. When this is not the case, students may suffer. The interviewees were aware of many such labs, often giving a specific example of a lab that was explicitly run as a production site, with training as a subsidiary goal in the lab director's eyes.

Unlike the three types of training labs to which we turn shortly, young scientists in this lab type were "extra hands" in the lab head's race for priority. When labs are instruments of the lab directors' pursuit of personal success within the larger field, students execute one piece of a larger research agenda defined by the lab head—hence the term *extra hands*. A lab is organized in this way to get the director's work done as rapidly and efficiently as possible. One Lewontin G2 contrasted himself and his mentor with lab heads who have "a very, very focused research program." The G2 explained, "Everyone they hire has to fit into that in a very specific way, [and] you keep very tight reins on what people are doing from day to day. And that's a very successful model." Success in this context is measured by maximizing the lab's productivity or prevailing in races for priority against other labs. Students in such labs tend to be exposed to a view of the wider field as a competitive, zero-sum social system.

It is possible for students to admire the heads of such labs and for the lab atmosphere to be congenial. One G3 recalled an experience in a nonlineage lab quite favorably and admired the lab head: "He's brilliant, absolutely brilliant. . . . It's amazing what has been done under his guidance. He's so knowledgeable. . . . But the thing is that when you work for him, you don't get to see him very much, although, interestingly enough, his lab functioned fine even though he wasn't there. . . . But he doesn't really take a personal interest in who works for him. Someone once described that he thinks of the people in his lab as tools to achieve specific ends, and in a way that's true. But he's very up front about it . . . he's a very pleasant person to work for."

In such labs, students may acquire technical skills, learn protocols, and even develop a sense of how to do big science effectively. Students may have a clear view of the overall research program that they are serving. Or they may have a limited understanding of the lab head's goals. They certainly do not select and pursue their own research projects, and their development as independent scientists is not a major consideration in defining their role within the lab. None of the lineage heads endorsed this model as an educational paradigm or a reflection of good science.

Turning to labs run by scientists who emphasize training as well as their own productivity, and craft the relationship between microcosm and wider field with attention to student development, it is helpful to use two dimensions to characterize different lab types. One concerns the lab head's images of the wider field and the lab community. Of particular importance with respect to good work is the degree to which professional relationships within the wider community on the one hand, and within the lab community on the other hand, are seen as competitive (that is, zero-sum) versus cooperative (that is, "nonzero"). A second important dimension is the balance of independence and control that lab heads consider necessary for development as a scientist given their images of the wider field. Combinations of these dimensions define very different kinds of training-oriented labs, of which we describe three.

Survival of the Fittest Now, and Later. In one type of training lab, the students may enjoy considerable autonomy, but the atmosphere is sink or swim, and there is no incentive to cooperate with labmates. The senior scientist sees research as a competitive race and actively seeks to replicate the field as a competitive arena within the microcosm of the lab.

At least in the first half of his career, it has been said that James Watson's goals and view of the field led him to embrace this form of social Darwinism. His practices communicated the message that survival of the fittest prevails beyond the lab, so it should prevail inside too. The measure of fitness is speed, or priority: being the first to make a discovery. The defining training practice in this kind of lab is to pit two lab members against each other in a race to solve the same research problem; the practice promotes an intensely competitive culture. Only the student who finishes first receives his or her Ph.D. for solving the problem. Peers become rivals, just as it is expected that they will compete against other scientists when they enter the wider field. Lewontin disdained this model, spontaneously criticizing it during his interview. Gall concurred:

> You could certainly have a very productive lab where there's a lot of dissension and a lot of unhappy people. . . . Students come and ask me about doing postdocs in those labs. I warn them and say, "[If] . . . you're willing to put up with a cutthroat attitude or somebody else in your lab being given your project at the same time so that you two can compete, okay. But do it with your eyes open." I mean, that's the sort of thing I would never do. I would never put two students on the same project to see who could get

to the answer. I might put two students on the [same] project
if they were willing to work and cooperate and share the aspects
of it.

Arming for Survival. If the senior scientist sees the larger
field as an intensely competitive arena, replicating this is not
the only possible relationship of lab to field. One G3 described
a second kind of training lab. The well-intentioned lab director sought to insulate the lab from the larger field, protecting
students and equipping them for later success. His view was, "It's
a tough world, and I'm going to guard the door while you guys
grow up." This lab was structured to foster students' success. The
lab head appeared to introduce no barriers to cooperation inside
the lab; however, he took it as a given that beyond the lab door
lay a battlefield, and students' freedom in the short term had to
be sacrificed to their competitive edge in the long term. Each
student's graduate experience was heavily programmed by the
mentor to produce good academic performance, get articles into
good journals, and complete the degree rapidly. And yet while
the mentor did all this as a means of supporting his students'
professional prospects, some other qualities were lacking: the
cultivation of independent initiative, "the more idealistic and
the broader view" of a life in science, and the pleasant atmosphere that the G3 associated with the lab in which he himself
had trained. The particulars of this case may be unique, but the
strategy of arming for survival has general applicability.

These two types of training lab share a fundamentally competitive, zero-sum image of the wider field but illustrate very different ways of organizing the lab in response to this perception.
In the first, competitiveness becomes a key meme embedded
within the structure of the lab and the student's role in it; in
the second, the student is armed for eventual battle, but the lab
itself may be a cooperative setting. Furthermore, training in the
first type of lab encourages independence, while training in
the second does not.

Cooperating Now, and Later. In the last type of training lab, illustrated by the study's lineage heads, the lab community is organized to operate on cooperative principles, and it is felt that the larger scientific community also is—or should be—characterized by a spirit of cooperation. In addition, students' ability to work independently may be a criterion of admission to these labs, and the organization of the lab supports its development.

Gall appeared to view the wider scientific community as an ideal social system still significantly characterized by long-standing norms. Merit is generally rewarded. Despite the expanding presence of business interests in science, openness and cooperation continue to be viable, if threatened, principles, consistent with the traditional scientific ethos. Gall maintained a lab community governed by this ethos. While he warned students to enter cutthroat labs with their eyes open, he prepared them to expect that by and large, the norms governing his lab would apply in the wider field as well.

Lewontin, a self-described "orthodox Marxist," described his lab in more activist terms. He juxtaposed the kind of community he has sought to create in the lab to both society as a whole and some parts of the scientific community. According to a former student, Lewontin had been drawn to the "gentlemanly" and collegial culture of their subfield. Later, there had been a time when he and a colleague tried to organize the lab on the model of a communist cell. As one observer put it, "He was trying to create a society in the lab that matched the society that he wanted to live in."

Both risks and possible gains attend this approach. The risk is that students trained in cooperative labs subsequently will be derailed by ruthless, zero-sum social dynamics in the increasingly high-stakes field of genetics. The potential gain is that if scientists continue to live by the practices acquired in these training labs when they enter the wider field, interacting collegially with other scientists and establishing the same kind of lab themselves, they will help create a more cooperative scientific community (compare with Cohen & Taubes, 1995).

Memes Transmitted by the Lab Structure

The organization of the lab is a particularly powerful means for transmitting certain memes, including independence or, alternatively, top-down control. This is because graduate students to a great extent learn by doing, and the lab head determines how much freedom to grant to students, or how much control to impose on them, in conducting their research. In G1 labs, the student role was structured to require and foster independence. Students were given freedom to select their own research projects in sharp contrast to other lab types described earlier. While Lewontin and Gall considered themselves accessible, they did not closely monitor students' work. Because of both the competing claims on their time and their pedagogical beliefs, they expected students to motivate themselves and attempt to solve their own problems.

The organization of the lab is also a particularly important and effective means of transmitting the meme of cooperativeness—and its alternative, competitiveness—because these can be practiced only in interaction with fellow scientists, as occurs in the lab on a regular basis. Gall and Lewontin each used distinctive practices. Gall deliberately spread students out in his lab so that their research areas did not overlap, and students often worked with an organism (model system) that no other lab member was using. This signature practice (the norm is to use the same organism for all research conducted in a lab) facilitated openness and cooperation while showing the value of Gall's distinctive breadth of scientific knowledge, on which the practice hinged. Gall's students remembered their labmates as helpful, especially the senior peers from whom they learned technical skills and protocols. The "freedom from [rivalry]," combined with certainty that neither outright harassment nor gender bias would be tolerated, made the lab a safe environment.

Lewontin imparted cooperativeness in a somewhat different fashion. He organized his lab on Marxist principles, with nonhierarchic and collectivist relations as the goal. Resources and responsibilities were shared; for example, everyone shared in cleaning the lab. He described deferring to his students in making a decision about whether to accept an applicant into the lab, on the thinking that "if they don't want to live with this guy, they shouldn't have to." Lab members developed collaborative projects without Lewontin's direction. In a lab where the debates could be lively, Lewontin intervened primarily to make it a safe environment: "I try my best to have a group operate in such a way that people's egos are not under assault. . . . I spend a certain amount of my time hand-holding if I think that people are being put off by other people" and doing repair work if "[I] tread on people's toes unconsciously."

What guidance do these examples offer about creating a positive lab environment and atmosphere? As discussed, student-selection criteria are not a trivial consideration. Undoubtedly the lineage heads' strength of character and personality (quiet in one case, charismatic in the other) were also factors. The multiple pathways that the lineage heads used to communicate their values and practices were mutually reinforcing; consistent modeling, intermittent conversations, and the lab culture conveyed the same messages. Senior graduate students and postdocs complemented the mentor's role, teaching technical skills and knowledge that the mentor did not. They also amplified the mentor's formative role, reinforcing his values and practices. The lab's physical layout and specific training practices also mattered. Finally, particularly important was the recognition that the lab is a social system and a microcosm of the larger field, the organization of which has significant consequences for the scientists educated there.

The Student as a Selective Agent

In Chapter One, we cautioned that the theoretical lens of cultural transmission could appear oversimplifying and mechanistic if mistaken as a characterization of the social-psychological processes of learning and development. Focusing on the formative influence of the mentor and lab community should not obscure the role that students play in this process. Students are active participants in their interactions with the mentor and labmates, not passive receptacles of transmitted knowledge, values, and practices.

At least for the students of these exemplary scientists, learning by apprenticeship proved not to revolve around assisting in a master's work and certainly was not a matter of receiving didactic instruction. Instead, like the process through which we acquire our native language, it is best described as actively learning by doing within a community of practice. In Lewontin's and Gall's cases, the community was defined by the mentor's lab and in Motulsky's case extended to the training program that he created. Participating in this type of community and learning by doing required the student's initiative, however. Other means of transmission also required students' initiative. First, Gall and Lewontin expected students to decide when to initiate the informal exchanges about their research. Second, all three lineage heads deliberately exposed students to the way that they approached science themselves: teaching by example. However, the mentor's modeling depends on the student's active observation to be effective.

Even when a student actively admires and emulates a mentor in many respects, the transmission of memes is not a process of wholesale replication from one generation to the next. Various factors—goals, capacities, temperament, orientations grounded in earlier experience—inform students' selective retention of some memes and rejection of others as they construct their own distinctive approaches to a life in science. Sometimes a mentor's admired qualities, such as originality, may resist emulation. In other cases, a mentor's values or practices appeal to some students but not others, and the latter do not absorb them. One student may admire her advisor's work ethic, emulate her habits, and encourage them in her own lab; another may chafe under the advisor's workaholism and establish a different balance of work and nonwork life as soon as he is on his own. One student may luxuriate in the independence allowed by a mentor; another may be shaken by the same mentor's lack of solicitude and counsel. The first may go on to reproduce the mentor's light hand with students; the other may take care to meet on a weekly basis with each student.

Students' alternatives are not limited to rejecting or accepting a mentor's memes. Students may inflect an influential mentor's memes with their own qualities or introduce altogether new memes. For example, Lewontin's students tended to admire and emulate his integrity with respect to authorship credit and transmit it to their own students; at the same time, they manifested their moralism in other spheres. We saw that one student in the Lewontin lab lastingly impressed a peer because he shared the lineage head's moralism but expressed it in his stringent standards and seriousness about science.

Furthermore, almost every scientist encounters multiple influences during the course of professional training. We asked interviewees who had been most important in shaping their approach to science over the years. Every scientist cited two or more significant professional influences; some recalled as many as half a dozen. Those identified were primarily teachers, especially advisors at the college, graduate, and postgraduate levels, but also fellow students and labmates. How do students selectively reproduce certain influences over others? One major factor is the sifting and appropriating that is actively (even if in part subconsciously) performed by the student. In the face of multiple influences, individuals play a large role in their own professional formation because they are obliged to select, reconcile conflicting examples, and construct a model of the kind of scientist they would like to be.

Finally, norms about creativity affect novices' receptiveness to and acknowledgment of influence by others, and these norms differ from one profession to the next. For example, modern dancers interviewed by Keinänen and Gardner (2004) were quite resistant to acknowledging any senior figures or former teachers as significant influences on their approach to dance. One likely reason is that the way a dancer approaches dance is viewed as a measure of his or her creativity. In contrast, creativity or originality is highly valued by research scientists but is judged on the basis of a scientist's choice of problems and quality of solutions, not the scientist's approach to research. Some scientists we interviewed resisted singling out one person as the strongest influence on them; however, most were not reluctant to see themselves as having been influenced by mentors, and certainly not with respect to technique, standards of excellence and integrity, mentoring practices, or even signature aspects of their scientific approach. We did not encounter any scientist in the sample who claimed never to have been significantly influenced by a senior figure.

Conclusion

Contrary to our original expectations of intense, personal, one-on-one interaction, the senior scientists influenced their students' values and practices by force of example and by shaping the culture of the training environment as much as through conversation. Every lab head decisively influences the small world within his or her lab. Mentors shaped the lab's community and ethos, such that their own direct influence was reinforced and complemented by group interactions and the lab culture. These magnified the mentor's influence so that the lab became an embodiment of the mentor's values. Students actively participated in the learning process, keenly observing and selectively emulating the mentor, and integrating the mentor's influences with those of other formative figures.

Up to this point, we have not focused on the nature of the relationship formed between mentor and student over the course of an apprenticeship in science. In the next chapter, we examine the key features of the relationship between mentor and student to see how the quality of the relationship serves as context for the transmission of values, practices, and knowledge.

7

SUPPORTIVE RELATIONSHIPS AS THE CONTEXT FOR INTERGENERATIONAL INFLUENCE

Ours is a selective sample, as we have pointed out. The lineage heads were all well known as effective mentors as well as elite scientists, and the subsequent generations of students descended from them were also highly successful scientists with notable career achievements. In addition, as we saw in Chapter Five, each lineage can be considered successful from the point of view of meme transmission through the generations. Beyond these general benchmarks of effective mentoring, interview transcripts were coded for negative advising experiences (for example, abuse or neglect) and for positive advising experiences. An individual could report both positive and negative advising experiences.

Mentoring Relationships: Negative Aspects

Some limited yet revealing negative aspects of mentoring relationships were reported by the scientists we interviewed. It is perhaps no secret that mentoring relationships can provide a fertile breeding ground for disputes and difficulties, including conflicts over intellectual property and authorship, feelings of neglect, exploitation, gruff treatment, lack of fairness in evaluation or resources, and resentment at the advisor's unreasonable or constant demands. At the extreme end, there is no lack of high-profile cases regarding alleged violations of intellectual property in the popular press, especially with publications or discoveries that are groundbreaking, award winning, or otherwise highly acclaimed. The president emeritus of Stanford University, Donald Kennedy (1997), noted that most of the grievances concerning authorship and intellectual property that he dealt with were in the sciences, partly because scientific discoveries sometimes hold great economic value, particularly in the modern era of genetic discoveries and biotechnology.

We investigated the following questions: What were the reasons for disappointments or dissatisfactions with mentoring relationships? In particular, what were the most common causes of rifts in the relationship from the student's point of view?

Abuse and Extreme Self-Interest

Given the selective nature of the sample, the number of problems encountered in mentoring relationships is necessarily limited and possibly skewed with respect to severity. We expected there to be fewer problems reported than in a random sample of graduate advising relationships, and this was most likely the case. To be sure, issues of authorship and intellectual property did arise in a fair number of interviews. Most such conflicts appear to arise because the advisor expects to be identified as an author on a paper primarily conceived, conducted, and written by the student while guided by the advisor and using his or her data, equipment, or other resources.

Beyond authorship issues were several instances of what appeared to be poor judgment on the part of mentors in putting their interests so far ahead of their students' that they essentially shunned responsibility for them. In the worst instance, one respondent shared an episode in which he interviewed for an academic job and named his advisor as a reference. When the prospective employer called, his advisor did a wonderful job of promoting—but not on his student's behalf. His advisor ended up taking the job himself! In another case, an advisor was reluctant to relinquish a student who had graduated, even after the student accepted a new position. In graduate mentoring relationships, there can often be a tension between the growing independence of the advanced student and the faculty member's need to enlist his or her help and talents.

Most instances of poor behavior, however, occurred in the course of day-to-day interactions. There were several reports of a mentor who had lost his or her temper or intimidated students. Mentors may not realize what a lasting impression such negative experiences may make on advisees, particularly in the absence of counterbalancing praise or positive feedback.

Some examples of harmful behavior involved public intimidation, embarrassment, or humiliation. This occurred most frequently in classroom situations when advisors asked questions that students could not answer, made insulting comments in front of peers, or were otherwise perceived as intimidating. While some students might be able to roll with the punches, others find such behavior genuinely terrifying.

In this sample, it was not what mentors did that the students complained about most, but rather what the mentors did not do. When it came to descriptions of negative aspects of their mentoring relationships, there were only scattered reports of abusive or other poor behavior; in contrast, there were upward of thirty complaints of neglect in one of various forms, an average of almost one such report per respondent.

Neglect

Among other things, students complained about advisors who did not offer enough advice or guidance, challenge them enough, help them to publish soon enough, offer opportunities or forums to talk about students' work, offer enough feedback (especially positive feedback), take enough interest, spend enough time thinking about their students, monitor lab dynamics closely enough to resolve internal disputes, offer enough professional connections, explain how to navigate the field, or provide enough help to get a job.

This is a lengthy and varied list, with each respondent usually generating only a single complaint. Anyone who has held a faculty position or led a lab can probably sympathize with the targets of such complaints. After all, these are demanding positions, and those who run labs may have as much difficulty as anyone else in being all things to all people. Since nobody is perfect, they would soon burn out if they were overly sensitive to criticism. However, these grumblings made up only about half of the reports of neglect. The other half were instances in which the advisor left the student completely alone, rarely or never checking on the student's progress. A classic example comes from Lewontin's training. His advisor while at Columbia, Theodosius Dobzhansky, gave the young Lewontin an experiment to do and then went to Brazil for a year, never checking on him. Lewontin recalls, "And I didn't do the experiment. He came back and said, 'How did the experiment go?' And I said, 'Oh I tried it, and it didn't work.' Which was a lie; I never even tried it." Lewontin did another experiment instead; it eventually became his thesis, which Dobzhansky accepted. The brilliant and independent Lewontin did not experience this as a major problem, but of course, he is not a typical case.

The overriding sentiment among students who felt neglected was that their advisors were too busy for them and should be left alone. This can be a difficult situation for students in need of guidance or feedback. Imagine a student who has never asked his advisor any questions for fear of disturbing him. Finally he reasons that he has been in the lab for a long time without bothering his advisor, and now really needs his advice. When he goes to the advisor and poses a question, however, he is told he can figure it out on his own. In the rare instances when we heard about experiences of this kind, they were clearly upsetting to the student and could color his or her perception of the whole educational experience.

Professors are extremely busy people and juggle advising responsibilities with research, teaching, and university service. In fact, many professors probably do not even suspect, let alone fully understand, how students may experience an absence of their attention. One scientist told a story about a graduate advisor who "wasn't always the most pleasant person." A fellow student broke his leg and returned to the lab on crutches with a big leg cast; he happened to be at "a critical stage in doing his experiments." On his return, the advisor came to the lab, looked at the injured student, and—interested only in the fate of the experiment—said, "*So?*" The interviewee concluded, "He didn't take much personal interest in people."

Students quickly pick up on how their advisors perceive their relationship and how much they are respected. As one student reported about an advisor, "He didn't take interest in people's personal lives. . . . He wanted to depersonalize the relationship between people. He didn't fraternize—and he once said that the reason he doesn't is because he has nothing in common with his students." Undoubtedly observations such as these indirectly communicate something to the student about his or her place or status in relation to the advisor. If students feel that they are spending a good part of their lives on the same work as their advisor and yet the advisor feels that they have little in common, then they may infer that the main source of separation in the advisor's mind must be his or her superior stature. In cases like these, potential role models instead became "antimentors," a term coined by Howard Gardner in the course of the GoodWork Project for individuals whose instructive significance stems from providing an example students do not want to emulate. In most cases, students' experiences with an antimentor were too bitter to inflict the same treatment on their own future students. The positive qualities of antimentors might be recognized, but often were not absorbed.

Mentoring Relationships: Positive Aspects

The quality of the mentoring relationship may play a key role in whether a student absorbs the mentor's values and practices. Indeed, there was a strong correlation between our ratings of overall quality of the mentoring relationship and how important a mentor was perceived to be to the mentee's career ($r = .67$, $p < .001$, $N = 35$). Perhaps even more meaningfully, there was also a significant association between the quality of the relationship with a mentor and the number of memes absorbed from that mentor ($r = .50$, $p < .01$, $N = 35$). Although these data cannot establish causality, the pattern suggests that students are more likely to be influenced and carry forward a mentor's memes when the overall relationship is positive.

Admiration for the Mentor

The most frequently mentioned aspect of positive mentoring relationships was the student's profound admiration for his or her mentor. In fact, twenty-five of the thirty-six participants—over two-thirds of the sample—described deeply admiring their mentors. This high frequency was all the more noteworthy because we did not explicitly ask about such admiration; the participants volunteered these descriptions.

Respondents described intense admiration and respect for their mentors' impressive qualities. Many stood in awe of them, as if interacting with a living legend. Certainly all three G1 scientists were described in such terms by students. A student of Richard Lewontin enthused, "He's just extraordinarily well read and broad thinking . . . also extraordinarily bright, the brightest guy I've ever met. . . . I was just so amazed at this guy. I thought, if I can hang around with him, it doesn't really matter what I do. He's just so bright, I'll learn something."

One of Arno Motulsky's students said of his mentor: "[He] brought out the best in you. . . . He was very fatherly—like in the sense that I think all of us wanted to sort of win and earn his respect. It was something that was valued because of the esteem in which he was held both locally and nationally. . . . Very unabusive, gentlemanly, scholarly. . . . You just felt if he recognizes me as doing something good or useful, that's positive. I want to have that feeling."

Asked to describe her image of an ideal scientist, one of Joe Gall's students responded: "I think it would be pretty close to what Joe Gall is. . . . Just being around him, to this day, it's the closest thing I ever come to, to being high on drugs. . . . It's just so much fun. . . . He has just an amazing mind and he was a very kind and patient mentor. He explains things so clearly and tests things so thoroughly. He's just great."

We might expect such heartfelt declarations from the students of the three eminent lineage heads. There is little doubt that the admiration these respondents expressed often stemmed at least in part from their mentor's strong record of accomplishment and success. Interestingly, however, there was no major difference in the frequency with which admiration was reported by the G2 participants (nine of twelve, or 75 percent), who were describing the lineage heads, and the G3 participants (fifteen of twenty-one, or 71 percent), who were describing mentors in Generation 2. This suggests that the G1s' eminence was not the only factor underlying such awe. In fact, mentors were admired for many traits, including honesty and integrity, treating others with respect, and fairness.

Supportiveness: A Deeper Look

The defining characteristic of positive advising relationships was supportiveness. In discussions of such relationships, support dwarfed other attributes; it received at least three times as many mentions as any other aspect. One respondent captured this sentiment in stating, "I would define a mentor as somebody who's very supportive and constructive and patient." The importance of supportiveness is confirmed by research on the positive impact that supportive mentors and coaches have on children (for example, Smith & Smoll, 1990) and by prior research on graduate school mentors (for example, Tenenbaum, Crosby, & Gliner, 2001). By itself, the importance of supportiveness may not be surprising. Everyone knows that providing support is an important part of mentoring, teaching, parenting, or any relationship in which an elder takes responsibility for nurturing a younger person. Why is it, then, that even well-intentioned elders are frequently perceived as unsupportive by the younger? Are our ideas of support overly simplistic?

In order to gain some leverage on these questions, we made a distinction between relationships that appeared to be particularly strong and those that were weaker. In global assessments of each transcript, we rated the overall quality of the mentoring relationship as described by the mentee. Relationships rated 4 or 5 on a five-point scale were classified as strong, and those mentors are described as effective ($n = 25$); those rated 3 or below were classified as weak, with those mentors described as less effective ($n = 11$). In our analyses, we compared relationship characteristics of the stronger and weaker mentoring relationships. The comparisons did not always yield interesting or significant results, but they did help illuminate the multidimensional nature and far-reaching effects of a mentor's supportiveness. In fact, we found at least six related but distinct components of supportiveness: consistent availability and involvement, a balance between freedom and guidance, an atmosphere and resources fostering supportiveness, frequent and specific positive feedback, treating graduate students as respected collaborators, and individualized interest in the student.

Availability and Involvement

At minimum, effective mentors were accessible and available. One lab director stated that she sought to be available to her students and to help each one develop into an independent scientist. "Mentoring," she summarized, "mostly involves a commitment of time and thought to what the student is doing." This kind of commitment of time and energy depends on a perception of mentoring as important. This perception is critical, since time limitations were repeatedly cited as one of the greatest obstacles to effective mentoring.

Perhaps one of the most basic distinctions between effective and less effective mentors resided quite literally in being present, usually on-site. Physical presence occurs as a matter of course for advisors who actively work at the bench or have an office in the lab, regularly putting them in close proximity with their students. One G2 observed that because his office was literally in the lab, "I'm always there, walking by people doing experiments."

One obvious function of graduate advisors is to be available for necessary help, guidance, and expertise with academics. Many graduate students enter their doctoral program with a fund of knowledge but without a specific approach to solving research questions. While providing academic help is assumed to be integral to the graduate advising relationship, significant help is not always forthcoming. Those who provided effective academic help successfully communicated that they were there for the student when needed. One scientist remembered her advisor as always making the time to help: "She would always be there if I had questions about patient-related [issues]. If I was interested in a piece of research, I could always rely on her to look at ten drafts of whatever it was I was doing and make useful comments."

The frequency of interaction was not always determined entirely by the mentor, however. The student needed to make the effort and the time as well. Beyond the routine asking of specific questions, students needed to be proactive about asking for a meaningful amount of time and attention, if not pressing for it. One student recalled, "My advisor would sort of come through once a year routinely and sit in your office and say, 'So tell me what we're thinking about this year.' If I didn't initiate something, that could be it for the year. That really could be it because—for me that was good because I'm very self-motivated, so I'd just push him when I needed him, and he'd always be there and respond."

True availability required being approachable, so that students felt they could turn to the advisor when needed. Advisors who had been highly available to students were remembered with gratitude and with the recognition that it is not always the norm. A theoretician recalled that one advisor "was tremendously accessible to his students. . . . He would stop in the corridor and stand there holding a pile of papers and get into an intellectual discussion. You could interrupt him, and he was tremendously tolerant of that. . . . He almost never said, 'I'm sorry, I'm busy now.'"

In contrast, and making clear that physical presence cannot always be equated with availability, he had a second mentor whom he felt could never be interrupted, and thus had a way of being inaccessible even when they were in the same room. More than they may realize, advisors who had been generous with their time and attention were remembered with great appreciation and admiration. For example, one G3 recalled with amazement that his advisor was always willing to talk with him when he had questions. He could not recall a single instance in which he had walked into his advisor's office and his advisor did not drop what he was doing in order to talk, for hours if needed. The student felt this attention was critical to the formation of his research interests.

Students with the most positive experiences reported that their mentors were more than just accessible; they were actively involved with members of the lab. We encountered numerous examples of effective mentors actively intervening to maintain a positive lab community and climate. The more involved mentors set limits and put their foot down when needed. Of course, setting appropriate limits and demands may be considered part and parcel of an effective, optimal style of teaching or parenting. According to the theories of Diana Baumrind (1989; see also Evertson, Emmer, & Worsham, 2003), the ideal parenting style is "authoritative." It is neither restrictive and punitive, nor permissive. Rather, authoritative parents effectively set and enforce limits in the context of a responsive and caring relationship. However, limit setting may be less common than is needed in university lab settings due to the degree of involvement required if the lab head is to be aware of lab interactions. Mentors who maintained an active presence regularly monitored students' progress and the climate of the lab. One young scientist noted that she was aware of exactly what everybody in her small lab was doing. At this stage in her career, she was not out of the lab doing administrative work, but in the lab all the time to "see what [was] going on." Other scientists interacted with every student in the lab on a daily basis to at least check in.

In general, then, effective mentoring was enhanced by remaining attentive to students as learners rather than as extra pairs of hands, and treating the lab as a training environment rather than as a production site. Investing a great deal of attention and involvement is not categorically effective, however. High involvement may also lead to intrusiveness and tight control. Effective mentoring, rather, results from being present and involved without becoming overly controlling.

Particularly because students need the mentor's involvement less and less as they move through the training process, optimal involvement is not necessarily maximum involvement. While ongoing involvement is important, it should not be so great as to compromise students' development as independent researchers. One distinguished scientist working primarily with post-doctoral students noted that the lab head virtually lives with members of the lab "day in, day out." Though he considered an open door policy important for remaining accessible to his students, he cautioned, "Part of being independent is you learn how to solve some problems for yourself. So there's a certain balance." In another example of striking that balance, a G3 said that his own serendipitous lack of availability following several years of very active involvement was key to the success of one of his students. Whereas initially the student lacked originality and was afraid to think "outside the box," he became more thoughtful once he realized he was on his own. The G3 related, "And so not having anyone around really caused him to raise the level, and he's doing really well now."

The Balance of Freedom and Guidance

Despite the importance of accessibility and involvement in supportive mentoring relationships, the interviewees as graduate students had greatly appreciated the freedom to become independent. They spoke as much about the importance of freedom and independence as any other principle of supportiveness, perceiving it to be essential to their growth and development. One respondent told us that what she appreciated most about her mentors was the absolute freedom to do what she was interested in doing.

Multiple pros and cons may need to be weighed when determining the extent of one's involvement as a mentor. For example, one respondent said that his advisor was very "hands-off" and did not "look over his shoulder." Unfortunately, the student's first few projects failed. Perhaps his advisor felt that it was valuable for the student to learn what succeeded and failed on his own, but the student could not help feeling that the amount of time he wasted was excessive. It is always difficult for teachers, advisors, and parents alike to know how much to intervene in the development of someone junior. There is a sense that people do need to discover things on their own, that the path to learning and growth must be a natural one. For example, some advisors like their students to do all of their important lab work independently; others guide students so that they can eventually learn to do it on their own.

The issue is complex. Providing freedom can be productive; neglecting students can be destructive; and there is a fine line between the two. Undoubtedly there is a delicate balance to be struck, providing an appropriate measure of freedom along with the needed guidance and structure. Finding the optimal balance is not easy, however. In light of our findings about the damaging impact of perceived neglect, one important question becomes: How do successful relationships provide freedom in such a way that it is not experienced as neglectful?

Mentors who were appreciated for the freedom and independence they allowed had subtle but important ways of staying involved with their students. In some cases, they checked in only periodically, but made themselves available to provide guidance at the student's initiation. Other advisors were equally accessible, but rather than checking in periodically, they monitored their students' progress well enough to intervene when they thought that a student was not on track to succeed. Others followed the model of "leading a horse to water but not forcing him to drink." They would push the student forward initially and then back off; they would suggest the importance of certain work, but ultimately would seek signs of self-motivation rather than insisting a student work in an area that did not inspire interest.

Appreciation of freedom frequently centered on students' being allowed to pursue their own research project, particularly for their doctoral thesis. Such a practice may seem basic since a doctoral thesis by definition is a piece of original work that significantly contributes to a domain of knowledge. However, an advisor might strongly encourage students to pursue a topic that furthers his or her own career rather than the students' training. Practices like this provide all the more reason that intellectual freedom is so appreciated when received.

This is from the perspective of students, however. Some of the most valuable insights regarding how successful mentors approached their students came from Generation 1 and 2

respondents speaking about how they seek to mentor their students. Some spoke directly of the need to balance freedom and
guidance and took different approaches depending on the student: "I do give [my students] a lot of freedom. . . . I mean, I do
give them guidance, but I am not telling them every step of the
way what they should do."

Another mentor grew to learn the importance of backing off
and providing freedom over time but still took several measures
to provide guidance:

> I was really hands-on with all of them the first five years, and
> now I've found that they actually do better if I step back and
> let them fail a bit on their own or succeed a bit on their own.
> So now we always talk a couple times a week. And they quite
> often come in my office on a daily basis during bad times. So it's
> more like the style I've taken from my advisor. . . . We have a lab
> meeting, and everybody talks about their work every week. And
> then I try to have a personal meeting one on one with everybody
> once a week. But I can let that slide if somebody is obviously
> doing well and looking happy, I won't bug them about it. But if
> they're not looking happy, I insist.

In a process similar to scaffolding (Vygotsky, 1978), one
mentor explained her tendency to provide structure early on,
when it is most needed, and to gradually withdraw it as students
gain independence over time. Early on, "[advising them] will
mean designing a project, directing them to the correct reading,
talking to them about it, making sure they understand, giving them protocols, standing next to them at the bench, and all
that kind of thing." Later, "as they become more independent, it
may mean just talking to them every few days or once a week or
whenever they have a question."

Recommending a good research project or topic to pursue
constituted one of the more common forms of faculty guidance. An advisor gave a detailed account of balancing such

guidance with allowing students to choose and pursue their own projects: "I talk to them on a regular basis, hopefully once a week. And then I kind of discuss what is going to have to be done in the next one or two weeks. And then I'll see how they have progressed. . . . So it's basically general guidance. I have usually more ideas than they do. Not always. So I tell them this might be interesting to look at, that might be interesting. I try to tell them why I think this is the case. But eventually students and postdocs come up with their own ideas that they pursue independently."

The extent to which effective mentors provided ideas was often based on a student's need for structure versus independence. Students with the ability to come up with their own ideas for research topics and experiments were often allowed to do so. The same scientist explained:

> In the beginning, when a student comes, usually I discuss various possibilities of topics. . . . But then after [they take basic courses], I propose certain topics, and a student may then pursue one of these topics, or he or she may come up with a topic of their own. This has happened actually in the majority of cases. I had one student who came and said, "I want to work on neural networks." At the time, I didn't know what this was; he had to take classes and do some basic work first. And then it turned out, I learned myself about neural networks, and I learned to see how they could be used. And now he really did beautiful work. This has turned out to be a very important area of research. This was his idea. I think more than half of the cases, people have come up with their own ideas.

What many reports from mentors suggest is the tremendous value of guidance and knowledge from someone who has already traveled down the same path on which a student is now embarking. Someone who has already traveled the path is in an ideal position to point out the ins and outs, dos and don'ts, opportunities and pitfalls. Mentors were particularly support-ive in dealing with fairly inevitable failures, for example, as promised by the high rejection rates of journals. One advisor talked explicitly about his role in providing perspective at such moments. When their papers were rejected, for example, most of his students wanted to know what they should do. The advi-sor was able to calm students down, provide perspective on what the rejection really meant, and encourage students to revise and resubmit their manuscripts using the feedback from reviewers.

A Supportive Atmosphere and the Provision of Resources

While the appropriate balance between allowing freedom and providing guidance sets the stage for a supportive relationship, there are many other dimensions of mentor support. For exam-ple, many grateful students spoke about their good fortune in working in a supportive environment. This usually referred to being surrounded by others in the lab who were generally help-ful. In some cases, support was the tacit feel of the environment rather than what was overtly expressed—a comfortable atmo-sphere of the lab. Although the whole environment was felt to be supportive, the lab head played a pivotal role in setting the tone for the lab, as described in Chapter Six. For example, one student observed that her mentor would not settle for less than absolute respectfulness in the lab: "She was responsible for providing an atmosphere in the lab that was conducive to feel-ing comfortable about expressing your ideas. I think this is very important, because I think [a] lot of heads of labs aren't really in touch with the dynamics that are established in the lab."

Mentors support students not only socially and behaviorally, but also financially. At the simplest level, the mentor may liter-ally hire a student as a research assistant. Providing necessary resources was an essential aspect of strong mentoring relation-ships. In most university settings in which graduate advising revolves around research, financial support and resources are integral to mentoring. One of the most distinctive features of weaker mentoring relationships was that the mentors provided the necessary financial support and resources, but the support appeared to end there. In the stronger mentoring relationships, mentors not only provided financial support and resources, but also did it in a way that communicated their intellectual, social, and emotional investment in the student.

Several of the students in our sample commented that they felt a certain amount of trust was invested in them by virtue of being hired, particularly when the student lacked substantial experience. In the more supportive relationships, the mentor not only "took in" the new student, but the new student was then warmly accepted by others in the lab. For example, one of Motulsky's students felt that the senior members of his lab took her "under their wing" and included her in social and professional opportunities. She was treated as a "little sister."

Giving a student a job and taking her into the lab usually communicates a high degree of interest. Occasionally a mentor may not only invite collaboration, but also go to great lengths to secure it. One of Lewontin's former graduate students recalls his mentor's unusual show of support from the beginning of a summer job with him: "He said, 'Would you be interested in doing graduate work with me?' and I said, 'Yes.' He said, 'I'm moving to the University of Chicago, so you should apply to the University of Chicago'. . . . He talked to the department there and said, 'You will admit this student. Don't ask questions. Don't worry about evaluating him, just admit him.' And they said okay, they would do that."

Hence, a student's salary not only supports his survival, but can also represent more in terms of the mentor's trust and investment. In addition to funds, mentors provide the physical resources and tools for conducting experiments, which are essential to most research in the biological sciences. Such tools can communicate the same sense of trust and freedom when given for use at the student's discretion. One of Lewontin's former students recalled:

> Lewontin took me down and got me keys. And then I asked, "Where's the lab?" And he opened the freezer and he said, "Here's all the reagents.". . . [Before] I literally had to go and steal little bits of reagents from other people so I could do my experiments. And Lewontin has a freezer full of this stuff. And he said, "There's NAD [nicotinamide adenine dinucleotide] and TPN [triphosphopyridine nucleotide]. The enzymes are all over here." And I was kind of dumbfounded, and I said, "I can use them?" And he looked at me and said, "Of course. What do you think they're there for?" And at that instant I realized that this was going to be fun. That was the way that lab was. All the resources are there, and anyone can use them for whatever purpose, and no one's going to [keep] tabs on how much you're using of what. Just go; do what you think is interesting.

Resources and funding were sources of support in their own right, and in cases like this, they were also a symbol of the mentor's investment. Such mentors saw their ability to provide necessary funds as an investment in the growth of a student toward a level of professionalism that they were committed to seeing the student reach. Of course, many excellent mentors also realized that the success of their students was one tangible measure of their own success. One mentor coupled the funding of students with seeking assurance that the students would capitalize on the investment by finding career opportunities:

> [My students] basically have put their careers to a large extent in my hands when they come to me in many ways. Obviously they're their own people, and whether they succeed or fail is their problem, but I feel like if they come to me, I'm going to fund them throughout. I'm not going to let them all of a sudden find themselves without funding. And I always assure them that

the day they say they want to be in my lab, I'll guarantee them five years' funding. However I do it, I don't know, but I'll do it. And they don't ever have to worry about that. They'll have to write grant proposals, but that's more of a game in a sense. It's not because they have to. And the other reason I make them give talks, and basically I make them give talks every year, is because I really feel responsible for getting them their next job. And [in the] beginning of their fifth year, I make them go basically start interviewing for postdocs.

In mentoring relationships such as this, resources represent professional opportunities. This is perhaps nowhere clearer than in the case of travel funds to send students to professional meetings and conferences, a resource that respondents mentioned gratefully. Mentors see spending such funds as an investment in both the student and the student's research. Those who were treated generously in turn made the same investments in their own students. One of Lewontin's students reported that he liked to be able to support his students financially, just as his mentor had done.

What is actually learned from one's mentor leads us to another critical type of resource: intellectual. Mentors are often considered the source of the intellectual framework and structure on which all lab activity is built. They are the idea generators. Some respondents felt that one benefit of having a highly creative and well-connected mentor was constantly receiving information about new directions, discoveries, and important developments occurring in the field as they unfolded. Students considered this type of resource invaluable for their professional growth. One commented that such an experience "changed everything."

The Role of Frequent and Positive Feedback

Outside of providing the right kind of atmosphere and resources, support resided chiefly in the things that mentors said—or did not say—to their students. First, mentors perceived as supportive did not denigrate. Although this may seem somewhat obvious, it is worth mentioning because degrading comments to students in highly pressured research environments are common enough that simply treating students with respect is often felt to be supportive. Beyond the absence of negative comments, supportive mentors were liberal in offering positive feedback. That positive feedback was a common feature of supportive mentoring is hardly surprising; nevertheless, expressions of encouragement were an important and frequently mentioned aspect of supportive mentoring relationships. Comments as simple as, "Good work!" and "Glad to see things are going well!" communicated support in a way that did not occur with mentors who insisted that their students had not proven anything until they ran three more experiments. Mentors also encouraged students with emphatic responses to large and small accomplishments. They were prone to making enthusiastic—even corny—comments such as, "Fantastic!" "This is great!" "That's really interesting!" and "Wow!"

Many intelligent people have the analytical skills to dissect a situation and determine what is wrong with it. It takes a higher level of leadership and mentoring skill to be able to assess a situation with the question, "What is *right*, here?" (Seligman, 2006). Providing positive feedback effectively requires conscious effort and skill. One must actively look for areas in which students are doing well. An important aspect of positive feedback is the need for it to be specific. Mentors not only noticed that students had done good work, but also explained specifically why it was good and what could be made better. They tended to celebrate what others might consider small accomplishments and did not hesitate to share their enthusiasm with others. As one mentor explained with respect to positive feedback, "I try to do that in my lab. I try to do it with students. I try to always find cool things that they've done, even if they're pretty modest, just to say, 'This is a cool thing, and you should be excited about this.' And to tell other people, 'You know what Becky did today?' Or, 'You know what Andrew found? This is really cool, and this is why it's cool.' That sort of stuff."

A less recognized aspect of positive feedback illuminated by these scientists is that supportive mentors use it more frequently than one might think. While many advisors may come to believe that giving a few compliments will let students know that their work is valued, more effective mentors appear to use it much more frequently. One student remembered his undergraduate mentor: "It was day-to-day looking over your shoulder. 'Oh, that looks good. Yeah. Very good work.' He was very much into the positive reinforcement thing. Oh my God. He was constantly—I was really, I came out of there with a really swelled head."

One particularly valued form of feedback was the written feedback provided on academic work. Here, there is obviously the need for constructive criticism as well as positive feedback. Providing an optimal balance of the two appeared to require a high degree of skill: the ability to comment on students' drafts of writing in an interested, insightful, and supportive way with attention to specific strengths and weaknesses. This skill becomes especially important while students are writing their dissertations, when the advisor may be the primary source of feedback for a significant period of time.

Particularly at times when students would naturally doubt or lose hope, encouraging mentors played an important role. One graduate student recalled, "There were wonderful people there. I learned a lot. I had a lot of freedom to do what I wanted to do. She was very encouraging. I had a project that had a long dry spell in it, and she was very encouraging during that entire time: 'Just keep trying. Just keep trying. Just keep going.'"

Mentors have the power to uplift by offering needed encouragement such as, "You can do this. I know you know how to do this." Such encouragement can help a student to persevere and stick with the program where a lack of support could lead to dropping out. One respondent said about her advisor: "My graduate school experience was not a smooth road, so I would never have stuck with it if I hadn't had his support. He was always there when things got really bad, which they did frequently. . . . So it was bad, and he just kept me going. He kept saying, 'You can do it, and I want you to be here, and I value your contribution.' . . . He always believed that I would get through it."

Mentors were sometimes surprised by the extreme reactions of struggling students to their sincere offers of encouragement. One mentor shared the reaction of a student having problems in her program, after she demonstrated concern for the student's welfare: "I've just met with her and expressed what I believe, which I think nobody says, which is, 'The program's not there to have you fail, the program's there for you to succeed. And we want you to succeed.' Well, tears came to her eyes, and she said, 'I didn't think anybody cared about me.'"

Some mentors noted that, in contrast, an unkind or overly critical word from a professor to whom students look up can be damaging to self-esteem. One mentor's approach was to share the self-doubts with which he himself had struggled so that students would understand they are not alone: "To give you the notion that, yes, I struggle; and yes, I didn't know whether I would get the grant; yes, I had career crises. So you try to share many different things that are going to allow somebody to make it. Now you can't make someone make it. If they are crippled emotionally, they are going to be crippled emotionally. But you can at least try to diminish the number of impediments by telling them that they are not alone. It's the old story for support groups."

Treating Graduate Students as Respected Collaborators

One of the most frequently mentioned aspects of highly supportive mentoring relationships was that the mentor listened to, respected, and treated his or her students as equal colleagues or collaborators. Students of such mentors indicated that their mentor respected them as scientists. This perception was usually based on a trusting posture toward the students, in which they were not given orders, "told what to do," or constantly prodded. From our interviews with effective mentors, it became apparent that such a posture can entail a conscious effort. As one mentor stated, "All the work, all science, is done as a team, and you have to make sure that every member of the team feels like they are a full participant." Other effective mentors told us that their relationships with students were characterized by both respect and friendship. They were personally happy or excited by the expertise that individual students brought into the lab.

Some mentors felt that the most important aspect of teaching was to help students develop self-esteem by listening to them and respecting them as scientists. One mentor told us:

> So I never look upon someone who knows a great deal less than me as being less able. If you treat people as peers, that will firstly develop self-esteem, which will allow them to function later on. Self-esteem is very important in my view. . . . [Paramount is] to convince them that they actually are good and able, and if they put their minds to it, they can answer these questions and these issues. . . . So, yes, mentoring is very important and it involves trying to help develop values—the values necessary to become a successful scientist—curiosity. So you mentor them by listening to them. You mentor them by encouraging them. You mentor them by showing them how you respect their individuality and autonomy.

Effective mentors also gave due recognition and credit to their students for their contributions, while minimizing and discouraging a climate of competition. Some students spoke explicitly about their mentor's lack of ego or possessiveness as a factor in the quality of their experience. One respondent greatly appreciated his experience with two mentors who both focused on ideas rather than on fault or credit. Realizing how rare this quality can be in academia, he felt extremely fortunate for his experience with them.

An Individualized Interest in Students and Their Work

The mentor's demonstration of an active interest in a student and his or her work may be one of the most valuable aspects of a mentor's support in terms of making a profound difference in the professional life of a student. However, being interested in the student's work and being interested in the student were not always the same thing, even if they were intimately related. Being interested in the student's work was of course perceived as supportive by the student. In many cases on the graduate level, the student's work was related closely enough to the advisor's own that such interest would be natural. Taking an interest in students' well-being or professional growth in many cases made perhaps a greater impression. The sense that one is not getting lost in the crowd, but rather is noticed by one's advisor, may lie at the heart of a satisfying and rewarding relationship from the student's perspective. As one scientist commented, "[My advisor] was very kindly to me. He was always looking out for things to apply for, or bringing things up. . . . I felt very much that he was interested in me and what I was doing. But I actually think all of his fellows would have felt that way."

Does a mentor's enthusiasm and active interest in a student affect the likelihood that a student will absorb the mentor's memes? Many scientists suggested that this was the case. In speaking of three influential mentors, one scientist said, "I feel each of those three people demonstrated to me [that], first of all, they were interested in me. Second of all, they were excited about the field. Thirdly, you just absorbed how they went about business." As the scientist suggested, a mentor's interest in the student and enthusiasm for science were frequently integral to a relationship conducive to the absorption of the mentor's memes.

As a general practice, investing individualized attention in students is an important aspect of effective mentoring. One G3 described with amazement the mentor's capacity to remember key details of a student's project months later. Skillful mentors discerned and accommodated differences among students, and in so doing, they fostered the student's development. Each of the G1s was recalled as individualizing his response to students in some respect. For example, students of Lewontin recalled his great capacity to respond to their unique interests, personality, and needs, maximizing the impact of his infrequent interactions with them. One G2 recognized the high level of complexity at which Lewontin operated in adapting his approach to the specific situation. Each student was treated quite differently. He "would be very gentle and tender if somebody was emotionally weak. And he could be really hard-core with blustery guys who thought they knew everything." He was able to work at "many different levels."

The G1s were also mindful of the training environment that their habitual style created, and they selected students most likely to thrive in it. Beyond this initial matching, what characteristics of students did mentors recognize? Most commonly, advisors mentioned attempting to capitalize on students' distinctive capacities and strengths, especially intellectual abilities. They frequently mentioned scientific interests, which, in conjunction with aptitudes, proved to be intimately connected to the student's self-realization as a scientist. Mentors also emphasized the importance of recognizing and accommodating students' personality traits, needs, learning styles, and other personal qualities. Some interviewees mentioned cultural and other aspects of students' backgrounds. Finally, some mentors highlighted the importance of being responsive to students' unique situations—such as a student's level of expertise at a given point in time in undertaking a specific research project.

Being responsive to individual students demands both a certain attitude and capacity. In light of our attention to intellectual legacy and the relationship between apprenticeship and cultural transmission, it is noteworthy that many of the mentors interviewed were not interested in, to use genetic imagery, cloning themselves. They might desire that their students absorb their standards, values, or general approach, but effective mentors did not expect their students to carry forward their particular research interests or even pursue a career in basic academic research. One scientist observed that she provided an example to her students, but noted, "It's not that they have to end up the way I am." Another scientist explained that his lab has a distinctive style that "lab members can pick up if they want to," but "everyone's an individual, too, so they modify it and make their own hybrid when they're done," believing the hybrid is what they carry forward. He continued, "It doesn't matter to me if they follow exactly the same style, as long as they are successful. I take pleasure when someone who was in my lab publishes a nice paper. . . . I feel more science is coming out of this, and maybe I had a piece of that somehow." Another senior scientist observed that students "don't all fit one mold. A lot of people talk like it's a failure if all your students are not professors at top-tier universities. But you know, there are many ways to succeed, and this could include careers in teaching, law, or public policy."

Some respondents cited a practical reason to avoid the temptation to "clone oneself" and instead support career choices diverging from one's own: survival in a field and an academic job market that is sure to change. For example, in addition to endorsing students' pursuit of their own interests, an older G3 recognized the adaptive value of diversity:

> There's not going to be fivefold replacement of Drosophila college professors, right? . . . You're not doing your mentoring well if . . . all you're doing is creating clones of yourself because there's not going to be that kind of growth. . . . When you're mentoring, you have to be thinking in terms of what does that person really want to do. And what is realistic for that person to

do, and how can I help them do that. And that probably won't be the same thing I'm doing. . . . I want them to follow their curiosity; that's absolutely not a problem. I don't have any arrogance that I've chosen . . . some fundamentally more interesting research field than others that they may choose.

Experienced mentors sometimes took their cues for action from their students. One mature scientist described a student who made it clear that he wanted a lot of ownership of his work: the autonomy to find his own solutions and publish on his own. Others preferred to collaborate with their mentor on papers. The mentor generally based his involvement on the student's need: "I've really taken it on a person-to-person basis, how I contribute to their development, what they need, what they want. I really try to let them guide me." He acknowledged that his approach worked well with students who were very clear about what they wanted but was challenging for those who were less clear.

Were Supportive Mentoring Relationships Personal?

The ability to recognize a student's individuality in order to accommodate individual needs requires a genuine perceptiveness rooted as much in human caring and compassion as in skill or ability (Shernoff, 2001). Since many educators derive satisfaction from providing such care, individualizing one's mentoring approach can be enjoyable and yield rewarding outcomes. Each mentor may struggle with the appropriate boundaries of care and involvement. Mentors vary a great deal with respect to their comfort level in forming personal relations with their students, which can extend beyond the strictly professional to the social and personal spheres. For example, collegiality and socializing were part of many of the strongest lab cultures; labmates formed close and lasting friendships and felt they were part of a community in which the mentor played an active role. Several subjects in strong mentoring relationships reported having meals with their mentors (often with a group of students), or visiting their mentors' homes. In such cases, the boundary between personal and professional becomes somewhat blurred.

An interesting question thus became whether effective mentors were more likely to cultivate close personal relationships with their students. One might conjecture that knowledge of the student's life beyond the lab strengthens the apprenticeship. In this sample, however, there was no strong correlation one way or another. That is, there were at least as many effective mentors who did not form personal relationships with their students as mentors who did. Therefore, it did not appear that effective mentoring was associated with a pattern of socializing on a personal level beyond the working relationship. In fact, two of the three lineage heads, Gall and Motulsky, were relatively formal in their relations with students—at least until after graduation—and were nevertheless extraordinary mentors. Some students described positive relationships with mentors who were "very private." From the mentor's perspective, as one scientist observed, "I've had students who have come into my lab, they want to be my best friend, and I'm sorry, that's not the relationship. . . . I've ended up putting a little bit of distance between me and them, saying, 'No I won't tell you my opinion of this or that. That's private.'"

One of this scientist's mentors set "limits to what you could talk and joke or inquire about," while the other was "much more willing to just lay his life out in front of you." Closer to the first type, one female G3 told us: "Mentoring, to me, sounds very invasive. I'm not an invasive person. Like I said, I let people make their own decisions. If somebody asks me for advice, I will give it to them. But I don't listen to problems and tell people what they should do. I just don't do that kind of thing. I just never have. I'm just not that kind of person."

Once again, dispositions such as this did not keep advisors from being effective mentors. Even beyond predispositions, scientists differed about what they considered to be the wiser course from the standpoint of students' well-being. One G2 explained her judgment that it is better to know about students' personal lives, while noting that many of her friends question this stance:

> I care a lot about people's emotional states in the lab. So I sort of watch and if somebody looks distant and not happy, I usually ask them to come in and just tell me. "Do you want to talk about it? Is it lab related? Is it personal related?" So I at least try to provide a forum for that, which a lot of my friends tell me is crazy, because then I end up being [a] therapist. But I don't know, these people are—they spend more time with you than they do with anybody else. And if you can't connect about some of this stuff, you never know why they're not happy or productive, and some of it makes such obvious sense once you do understand that and you realize it's not a long-term thing. It's that they just broke up, and in three months they'll be back to their regular selves, and that kind of stuff really makes it easier to deal with the fluctuations in people that we all have.

While some advisors actively counseled their students to "stay away from the personal lives" of their students, others differentiated between personal involvements that were benign and those that may be deleterious. This latter reasoning suggests that relationship building may be appropriately limited when it has the potential to lead to a student's harm. For example, an emotionally dependent student may be hampered in the long run by becoming overly attached. On the other hand, a student clearly not interested in a personal involvement might feel invaded if forced into one. Thus, establishing a personal relationship may pay dividends for the student—but only within the parameters of the mentor's and student's predispositions. A mentee who requires a personal relationship to flourish may not change the comfort level of an impersonal mentor. Hence, the mentee may need to adapt to the mentor's style for the relationship to succeed as much as vice versa, or else find a better match.

Conclusion

The most common difficulty in the graduate advising relationships we studied was neglect: mentors who failed to provide guidance and support. Outright abusiveness was much less common. The most common characteristic of the positive mentoring relationships was the initial admiration or sense of awe that students felt for their mentors. Despite the high expectations for success and independence, the hallmark of strong mentoring relationships was supportiveness. Because students were more likely to be influenced and carry forward a mentor's memes when the overall relationship with the mentor was positive, supportive relationships may be seen as the context in which effective mentors exerted a strong, positive effect on the future of the domain and the future field.

Six dimensions of support stood out in the data. The first and most basic characteristic of supportive mentors was availability to students and having enough involvement with students in the lab to understand the lab dynamics. Most effective mentors also maintained an active presence in the lab, which included consistent monitoring of lab activities and interactions. Second, supportive mentors effectively balanced the provisions of freedom and guidance, providing intellectual autonomy for students to make their own choices, while simultaneously supervising research projects and sharing their ideas, professional judgment, and broader perspective. Third, they provided a supportive atmosphere by maintaining the necessary awareness of the lab to keep it safe and comfortable for all members. They also provided numerous kinds of resources, with more effective mentors offering resources that communicated a sense of investment in and commitment to advisees. Fourth, supportive mentors offered positive feedback frequently, often showing enthusiasm about students' accomplishments. Their feedback was usually respectful, specific, encouraging, and affirming. Fifth, they tended to treat students as colleagues, valuing their contributions rather than pulling rank, belittling, or denigrating. Sixth, they took an active interest in students as well as in their work, individualizing their support and treatment of students, flexibly responding to the capacities, interests, personality traits, and backgrounds of individual students. While strong mentoring relationships were inherently caring, they were not necessarily personal in nature.

There is little doubt that these characteristics are important in their own right inasmuch as the quality of relationships has intrinsic value. Because mentoring is a key avenue through which a scientist can leave a living legacy and shape the future of the field, however, we believe that mentoring relationships are not only beneficial for the personal and professional lives of the mentor and student. The mentor-student relationship also appears to be a crucial mechanism in the evolution of a profession and the survival of good work.

Part Three

PROMOTING GOOD MENTORING

Part Three concludes the book by discussing some of the most important results of the investigation, and then offering concrete suggestions for the practice of mentoring and avenues for future inquiry.

Chapter Eight places the process of mentoring in professional contexts into the larger framework of an evolutionary, systems model. It then reviews some of the evidence with respect to whether mentoring served as a vehicle for the reproduction of good work and good workers through multiple generations. If so, how did this help young professionals navigate the pressures to cut corners or cause harm in an effort to get ahead? How did the lineage heads exemplify and propagate good work similarly and differently, and how did distinct influences manifest in the working lives of younger generations? Chapter Eight also summarizes conclusions concerning the pattern of transmission through the generations. The concept of good mentoring emphasizes the continuation of memes foundational for the well-being of a profession, such as honesty, treating others with respect, and, indeed, mentoring itself. However, how do memes change over time, and when do new ones arise? Finally, what conclusions can be drawn with respect to pathways for the transmission of good work and the characteristics of relationships providing the optimal context for intergenerational influence?

Chapter Nine presents some specific principles that the lineage heads and other effective mentors in our study modeled that might provide leverage for improving our own future mentoring interactions and practices. We distill from the data several principles for promising practice not only for mentors but also for mentees and institutions. In addition, we identify several avenues emerging from this investigation that appear ripe for future investigation. Future directions for inquiry include a more systematic appraisal of processes involved in students' active learning from a mentor's positive influence, mechanisms stimulating the emergence of new memes, the relationship between creativity and the acceptance of tradition, and the extent to which effective mentors must also be paragons or superstars. Finally, we consider the overall significance of good mentoring for the welfare of professions and for society at large.

8

WHAT HAVE WE LEARNED?

Mentoring has always been valued as a process that benefits novices in a community. In recent decades, researchers and practitioners have extended this focus on individual socialization and development in two important ways: examining how mentoring contributes to the well-being of the mentor and how it benefits the organization in which both work. This book has sought to broaden further the perspective on mentoring, examining how it affects the evolution and well-being of a profession over time. Toward this end, a multigenerational, multilineage research design was conceived.

Given the goals of breaking new ground where there was little science to build on, and illuminating the enduring effects of long relationships, we chose to conduct an interview study. For the purposes of this first-of-its-kind study, we considered access to an emic perspective, narrative richness, and the opportunity to probe responses in detail indispensable. In order to gain the benefits of in-depth qualitative accounts, we accepted some familiar limitations of interview research, such as a small sample and reliance on retrospective self-reports.

The design was motivated by the study's guiding questions. Being able to trace the survival of values, practices, and signature approaches to work across multiple generations required identifying successive generations within a research tradition and asking about their formative influences, guiding values, and defining practices as scientists, and what they have attempted to pass on to students. In order to determine which values and practices were distinctively handed down by a particular scientist and which ones were shared with other exemplary senior scientists, we also needed to compare multiple lineages. Past research on mentoring studied first individuals, then mentor-protégé dyads. The multiple-generation, multiple-lineage sampling design is a new tool to address new kinds of questions about mentoring.

Along with a suitable research design, we needed a conceptual model to analyze the perpetuation of good work over time. The primary concepts of the mentoring literature—functions, phases, motivations, and qualities—were informative but did not help in framing the study's central questions. We thus adopted a conceptual framework that spoke to these questions but to our knowledge had not been used to study mentoring before.

An Evolutionary, Systems Perspective

To study the evolution of professions, it was useful to adopt the concept of memes as a lens for viewing a profession's cultural domain (Csikszentmihalyi, 1988), the shared body of information (broadly defined) with and through which the profession functions. As we noted in Chapter One, the concept is drawn from Richard Dawkins's (1976) analysis of cultural evolution because of its heuristic value. It has the virtue of illuminating how ideas, beliefs, knowledge, stories, practices, tools, technologies, styles, norms, values, and many other things making up a profession that we think of as disparate nevertheless are similar with respect to the processes of interest here: the transmission and transformation of cultural resources for individual and collective action (see also Csikszentmihalyi, 1988; Heath, 1996; Inghilleri, 1999; Massimini & Delle Fave, 2000). Analogous to genes in biological evolution, Dawkins argued, memes carry instructions for action: consider recipes, laws, parables, or scientific procedures. Like genes, they are replicated, undergoing variation in the process. Some variants are selected and retained as part of the culture, while others die out. We were most interested in the fate of memes that support good work: for example, rigorous lab techniques, effective styles of clinical interaction, and practices for successful collaboration with others.

The notion of memes and the process of their evolution need to be understood in the context of a systems perspective. From the systems perspective (Csikszentmihalyi, 1988; Gardner, Csikszentmihalyi, & Damon, 2001) employed in this book, a profession can be characterized by three components. The first is the cultural domain, which comprises memes: specialized knowledge, practices, tools, standards of quality, orienting values, defining aims or mission. For Gall, this included the corpus of knowledge about cell biology, in situ hybridization, microscopy, and the practice of sharing information. The second is the associated social field made up of social institutions (for example, organizations, professional societies), roles, and the workers occupying these roles (for example, initiates, trained practitioners, and gatekeepers). Most salient among the practitioners comprising the field are the gatekeepers—licensing bodies, funding agencies, editors, and so on—that not only influence membership in the field, but also exert control over the domain by soliciting, encouraging, and rewarding some contributions while rejecting others. For Motulsky, the field included the American Society of Human Genetics, the pool of prospective medical fellows and faculty in his program in medical genetics, and the editors of medical and genetics journals. The third component is the individual practitioner qua member of the field: Lewontin in his role as an evolutionary biologist, for example.

Interactions among these subsystems affect how a profession evolves. Individual practitioners advance some work and ideas (conduct an experiment, fashion a product, stage a performance, counsel a patient, or otherwise provide a service) while forgoing others, and the field's gatekeepers then select some subset of these efforts for inclusion and retention in the domain moving forward. When the field's gatekeepers recognize, reward, and retain good work, individual practitioners are more motivated to pursue it, and members of the society benefit as the consumers of the profession's services or products. Good work may also be impeded by forces arising from these components: for example, an inadequate knowledge base for discovery (domain), an incentive system rewarding win-at-all-costs competitiveness (field), or an eroding commitment to the traditional mission of the profession (individual practitioner).

Forces within the profession are not the only ones that shape its evolution. The profession is embedded within a larger sociocultural matrix, which justifies its very existence. Genetic research, as one example, flourishes today because the broader society continues to endorse and support its contributions. The profession affects the wider culture, most directly (though not exclusively) through the work that it contributes—in the case of genetic research, advances in knowledge. It is equally true that the larger system affects the profession and its evolution in manifold ways. For example, many of the pressures that challenge researchers' ability to do good work arise outside the profession, in the changing society and culture. We return to these pressures shortly.

The evolutionary, systems perspective is particularly applicable to the sciences, where the explicit goals are discovery and innovation—the growth of knowledge, the improvement of tools—and there is self-conscious competition among alternative ideas or interpretations within the field (Campbell, 1976; Csikszentmihalyi, 1988, 1999; Simonton, 1999). However, it has heuristic value in thinking about the shifting conditions for advancing good work in any profession, not only in creative domains.

The Mentoring of Good Work

To an aspiring professional, entry to the field means mastering the domain: absorbing a body of knowledge, developing a specialized set of skills and practices, and internalizing the standards, values, and norms that define successful work. From the standpoint of the profession, the entry of newcomers presents an important opportunity for the domain's evolution to be steered in one direction versus another: at its extremes, toward the continued pursuit of good work as the profession evolves, or toward a compromising of the profession's societal value. We have argued that mentoring in the context of professional training is an important means by which this steering occurs.

While genetic instructions are transmitted in sequences of nucleic acids, the instructions contained in memes are transmitted only by a process of teaching and learning. Some teaching and learning occurs through classroom study or the writing and reading of books. However, we focused in our study on the role played by the practitioners responsible for hands-on training of novices or students. That is, we addressed the impact of mentor-student relationships on the survival of good work, focusing specifically on good mentors—those who care about good work.

At the outset of this study, we expected that good mentors would contribute to the transgenerational perpetuation of good work by transmitting memes that support it: novices who are mentored well may be better equipped to hold fast to those inherited values, practices, and beliefs even in the face of new and changing pressures. This expectation is consistent with Lapsley's conceptualization of the moral personality (Lapsley, 2005; Lapsley & Narvaez, 2006), which encompasses being a moral exemplar, possessing a moral identity, and having moral character. Research shows that moral exemplars embody virtues reflecting moral commitment and excellence (for example, they are almost universally honest and dependable; see Walker & Henning, 2004), modeling moral identity and character for others. Those with a moral identity hold moral notions and commitments central to their lives, the violation of which places their sense of self at risk. Moral character involves strength of convictions and persistence in overcoming distractions or obstacles; those lacking moral character often wilt under pressure or fatigue, become discouraged, or otherwise fail to follow through in behaving morally (Blasi, 2005). Therefore, modeling good work includes being a moral exemplar of moral character, and to the extent that moral character is emulated by mentees, they would be influenced to hold fast to their convictions even in the face of resistance or obstacles. Before reviewing the findings with respect to this issue, however, it is helpful to revisit briefly the types of pressures and temptations professionals confront and that might compromise responsible practice in the professions more generally.

The Professions Under Pressure

What current trends and pressures render the practices of good work and good mentoring increasingly difficult, and may continue to do so in the future? In *Good Work*, Gardner et al. (2001) discussed several general trends posing obstacles to good work, as well as ones that were specific to the field of genetics. Scarcely any profession appears to be immune to increasing market forces and the potential misuse of technological innovations. Sectors such as education have become increasingly privatized in recent years. One common example of market interference with professional mission is the doctor who cannot prescribe her preferred medicine or treatment because it is not underwritten by the health maintenance organization that employs her. Newspapers and other media companies are increasingly controlled by publicly traded corporations and can face pressures to sensationalize and even mislead in order to sell their product. Epitomizing these trends are cases of corporate executives who cheat, steal, or engage in other shady practices for personal profit.

Geneticists must also contend with a variety of rapidly evolving pressures specific to their field. In ways that the lineage heads did not encounter at the outset of their careers, tensions arise today from the expansion of industry in the biological sciences, accompanied by university pressure to start companies and patent innovations. At the same time, there are fewer and fewer academic jobs, and funding for research has tightened virtually across the board. For the young professional, this makes it more challenging to meet grant-getting and publication expectations. Some new practitioners alter their career path, accepting many years of postdoctoral work to improve their marketability or seeking employment within the growing biotech industry. Short of practices antithetical to good work (falsifying data, plagiarism, and so on), numerous practices pose threats to good work, including secrecy, unwillingness to share information and materials, and litigiousness. More commonly, young scientists feel pressure to publish prematurely, publish quantity rather than quality, compromise rigor, or use privileged information. We were told even institutions that have been bastions of faith for members of the profession may come to be doubted, such as the peer review system for awarding grants at the National Institutes of Health, which funds a great deal of genetic research.

Good mentoring, like good work more generally, faces significant counterpressures at the levels of both the institution and the wider field. Despite the establishment of formal mentoring programs and concrete incentives to mentor in some settings, the disincentives remain substantial in many fields. For example, much of what lawyers do early in their career is absorbed through informal mentoring from senior lawyers, yet many leading law firms would rather see partners record billable hours than devote time to nurturing new associates. Within academia, lab heads encounter considerable pressure to garner grants, be productive, and invest their time and energy in their own research, where the greatest rewards are promotion and tenure, as well as recognition by the wider field. Even beyond research, other responsibilities, such as classroom teaching and service to one's department, institution, and profession, are generally better rewarded than advising or mentoring students, which rarely receives formal evaluation.

This set of conditions led us to study senior scientists who were not only distinguished exemplars of good work but also effective advisors, having trained many productive scientists. Would these shining examples of good work also prove to be good mentors, inspiring their students to do good work as well? If so, how deep and enduring would their impact be? Would the students also become good mentors, and if so, would the senior scientists' influence transcend a single generation, being felt by a third generation of practitioners? The rest of this chapter reviews what we have learned about the nature and transmission of good work, including good mentoring.

Different Faces of Good Work in Genetics

Although the three lineage heads profiled in this book are exemplars of good mentoring as we have defined it, their divergent backgrounds, values, and mentoring styles suggest that there is not just a single pathway or approach to good work. With respect to background and formative influences, they varied markedly. Gall did not have the single, powerful influence that Lewontin had in his teacher, Dobzhansky, and Motulsky had many influences in a great variety of training settings. It is possible that Gall's early start in science lessened his susceptibility to mentoring. In any event, the three lineage heads illustrate that having a strong mentor is not a prerequisite for being a good mentor.

More salient, each lineage head illustrates a different variation of good work, suggesting that excellence and responsible practice, though united by the shared standards and ethics of a profession, find distinctive expression through individuality. Ultimately there are many ways to do good work. However, we suspect that one quality in particular made all three lineage heads both good workers and effective mentors: all believed that what they were doing was important and meaningful. This sustaining enthusiasm of the scientist can take many forms.

Gall's early love of nature developed into deep enjoyment of the scientific process. His curiosity fueled broad interests in science. Though such enjoyment was deeply personal for Gall, he believed that science is done only in a community in which collaboration and the sharing of information are vital. The values he brought to professional life found specific expression in a set of scientific commitments. Motulsky's early brushes with war and human atrocities gave rise to an unwavering humanitarian mission. For Motulsky, it was important that the insights generated by working on scientific problems inform the treatment of individuals with medical needs, and that, reciprocally, medicine inform science. Lewontin's longstanding Marxist beliefs undergirded his identity as social commentator as well as scientist. He came to be critical of mere careerists—professionals whose accomplishments were driven purely by personal ambition. We have described these variants of good work as emphasizing, respectively, the practitioner's relationship to the domain, the wider society, and the field.

As with other facets of good work, there are many ways to be a good mentor. For example, all three lineage heads mentored through modeling, informal talk, and the creation of an effective learning environment, but providing a model was especially important to Gall's approach to mentoring. Students learned directly from Motulsky in one-and-one meetings about research and by observing and talking about his compassionate interactions with patients during clinical rounds. Lewontin stressed the role of the lab and peer group, creating an intellectually exciting atmosphere characterized by the free and vigorous exchange of ideas.

The fact that each lineage head is committed to a distinct form of good work may help to explain why three good mentors could emerge from such different mentoring histories. If one cares about doing good work, one need not have had a good mentor oneself to have something one wants to transmit. One implication is that an established practitioner's relationships with novices can be positive and formative, and good mentoring can occur even if the practitioner's attention is not primarily student centered. At least in occupations where responsibility for novices is built into the mature practitioner's formal role, as it is in university-based science, good mentoring is not limited to individuals who possess nurturing personalities or ambitious generative strivings. Professionals who care deeply about the health of the domain, the associated community of practice, the broader social group, or some combination of these, will likely want to share these commitments with the novices in their charge.

Tracing the Transmission of Memes: Continuity and Change

In every profession, some forces support the continuation of existing memes at any given time, while others press for their transformation, extinction, or replacement. Because the existing domain represents the accumulated knowledge and wisdom of the field, transgenerational continuity of memes is important. And because times change (for example, the populations served by a profession evolve, the available technologies improve), transformation of memes through the generations is also important. In studying how a domain evolves, one might foreground either continuity or transformation. In the rise of a new school of thought, for example, change becomes figure, and continuity becomes ground. Because we anchored our study in exemplars of good work, the oldest of the three generations studied, the forces supporting survival of their memes became figure and the emergence of new variants of good work became ground. These are matters of accent, however. The underlying process is always a dynamic interplay between forces pulling for continuity and others pushing for change.

The Continuity of Memes

Concerning the question that animated this study, strong evidence was found for the transmission of values and practices through multiple generations. First, both the quantitative and qualitative data illustrate that not only do individuals place their own distinctive stamps on their approach to work based on temperament, strengths, interests, and experiences, but in addition, these characteristic memes may be perpetuated across successive generations. Some of these lineage-signature memes had the effect of helping to preserve the integrity of the domain of knowledge. Science is more likely to maintain its integrity when research is conducted for its own sake and when ethical standards for scientific research are met, as Gall was so effective in teaching. His focus on the domain itself was evident to students and influenced them. Some lineage-signature memes were passed down in order to help the mentee treat other members of the field, including their own students, ethically and respectfully. Lewontin's caution not to take credit from others is an example. This and other aspects of his engagement with the field impressed all his students and affected them. Still other memes were transmitted in order to help society or humanity in general. Motulsky's call to use science to treat patients and relieve human suffering exemplifies this. His students were keenly aware of his commitments, and many absorbed them.

Individuals are likely to place their distinctive signature on the relationship to the cultural domain, the social field, and the wider society and culture that the profession serves. In addition, different individuals may invest varying degrees of energy in serving domain, field, or society and derive differing degrees of satisfaction from their interactions with any of them. If multiple ways of doing good work exist and are handed down, this has practical implications for mentoring. It means that mentoring well does not necessitate working against the grain in order to fit into some monolithic mold or procrustean "good worker" bed. Individuals have their own characteristic ways of being a creative scientist, a caring nurse, a scrupulous accountant. Indeed, distinctive manifestations of excellence and ethics may evolve into hallmarks of a lineage or tradition within a profession, a source of pride that makes a given spin on good work more likely to persist. From the novices' side, this means that exposure to a single mentor may involve learning one variant of good work among many and that the path to becoming a professional may involve finding one's own expression of good work.

Evidence was also found for the existence of several good-work memes—practices and values shared and transmitted by all three lineage heads. In fact, good-work memes were handed down by all of the exemplary senior practitioners, whose students in turn handed the values and practices down to their students. These memes encompassed honesty and integrity in research, treating others equally and fairly, and two mentoring practices: providing intellectual freedom and guidance to students, and creating a lab structure that facilitates student development. Honesty in reporting research results is an important example of responsible behavior within the domain; the other memes concern positive and generative relations with the social field.

Mentoring as Inoculation: Learning to Do Good Work in Professions Under Pressure

We now turn to the question of whether mentoring experiences equipped new professionals to resist the pressures they encountered. The good-work memes that survived across generations in these lineages all faced some extinction (or "mutation") pressures from the field. The persistence of these memes in successive generations thus provides one type of evidence that mentoring well supports the rising generation's resistance to these pressures (see Tables 5.2 to 5.5).

In addition, some members of the second and third generations described specific instances when experiences with a mentor helped them later to resist pressures from the wider field. It was not uncommon for a mentor's example to give young scientists the strength to stand up for themselves when they found someone's behavior to be unethical or the treatment of others to be unacceptable. All three lineage heads treated others in the field fairly and respectfully. One striking illustration was provided by Gall's attitude toward educating aspiring female scientists in an era when women in science often faced discrimination. As a result, one of Gall's students was able to dismiss others' skeptical opinions about the abilities of women.

As we have observed, professionals frequently face pressures from the employing institution and the wider field to prioritize other job responsibilities over mentoring, let alone good mentoring. Providing freedom and guidance to students may be ideal for the students' professional training, but may be regarded as an obstacle to the lab head's own productivity. Granted freedom, the students may opt for projects that do not advance the lab head's own research agenda. Meanwhile, giving guidance to individual students and tending to lab dynamics require time and attention. With so many pressures competing with an investment in quality advising and mentoring, the example of one's own mentor is critical to support novice professionals in becoming good mentors when their time comes to do so.

Of course, not every meme survives unchanged as the pressures in a profession intensify or shift, and this pattern extended to cases in which the mentor deliberately sought to inoculate students against external pressures. The most important example in this study was the complex of memes encompassing cooperation, collaboration, and the sharing of information, which were much discussed but less widely perpetuated than the values and practices that we identified as good-work memes. The advice and positive example that mentors provided convinced many students to foster cooperation within their labs or accept the risks accompanying collaboration, and also provided them with ways of doing so successfully. However, even some students who deeply admired their mentors had difficulty embracing advice to share information with scientists outside the lab under increasingly competitive, industry-influenced conditions.

The Transmission of Mentoring Practices: Learning to Mentor

One of the study's most provocative lessons was unexpected. It is often said that parenting styles are inherited from one's own parents; this study suggests that at least some good mentoring practices tend to be inherited as well. As the Gall G2 profiled in Chapter Two put it, "I think of an apprenticeship as the way Joe Gall ran his lab, and that's the way that I would like to run mine."

This finding is significant for two reasons. The first is that mentoring is rarely taught during the transition to professional life. For example, in a national survey of doctoral students, a mere 16.5 percent of those intending faculty careers felt that their programs had prepared them very well to advise graduate students (Golde & Dore, 2004). Nor is such training typically received after graduation. One scientist ruefully told us that most young faculty feel poorly equipped to mentor students in crisis: "The first time there's somebody sitting in that chair in tears, it's like, 'Wait a minute. This was not in my job description, *anywhere*.' . . . That's when you dig down to whatever experiences you might have had by accident that weren't part of your training [which] will allow you to deal with . . . all these things that you were supposed to learn which you don't really have any formal training in."

This study suggests that one important source of these accidental learning experiences is the process of being mentored well. Good mentoring equips new professionals to do good work and provide good mentoring to the next generation as well. This finding is also significant because the lab is not just a training environment; it is simultaneously the site where the senior scientist's work gets done. Given the intense productivity pressures that lab directors face, students risk becoming extra hands in the advisor's research agenda. Graduate students in the sciences report greater exploitation than do students in other disciplines (Zhao, Golde, & McCormick, 2005). To avoid this outcome, mentors need to tend to their students' development while simultaneously staying productive. To accomplish this complex goal, a scientist must design the lab as a learning environment rather than as solely a production site, making the lab a beneficial environment for both mentor and student. Students in such labs are exposed to an approach to work that encompasses good mentoring, and they are themselves its beneficiaries. It may be that undergoing such experiences as a student both motivates and equips students to mentor well, inspiring a willingness to make similar choices later on behalf of one's own students and modeling specific ways to do so.

Conceptualizing good mentoring as the transmission of good work suggests that how a particular person mentors can be perpetuated across generations just like other good-work memes. Not only are the mentoring practices passed down, but they also have a multiplicative effect by equipping the next generation to transmit other good-work memes. For example, when a student learns to structure her lab as an effective training environment (for example, holding weekly meetings, creating an ethos of cooperation), she acquires a pathway for communicating other aspects of her approach to science to future generations. Mentoring practices may be transmitted in many occupations. It remains for future research to investigate to what extent other mentoring practices that we did not investigate *as memes*—for example, forms of talk, use of stories, types of modeling—also are handed down across generations.

Mentoring as Translation: Learning What Values Mean in Context

It is important to realize, and is not at all obvious, that individuals may endorse a value in their daily lives and routinely manifest it in already-familiar contexts without being able to deduce what course of action is the best expression of this value within the profession they enter. For example, while the basic virtues of honesty, fairness, and compassion may have been internalized long before a young person embarks on training for a profession, they may not know how these values translate into practice in the special context of science, medicine, education, law, or other profession. A moral imperative needs to acquire a specialized meaning for the student; "honesty," for example, must be translated into what it means to be honest in the context of a given profession. Among these scientists, mentors helped their students translate values into the professional context—for example, they helped them understand the meaning of honesty in the presentation of research, fairness in the allocation of credit, and compassion in the discussion of sensitive patient information.

One scientist described a graduate student from a collectivist culture who did not possess a Western notion of intellectual ownership. From the student's perspective, there was nothing wrong with representing what was in part a relative's work as her own. Students raised in the West may not encounter that particular difficulty, but they are quite likely to encounter others due to an analogous unfamiliarity with the specialized culture of the profession that they enter. Even norms that are universally agreed on within a profession may not be obvious to the neophyte.

One implication is that if work that shortchanges a profession's core responsibilities—compromised work (Gardner, 2007)—prevails within a field or even within the institution where training takes place, novices may absorb the prevailing norms and practices without ever having occasion to question the alignment of these norms and practices with their own extraprofessional commitments. Susceptible to the available social cues, they may tacitly learn from the wider field until or unless they encounter a respected model who questions and diverges from the common practice.

It is also the case that in some aspects of practice within a profession, there may be little explicit instruction and a whole range of acceptable standards. The lineage heads held themselves and their lab members to high standards of integrity, rigor, cooperation, and equal treatment of others. In another set of labs, other expectations might prevail that would become internalized.

For example, in a large-scale national survey of doctoral students across the sciences, social sciences, and humanities, only about one-fourth of students felt they had a clear understanding of "determining and ordering authorship on papers" (Golde & Dore, 2004, p. 28). Because rules for the allocation of credit usually are not formally taught, students possessing great clarity in all likelihood had derived their understanding through social learning. Many lab heads routinely put their names on papers produced in their lab—the work would not get done without the resources they provide, they say—and many students in the sciences undoubtedly accept this practice and go on to replicate it in their own labs without reflection. In contrast, Lewontin, who considered himself a "moralist" in his practice of science, both modeled and taught that the values of equality and integrity, translated into the arena of scientific research, dictate assigning credit based on intellectual contribution. We have stressed that signature memes often have personal roots, and this example also makes clear that local ways of translating an ethic into practice may be influenced by the background and commitments of the individual who establishes the practice. Lewontin was explicit and emphatic about giving credit where credit is due in the publication arena because he saw it as the translation of his Marxist beliefs about nonhierarchical relations and the ownership of (intellectual) property into the professional realm.

Attenuation and Emergence: The Active Roles of Mentors and Students

In the evolution of professions, both continuity and change occur. We have focused on continuity and the impact of good mentors on the persistence of memes supporting good work. As we discuss next, mentoring lineages also shed light on change—the dilution of an existing version of good work, the transformation of an inherited value or practice, and the emergence of new memes, as individuals evolve their own approaches to work and mentoring.

Attenuation

In Chapter Five, we saw that, almost universally, the memes most widely propagated by the lineage heads became less well represented from one generation to the next (see Table 5.5). This was true of both good-work and lineage-signature memes. In addition, a mentor's personal, extrascientific traits and beliefs were infrequently replicated, perhaps because the student was simply not able to emulate them or because the mentor chose not to teach them. Such qualities often did not survive into the second generation of the lineage.

Students absorb some of their mentors' memes and not others. In addition, few memes are absorbed by every student. Therefore, the next generation goes on to expose students to a smaller set of their mentor's memes than they were exposed to, and in turn the same is true of their students, the lineage's third generation. In other words, the impact of a mentor attenuates across generations. (Notice that in a strong lineage, this attenuation can coexist with the spread of a mentor's memes across generations. To the extent that the number of a mentor's "progeny" multiplies with each successive generation, the sheer number of individuals carrying a meme in subsequent generations can be higher even if a smaller percentage of individuals are influenced.)

As we have seen, one reason for attenuation can be competitive pressures or conditions undermining good work that weaken the influence of the mentor. From a systems perspective, conditions in the domain and characteristics of individual practitioners themselves might also cause memes to lose traction as new generations come on the scene.

The Active Role of Mentors and Students

The evolution of a professional domain is a process of both continuity and change occurring through the medium of intergenerational human interaction. The language of memes should not be read as implying that we view a mentor as just a meme's way of replicating itself, to borrow a trope. Equally, we do not see students as passive vessels for the values, practices, and knowledge of their mentors.

Mentors are active agents working within a profession, not mere carriers of memes. They form an approach to work through processes of self-definition and by absorbing selected influences from the environment; they select students rather than indiscriminately accept them; they make efforts to transmit some of their memes and not others; and they favor some means of doing so over others. In the same way, even while some formative processes may occur outside conscious awareness, students actively observe, select, reject, modify, integrate, and innovate as they shape their own distinctive approach to their work in the face of changing conditions.

Students bring a set of values and other memes to the profession (for example, basic motivational orientations were often possessed without crediting a mentor), and they learn in large part through their own active effort. Just as the craft apprentice or beginning martial artist learns to "steal with the eyes," as the saying goes, these students learned through active observation as well as by soliciting direct guidance. They then responded selectively to their mentor's memes. Lewontin's students, for instance, emulated his equal treatment of others, but they chose not to emulate his political views.

Furthermore, at least in science today, students select not only from among the multiple memes of a mentor, but also from among the memes of multiple potentially influential mentors. Virtually every interviewed scientist cited two or more significant professional influences. These multiple influences may reinforce each other, either because they are similar or complementary, or because the contrast is constructive. Alternatively, they may counteract each other, as when a positive influence buffers or mitigates a negative one. Students also actively disavow the values and practices of negative influences, or "antimentors."

Faced with these various influences, individuals actively and selectively construct their own set of values and practices and an image of the kind of scientist they want to become. Both mentor and protégé play active roles.

Mutation and Emergence

The sublineages in the study took on characters of their own based on the signature approach to work that the "sublineage head" had formed. A professional may create a variation on a meme absorbed from his or her mentor, whether by placing a distinctive spin on the mentor's approach, modulating the meme in response to new conditions, or expressing a meme in a different context, as when Gall's female students received equal treatment in his lab and went on to champion gender equality in the wider field. A professional may also transmit values and practices that do not come from their mentor at all, effectively introducing new memes into the meme pool of the mentor's lineage. New memes may express an individual professional's distinctive style and history, or reflect cultural changes entering the wider field through the new generations of mentors and students.

How Good Work Is Learned: Paths of Influence

Although the lineage heads differed in their priorities, they described three primary pathways for transmitting values and practices to students: informal talk, modeling, and shaping the lab so that it extended their own direct influence. If we distinguish between direct and indirect (or mediated) means, at least one of these two types of pathways is likely to be relevant for mentors aspiring to cultivate good work in any field.

Mentoring by Direct Means: Telling and Showing

Talk and direct dialogue was a less salient means of transmitting values and practices for these eminent senior scientists than we had expected, based on Niels Bohr's example. Certainly, the ways that mentors talk to their juniors mattered, and probably more than the sheer amount of communication. Forms of talk ranged from task-focused dialogues to wide-ranging group discussions, each having expressive as well as instrumental functions. In terms of personal impact, however, modeling appeared to be a more powerful mode of influence. To a great extent, the lineage heads affected students' values and practices as scientists-in-the-making through example. The majority of students reported that observing and emulating was an important means by which they had learned from their advisors. The effectiveness of modeling accords with a large body of theory and research on social learning (Bandura, 1985) that contends that much of human behavior is learned by observing a model perform.

Modeling is particularly important for the transmission of skills and knowledge that are tacit or embodied rather than readily articulated (for example, Gamble, 2001; Polanyi, 1958). In addition, seeing good work modeled on a consistent basis is likely to be an important influence in periods when forces undermining good work prevail. Under these conditions, exhortations to do the right thing are simply not compelling if the individual does not walk the talk. One might imagine that providing a role model means enacting an artificial performance—as by self-consciously striving to create a good example when students are in the vicinity. Rather, it appears that modeling good work consists in "living by one's convictions" in the presence of one's students, so that they can learn from one's example.

It may be ideal for the student when mentors use both of these modes, modeling and conversation, together. Certainly the way the lineage heads used them, they were mutually reinforcing—two pathways for conveying a consistent set of messages. As noted, advice carries more weight when echoed by action; students are not likely to be convinced by being told, "Do what I say, not what I do." By the same token, articulating one's practices and values, rather than only modeling them, helps to make the tacit lessons explicit so that their merits can be discussed.

Mentoring by Indirect Means: Crafting a Learning and Working Environment

An underrecognized way of mentoring is the creation of a learning and working environment that becomes an extension of oneself, transmitting one's approach to work. Contrary to what we expected, the Bohr model of intense, extended, wide-ranging one-on-one interactions, described in Chapter One, did not characterize many students' apprenticeships with the lineage heads. Rather, students absorbed their mentor's approach to science by becoming hands-on, active participants in the mentor's lab or program and learning by doing.

It was striking how much the lineage heads consciously shaped the structure, community, and ethos of their labs, or in Motulsky's case, the training program that he established. As a result, the environment tended to complement and amplify the mentor's direct influence on students. Gall and Lewontin in particular described creating what amounted to microcosms of the wider field in their labs, in which students rehearsed the approach to work and social relations that the mentors hoped they would go on to enact in their professional lives. The lab complemented the mentor's impact because novices learned technical knowledge and skills from lab members who were more experienced than them yet not so advanced in their skills that they could not be emulated, and who were present in the lab as much as the novices were (Vygotsky, 1978). The lab amplified the mentor's impact because its culture and structure embodied the mentor's values and made them part of the very matrix in which the students worked.

The acquisition of knowledge and skills by apprenticeship within a community of practice has been widely studied in adults (Lave & Wenger, 1991) and children (Rogoff, 1990). It appears that newcomers to a profession absorb memes associated with the mentor's variant of good work in part through this same process of participating in a community: *sine ecclesia nulla religio* (without a church, no religion). Moreover, this mode of influence may have special importance for learning to value and enact the social practices associated with good work—both the general (for example, collaboration) and the distinctive (for example, challenging discourse).

The lab as a community of practice is a viable pathway for the mentor's transmission of memes in the sciences, where novices typically learn through apprenticeship in a laboratory (for an example from space science, see Hooker, Nakamura, & Csikszentmihalyi, 2003). In other interviews from the GoodWork Project, journalists told similar stories about the pervasive influence of editors who deliberately engineered the structure, culture, and social dynamics of newsrooms, thereby shaping the formative experience of young reporters and editors. Similarly, educators described how small liberal arts colleges functioned as microcosms of the wider society in which civic and social responsibility were learned (Nakamura, 2007).

How Memes Survive: Long Apprenticeships

Memes were transmitted through working and living in the labs of good mentors. One basic contributor to the impact of the lineage heads is that in the sciences, training takes the form of a long apprenticeship. Undoubtedly, students are more likely to absorb the mentor's memes when exposure to them extends over a long period of time. This is also a reason that modeling admirable behavior cannot be faked—few acts can be convincingly sustained for years. While learning by doing throughout their training, novices can shape their own practices and put values into action under the guidance of the mentor. This is not the case for many other means of cultivating responsible practice, such as formal courses in professional ethics.

How Memes Survive: Positive Emotions

Equally important in cultivating good work appears to be the role of positive emotions. This factor was not anticipated or coded, but it recurred throughout the data. Good work in science requires working long hours with the possibility that an experiment will end in failure, helping patients whose situations seem hopeless, giving credit where credit is due even though personal success is derived from individual achievements, collaborating when doing so introduces risks of being exploited, and devoting resources to students when one might advance faster by treating them as resources. To encourage selfless behaviors, mentors might tell students that taking the high road is painful but necessary; although it entails suffering and may carry personal costs, it is good for the profession and society. Whether this approach would be effective, it is not the one for which the three lineage heads were remembered. Rather, one positive emotion or another smoothed the transmission of many of the most widely absorbed memes. This aligns with theory and research in the domain of positive psychology, which argues that positive emotions open us to learning new things (Fredrickson, 2001) and can make activities intrinsically attractive (Csikszentmihalyi, 1990).

For Gall, the long, uncertain hours in the lab were play, not drudgery, and his students recognized this. As one recalled, "He was obviously having a good time doing what he was doing." Interacting effectively with the family of a profoundly ill child, an unimaginable task for one of Motulsky's trainees before observing him in action, was revealed to be an opportunity to connect and show quiet compassion. Giving due credit became a point of fierce pride and an enduring source of group cohesion and identity for members of Lewontin's lineage. It produced the positive emotion of uplift that Haidt (2003) has called *elevation*. For Boyer and the students who trained with him, collaboration was so much "fun," so much a part of what made research worth doing, that the risk of getting mistreated paled in comparison. Gall's lab community was characterized by quiet harmony, in which individuals immersed themselves in their work in parallel with one another (Csikszentmihalyi, 1990); Lewontin's lab was known for vigorous exchange, in which individuals derived much of their enjoyment from challenging interactions with one another (Sawyer, 2003); and Motulsky created a community in which the rewards of caring for patients were joined to those of research.

In all these ways, mentors made ostensibly difficult values and practices attractive because enacting them was experienced as positive. It would be both glib and incorrect to say that the students absorbed values and practices that were easy and tension free. However, it was something of a surprise to see the extent to which virtues frequently carried their own rewards. In a study of higher education, a scholar of teaching and learning told us that, in his view, "Ultimately students have only one question of their teachers: 'Are you happy enough that I can stand to be like you?'" (Nakamura & Csikszentmihalyi, 2005, p. 66). As a student of Gall summarized, "He made it look like a very good life. It was very enticing." At the heart of this good life was good work.

It almost goes without saying that students' feelings of admiration for their mentors, as well as feelings of being respected and supported by them, were accompanied by positive emotions. In fact, it seems likely that students reproduce their mentors' generous and fair mentoring practices when going on to becoming lab heads in part because they directly experienced the positive impact of these practices during their own training.

The Context of Supportive Relationships

Identifying and understanding the mechanisms or pathways by which memes were transmitted was a primary objective of the study. To a great extent, the process occurred within the context of supportive mentoring relationships. The vast majority of the mentoring experiences described were decisively positive. Furthermore, it was in the context of positive relationships that students were most likely to admire, and therefore want to emulate, their mentors. In contrast, when mentors advanced their own interests at the student's expense, they were less likely to be admired and therefore emulated. This is not to say that behaviors like ruthlessness would not be emulated, especially if they led to desired outcomes like success. However, the overall quality of the relationship appeared to play a key role in whether the student absorbed the mentor's values and practices. The judgment of what constituted a strong mentoring relationship was made based on the student's interview. When mentees regarded the relationship as high in quality, we referred to the mentoring relationship as "strong" and these mentors as "effective." In strong mentoring relationships, students felt respected and supported, and they were given the freedom to grow and thrive as professionals.

While the three lineage heads were known for supporting students' independence, the primary quality characterizing strong mentoring relationships in the full sample was supportiveness. It included consistent availability and involvement, as well as provision of feedback, professional opportunities, resources, and counsel. Given that these relationships existed in leading research departments sometimes felt to be "boot camps," the amount of emphasis placed on supportiveness, as opposed to high standards and expectations for productivity, might be somewhat surprising. However, the adverse effects of outright neglect were felt and reported by students even at this level. In fact, in these relationships, the most common complaints registered about mentors concerned not actions that were horrible, such as outright abuse, but rather what the mentors did not do, ranging from lack of advice to lack of feedback or active interest. In half of the instances of neglect reported, the advisor was described as failing to check on the student's progress for an extended time.

Supportiveness: Balancing Freedom and Guidance

A pervasive dynamic of supportiveness, observed in all three lineages, was the allowance of intellectual freedom to frame problems and choose projects, combined with the mentor's guidance as needed. While consistent availability and involvement were essential, freedom allowed students to explore their interests, making them more likely to develop the independence needed to thrive as young professionals. In addition, a mentor's time to advance his or her own research was critical for creating the intellectual framework and resources of the lab. Effective scientist-mentors balanced their productivity with fostering supportive mentoring relationships. One strategy was to integrate these goals by collaborating on projects with students.

As with other aspects of mentoring practice, it became apparent that there is no one-size-fits-all way to accomplish the goal of providing a balance of freedom and guidance. Some mentors held regular meetings with students or checked in regularly; others did not. Some merely monitored progress unless direct intervention was needed, while others scaffolded student development by initially providing as much guidance as necessary and reducing it only when independence was demonstrated. Effective mentors often adjusted their style to fit the learning needs and styles of their students.

The pattern of providing both freedom and guidance to students extends to the professional domain our understandings of parenting styles and family relations. Baumrind (1989) conceptualized effective parenting as the combination of responsiveness (for example, love and emotional support) and demandingness (for example, discipline and limit-setting); Rathunde (1996) characterized optimal family environments as those that combine family support (for example, acceptance and affirmation) with family challenge (for example, high expectations). Although the role of the challenge and support dynamic in educational and professional settings is less understood than in the family context, it appears that it may be no less important (for example, Evertson & Weinstein, 2006; Wentzel, 2002).

Supportiveness: Making an Investment

A variety of other characteristics of supportive mentoring relationships suggest constructive mentoring practices within the professional context, especially in graduate education. Most of these characteristics amount to making a meaningful investment in students' professional growth and well-being. Effective mentors treated students as equal collaborators, helped students secure funding during graduate study (and sometimes a desirable position afterward), offered encouragement, provided counsel as necessary, showed their humanness and vulnerabilities by relating personal struggles similar to those of students, and assessed what was going well with students' work as well as what could be improved.

Like providing freedom and guidance, the ways in which effective mentors communicated interest or concern took a variety of forms. Some mentors were not only accessible but also generous with their time. However, it should be noted that there was no correlation between the stronger mentoring relationships and more personal ones in the sample of scientists as a whole. Whether the relationship was personal or not, effective mentors listened. As one scientist put it, "You mentor them by listening to them. You mentor them by encouraging them. You mentor them by showing you respect their individuality and autonomy." Effective mentors provide individualized attention where appropriate and recognize students' distinctive aptitudes, interests, needs, styles, and personal qualities. They are responsive to the unique situations that students present.

Graduate advisors and other busy professionals may wonder why they should bother investing time and energy in mentoring relationships. This study has shown that, like teaching, mentoring is a powerful vehicle for creating change and nurturing others, and the influence can extend across multiple generations. In addition, like doing good work, investing in meaningful relationships holds intrinsic rewards. Relatedness is viewed widely as a fundamental human need (Ryan, Deci, & Grolnick, 1995). Positive relationships are critical contributors to subjective well-being (Peterson, 2006), and helping others benefits the giver as well as the beneficiary (Piliavin, 2003).

Mentoring and the Evolution of Culture

Almost always, mentoring is thought about only in terms of its impact on the student's career success. We have argued that its implications are broader.

If a professional strives to do important work but does not mentor well, the capacity to contribute to the field ends at retirement. The individual is productive—but not *reproductive*. As one distinguished researcher eloquently put it, "All famous scientists publish great papers, right? That's sort of self-defining. But if you look at their offspring, their children—[that is,] their students, their postdocs—a surprisingly large number of them don't *train* well. . . . I think it's one thing to be a kind of a comet, a burning shooting star, and make a lot of light for a little while. But the bottom line is, if you believe in some sort of continuity in all of this and you're not a good mentor, you don't train well—it dies with you."

Even more than this, to the extent that students inherit and in turn transmit values, practices, standards, and other memes that affect the fundamental character and health of the profession, the mentor-student relationship can be a crucial mechanism in the evolution of a profession and the survival of good work. Thus, we all have a stake in good mentoring. As John Dewey (1916) recognized many years ago, social life within the professions and beyond is renewed through the process of transmission that good mentoring epitomizes: "Society exists through a process of transmission quite as much as biological life.

This transmission occurs by means of communication of habits of doing, thinking, and feeling from the older to the younger. Without this communication of ideals, hopes, expectations, standards, opinions, from those members of society who are passing out of the group to those who are coming into it, social life could not survive" (p. 3).

9

WHERE DO WE GO FROM HERE?

Being a good mentor does not enjoy nearly the standing that high productivity does at most institutions and, indeed, in most professions. For this to change, leading practitioners need to make good mentoring a central concern in their own careers and act as advocates for it, and researchers and educators need to continue refining the understanding of how to mentor well. This book has provided examples of good mentoring in the sciences that can be applied in a variety of other settings where the transmission of important skills and values requires personal interaction between mentors and mentees. How to apply these suggestions will vary, of course, depending on a number of situational factors. Some general advice might hold across the majority of situations, however.

To begin with a pervasive concern, one may wonder how busy professionals can find time for good mentoring. In our studies of good work, interviewees repeatedly identified lack of time as the primary obstacle to good work. Among journalists, it was "by far the most common complaint" (Gardner, Csikszentmihalyi, & Damon, 2001, p. 139). Three-fourths of high school teachers and 90 percent of medical interns and obstetrician-gynecologists spontaneously lamented the time pressure under which they worked (Solomon, 2007). In hectic newsrooms, it kept established journalists and novices alike from feeling that they had sufficient time for mentoring relationships. Indeed, most professionals report feeling stretched by a relentless time crunch (Hochschild, 1997); there are few other practical considerations as thorny. How can busy professionals find the time to mentor well? There is no simple solution, and each individual must devise strategies in accord with his or her own schedule, time demands, and mentoring style. However, several key mentoring practices shared by the lineage heads and many of their former students may make it inherently easier to mentor well even with significant time constraints.

In apprenticeships, novices learn by observing and doing. Their training is an integral part of an ongoing enterprise rather than a separate task. Even without a lab environment, it is possible for a senior professional to work collaboratively with novices, thereby aligning work goals and activities with training goals and activities. Providing a collaborative model means that the mentor can attend to a full range of responsibilities, and at the same time pass on valuable examples of professional behavior to students. An environment that embodies the mentor's values, is inhabited by young practitioners with varying levels of training, and is ruled by a spirit of collaboration can become itself a powerful adjunct mentor.

One of the most important and more generalizable elements of time management relates to the principle of providing freedom and guidance. In the labs described in this book, it was not necessary for mentors to monitor students closely, hold regular meetings, or otherwise maintain constant contact so long as they demonstrated a genuine interest in students' ideas and their activities, watched for signs of derailment, and provided guidance orienting the students within the field. The quality of interaction was as important as the quantity. Single meetings with Lewontin changed careers. Gall for the most part expected students to come to him, but he kept his door open, and students remembered their interactions with him vividly. Although Motulsky seldom worked directly with his students, they were able to perceive his abiding interest and warm support of their research and his willingness to provide feedback when requested. Virtually all former students recalled time spent with the lineage heads as highly meaningful and memorable. For all its virtues, the traditional model of mentoring through intense,

regular, sustained—hence time-demanding—one-on-one interactions is not the only model for mentoring well. Below we offer
several additional suggestions based on what we have learned.

For Mentors

- *Know yourself.* Individuals receive little support for reflection about good work, let alone good mentoring, in many
  professions. Nevertheless, the senior scientists in this study
  readily articulated their approaches to science in terms of
  basic motivations, key principles they have lived by as
  professionals, and the kinds of scientific work they value.
  They also easily and clearly described the kinds of students
  they like to work with in terms of motivation, degree of
  independence, and interpersonal style; what they have
  sought to transmit to trainees (and what they have chosen
  not to transmit); and how they have gone about doing so,
  including the kind of lab or program they have attempted
  to run. Mentoring well—and doing good work—proceeds
  most fruitfully when action is grounded in self-knowledge
  of this sort. Professionals in all fields will be well served by
  insight into their own temperament, signature practices,
  and strong commitments. As mentors, this self-knowledge
  can help in determining what sorts of students or novices
  are likeliest to thrive within the learning environment that
  they create and in monitoring whether their practices as a
  mentor are consistent with their commitments as a practitioner. Developing a personal mentoring philosophy, like
  articulating a personal teaching philosophy, is encouraged
  now by some innovative graduate programs before the outset
  of the career. Within such practices exists an acknowledgment that there are different ways of mentoring well. One
  factor not specific to science is the way that the resources
  for mentoring, and thus the nature of good mentoring, tend
  to change over the course of a career. Early in the career,

mentors may draw on direct and active involvement in the learning environment, a sense of adventure, and the potential affinity arising from closeness in age and recentness of their own student experience. Later in their career, mentors may leverage accomplishment; breadth and depth of experience, including relationships with earlier mentees; accumulated social capital; and other resources stemming from a productive career.

- *Work with young people who are a good match*. As this study revealed, a close alignment of values and motivational orientations can stack the deck in favor of creating a strong and influential mentoring relationship. For example, Gall sought students who were intrinsically motivated to work on scientific problems because this was congruent with his own priorities. The alignment may have been an important key to fostering not only successful mentoring relationships, but also a lineage that propagated many of his values and practices. A prospective mentor might wish to ask: Do this younger colleague and I share essential values? What other strengths and interests does he or she bring to the table that will be compatible with my own—or incompatible?

- *Address individual differences*. Just as differences among practitioners mean that there is more than one way of mentoring well, differences among novices mean that one way of mentoring will not serve all students well. We have seen that one way of maximizing positive impact as a mentor is to select students or trainees likely to thrive in the learning environment that one creates. However, in addition to the key attributes that might properly form a basis for selection, such as independence, there are other factors such as background that typically do not or—in the case of gender, age, ethnicity or race, and disability—legally must not influence selection. Furthermore, we have seen that even the same student or novice tends to have different needs over the course of his or her development as a professional, requiring varying degrees of guidance, for example. Would-be mentors need to attend to individual differences, should encourage students to come to them when their needs are not met, and must be prepared to monitor student progress and intervene if a student is floundering.

- *Enact key values and practices in plain view.* Values mean more if they are visibly enacted rather than merely expressed. Students can emulate only models that they can see. A mentor might wish to ask: What aspects of my conduct as a professional am I proudest of? What qualities or practices do I have as a member of my profession that I value and wish my colleagues shared? What do I find rewarding about my work: the excitement of discovery, the pleasure of organizing and presenting ideas clearly, the fun of collaborating, the stimulation of intellectual exchange? It may be particularly important to provide a visible model in fields where exposure is typically more limited. Again, a mentor to a younger colleague may want to ask: To what extent are my mentees able to see the reasons that I love what I do—or do they only see me reacting to the daily hassles that come along with the work?

- *Think out loud.* A practice several mentors mentioned can be viewed as an extension of providing a visible model: the habit of thinking work-related and scientific thoughts out loud, giving students access to how the mentor's mind works. An intimate understanding of how a seasoned professional reasons through problems and comes to make certain decisions can be of real benefit to novice practitioners. Moreover, this practice costs the mentor little in terms of time; rather, it makes better use of the time spent together.

- *Create a community that complements and amplifies the direct transmission of knowledge, values, and practices.* Prospective mentors might want to ask themselves questions like these: What are the values I hope to pass on to those I mentor? How are these values expressed—or contradicted—by the use of space, the way projects are selected or prioritized, the allocation of resources, the interactions I encourage versus frown on, the standards and principles I model and ask novices to live up to? The selection process significantly affects the character of the community and the success of the novice's experience in it. Heads of learning and working environments may want to ask themselves: Along with showing promise, can this young person fit into and flourish in this community? Lab heads might ask themselves: Do young people feel comfortable coming to me if there are problems in the lab? Do I find time to provide a constructive model in the lab, particularly if the work is not going well?

- *Help students learn by doing.* Students learn by doing—whether independently or collaboratively—within the context of a knowledgeable and cooperative community of practice (Lave & Wenger, 1991). Mentors may ask themselves: With what projects can I involve my students, and what role can I give them that is appropriate to their level of skill and experience? The answers to these questions must be based on careful observation, but the payoff can be large when students are working toward a common goal on tasks well suited to their respective talents and interests. The more responsibility students take, the more their mentors can learn about their strengths and needs, and the more the collaborative work can be expanded and refined.

- *Facilitate students' building of social capital.* Of all the resources that mentors provide, social capital was mentioned most frequently. Effective mentors help their students connect with others in the field. According to one respondent, a mentor is someone who "introduces you to other people and paves the way for you." Beyond providing the financial support to attend conferences, helping students enter social networks within the field can be an invaluable contribution. The senior scientists in our study were unusually rich in social capital; in any case, however, most mentors will be better established than their protégés within the professional community. Thus, while some mentors have greater social capital than others, most are in the position to catalyze the beginning of their students' integration into the professional community.

For Mentees

- *Know yourself.* Most students and novice professionals recognize that it is important to clarify their professional interests, understanding that these will determine the kinds of specific knowledge and skill they seek to acquire—the area of research or scholarship they pursue, the legal or medical specialty they select, and so on. With respect to being mentored well, however, it is important for students and novices to ponder not only their areas of interest but also their values, strengths, needs, and inclinations (for example, their learning style and interpersonal orientation). What motivates me? What has brought me to this profession? What values are nonnegotiable for me? Am I someone who needs a lot of support and guidance or, conversely, a lot of freedom? Do I learn best by working primarily on my own, or through interchange and collaboration with others? What kind of social climate stimulates my best work: Harmonious? Challenging? Actively pursuing this knowledge, and adjusting it on the basis of accumulating experience, will help students address the questions: What sort of learning environment will I most benefit from? What do I need from the environment, including from those who mentor me, in order to flourish? The same self-knowledge helps in evaluating prospective workplaces when entering the profession.

- *Seek a good fit in a mentor.* For newcomers in any field, mentors can have a profound influence on professional values as well as on career advancement. It is worth the time investment to find a good match. There can be little doubt that a strong match in terms of academic interests and goals is critical for students. However, satisfaction with one's mentor—particularly long-term satisfaction—may be affected by the match on a host of other human and personal qualities, such as working style, flexibility, sense of humor, expectations, and openness. Some may not unwisely regard a strong match with a mentor as the single most important criterion for selecting a graduate program or job. Graduate students in particular often spend several years working closely with a mentor. A prospective student might want to ask, for example: Is this a person I want to be like as a professional? If not, will there be opportunities to be mentored by others as well? Is this a person whose approach to advising will be a reasonable fit for me? Am I comfortable with the balance of freedom and guidance that he or she offers? If not, are compensating factors worth the trade-off?

- *Seek a good fit in a learning and working environment.* In choosing a mentor, a student in some professions is also choosing a learning and working environment such as a lab. Particularly in terms of specialized knowledge and technique, much of what graduate students in science learn will come from peers in the lab, who can heavily influence the quality of the graduate experience. Students may therefore want to learn about the social dynamics and ethos of the lab communities they are considering. While lab membership and social dynamics may change over a graduate career, the defining features driven by the characteristics of the lab head may not. Students may want to ask such questions as: Do students cooperate, share information, and collaborate? Is the climate too competitive, too combative, too quiet?

Have there been serious conflicts in the lab? If so, are compensating factors worth the trade-off?

- *Play an active role in learning from others.* Because there is little formal training, limited support, and few rewards for mentoring well in the sciences, and still less in many other fields, learning from others can be strongly influenced by a novice's own active efforts. For instance, in fields where learning occurs by apprenticeship and many effective mentors teach largely by example, being a keen observer of an admired model can be an invaluable skill. In addition, actively learning from and with peers is important in science labs and also in many other environments. Because so much learning of standards and ethics takes place tacitly, particularly in the first apprenticeship or other significant mentoring relationship, it can be important to make active efforts to articulate and evaluate the central practices and values that one is absorbing. This is not easy; however, it may be facilitated by exposure to multiple training environments and comparing notes with peers. Finally, while we hardly glimpsed apprenticeship's darker side in this study, other GoodWork Project interviews would suggest that playing an active role in one's development also may include gleaning lessons from the negative examples of antimentors ("Well, at least now I know what I *won't* do in these situations") or exiting relationships with outright "tormentors" (Fischman & Gardner, 2005).

- *Seek out multiple influences.* Due to differences of background, strengths, and interests, each person's version of good work will be unique in some respects. For mentors, we saw that one implication of this is the need to individualize the treatment of students if they are to flourish. For students, one implication is the benefit of exposure to multiple influences. That is, separate from its role in helping to make taken-for-granted practices visible through contrast and thus available for evaluation, exposure to multiple influences also makes it likelier that novices will get more of their needs met, and (in fields with a long apprenticeship, like graduate education) that they will identify a mentor whose approach to work and to mentoring is a good fit. Finally, it should be noted that many of the worst cases of mentoring gone wrong occur because in graduate education, a single advisor, or in some other fields a single patron, has a lot of control over a novice's professional fate. Seeking out multiple influences mitigates this hazard.

For Institutions

- *Support mentoring.* In graduate education and other fields, there are now routinely calls for increased attention to mentoring because it has been associated with outcomes ranging from degree completion to subsequent productivity to organizational commitment. This study has linked it to the perpetuation of good work. It is possible to maintain an island of good mentoring within a wider culture that is less hospitable to it, but it is not ideal. A supportive culture encourages students or novices to seek mentoring and encourages discussion among established practitioners about what it means to do good work and mentor well. It deliberately creates opportunities for novices to be exposed to mature practitioners at work. The examples are numerous. A major investment bank pairs novices and seasoned bankers on cross-country business trips, recognizing the apprenticeship opportunity built into the long plane rides and informal time together in which the meetings themselves are embedded. To improve the likelihood of making a good match, graduate students in the sciences increasingly undertake formal rotations, spending time in multiple labs before settling into one for their doctoral work. Less obviously, the physical layout of departments and work-places, like those of individual labs, can encourage formative interactions or discourage them. Those who already invest time and energy in mentoring may be the best advocates within an organization for the importance of mentoring.

- *Reward mentoring.* Individual institutions and the profession they comprise need to provide greater incentives for good mentoring—that is, the adoption of mentoring practices that cultivate the next generation's commitment to excellence and ethics. Indeed, prospective faculty members' desire and ability to mentor is largely ignored in university hiring even though the advisor-student relationship is central to successful graduate education. In academic psychology, for example, a systematic review of job ads stretching from 1981 to 2001 showed that mentoring and advising figured as "salient job components" in only 3.9 percent and 7.5 percent of the ads, respectively (Johnson & Zlotnick, 2005). The reward structure at most universities makes advising and mentoring activities appear costly to the careers of those who are in a strong position to mentor new-comers to the field: full-time faculty with research programs. In addition, whereas teaching evaluations increasingly receive attention, there tend to be few places in the administrative structure for advisees to have a voice about their mentoring experiences. Institutions need to recognize that as custodians of their respective professions, good mentoring is a sound investment of seasoned professionals' time, affecting the health of the profession and the larger culture in which they exist, as well as more directly affecting novices' satisfaction and commitment.
- *Prepare future mentors.* Individual institutions and professions need to initiate discussion of how to prepare students and novice professionals for the mentoring role. Increasingly, universities offer programs that prepare their graduate

students for classroom teaching. Analogous programs that prepare them to mentor are needed. The first of these are just beginning to emerge in the sciences, emphasizing learning by doing (Pfund, Pribbenow, Branchaw, Lauffer, & Handelsman, 2006). More generally the discussion of how to advise and mentor is entering the discourse about career development through the efforts of individual universities, professional associations, and government agencies (for example, National Academy of Sciences, 1997; Barker, 2002; Bonetta, 2004). In other fields, including business, nursing, teacher education, and law, establishment of formal mentoring programs has also raised awareness of the need to explore what it means to mentor well and prepare professionals to mentor.

Future Directions

The opportunities for applying the knowledge and insights that have been generated vary widely across fields. They are probably most relevant to the sciences. There, learning by apprenticeship is a well-established, central part of advanced training, and collaborative work is not uncommon. In other fields, where extended and wide-ranging relations with senior members of the field are not the norm, there has been considerable interest in establishing formal mentoring programs. What we have learned may inform such efforts. Scarce time and resources frequently create pressures to narrowly circumscribe the scope of formal mentoring relationships. This study, with its focus on long-term, informal mentoring, may help in comparing different forms of mentoring and their relative costs and benefits.

We also hope this book will initiate new lines of investigation using lineage structures to explore the sociocultural, transgenerational reverberations of individual developmental relationships. Because of the study's distinctive multilineage design and evolutionary, systems perspective, it opens up previously neglected questions that we hope will define avenues of future investigation and provide new guidance for mentoring practices. We offer several examples.

First, this book recognizes the active role that students can play in their own development, as suggested by recent developmental psychology (Brandstadter, 2006; Magnusson & Stattin, 2006), but does not foreground this role. Instead, attention focused on the good mentor's role, illustrating how he or she influences by affirming, modeling, talking, and setting up the small world in which the student learns to be a professional. While illustrating the student's active role in social learning, we did not systematically analyze how students select from among multiple influences to create new memes, potentially catalyzing cultural change, nor did we explore in detail the social, emotional, and cognitive processes through which students manage their side of the interface when learning from mentors. This work remains to be done.

Second, a related issue deserving more attention is how change (as opposed to continuity) occurs at the cultural level—how new memes are brought into the culture of a profession by the rising generation in response to new conditions. This study focused on the three exemplary scientists who served as lineage heads, tracing the fate of their values, practices, and other attributes through multiple generations. It might have focused instead on the youngest generation of practitioners, determining what memes they possessed that earlier generations had not, because of their exposure to evolving sociocultural conditions in and beyond their profession. To take one example of such a condition, we might have probed in detail how attention to women's rights in educational and work settings emerged in the wake of older traditions. In the future, the perspective and methodology introduced in this book should provide a useful lens for research on processes of emergence and renewal.

Third, as students, the interviewees worked in highly successful labs that produced cutting-edge work; the level of innovation and creativity was presumed to be high. Most of these students were receptive to the influence of their mentors. One might say that they exhibited a high level of "mentorability." However, if being a protégé involves "following" one's mentor, and creativity is fostered through independent thinking and resisting convention, what is the relationship between being well mentored and being creative? Related research on a lineage in modern dance suggested that some highly creative professionals value the role of the maverick who strikes out on her own without paying homage to the techniques or concerns of the rest of the field (Keinänen & Gardner, 2004). Those individuals may see themselves as too busy inventing their own techniques or working on their own problems. Others might argue that existing techniques or knowledge in the field needs to be mastered before going on to become truly creative in a way that would be accepted by the rest of the field. The issue will benefit from future examination: Can one who is mentored well become creative, and is a highly creative person "mentorable"?

Although we did not directly examine these questions, this study provides a platform on which future work might build. It showed that the transgenerational impact of an effective mentor can support the student's development as an independent scientist rather than a clone and simultaneously encourage the survival of traditional values and practices associated with good work. Mentors transmitted both continuity-supporting memes (for example, equality and integrity) through their example and guidance, as well as practices that supported independence (for example, provisions for intellectual freedom). Guidance gives students the benefit of the older generation's wisdom, and granting freedom allows self-expression, modification, and innovation to occur. Of course, there are also cases in which being strongly influenced does not support originality. The important question is: Under what circumstances can one be strongly influenced by a mentor and go on to become creative? More broadly, how do different professions balance the need to sustain traditional values with innovation, change, and new ideas?

Finally, a legitimate question is whether good mentoring is the sole province of stars and paragons, beyond the reach of most members of a field. Mentoring will be destined to play only a modest role in promoting the welfare of novices and the professions they enter if good mentoring depends on possessing boundless resources or the long list of exceptional qualities identified by some writers and admiring protégés. This study suggests that if experienced professionals are to contribute to the perpetuation of good work, there are some qualities that they must possess. Further research on other professions is needed to clarify these core qualities, but the good-work memes that were identified, such as honesty, integrity, and the fair treatment of others, offer a starting point. At the same time, there appear to be legitimately different forms of good work and different ways of mentoring well; thus, the conclusion is not warranted that a professional must have an exhaustive inventory of strengths and virtues and fit into a single mold in order to mentor well. Rather than conforming to some unitary ideal, we have suggested that mentors need to understand what they are best equipped to offer, just as students should understand what they are being offered.

Why Mentor?

The conclusions presented suggest the complexity of passing knowledge and values from one generation to the next. They also point to the many benefits of such a process. First and most obvious are the benefits that accrue to the novice who joins a profession: in many cases, young professionals feel adrift in their work if they are not exposed to the example and influence of more experienced practitioners. Less obvious are the benefits that accrue to the mentor. Yet as Erikson (1959/1980) postulated, and many scholars subsequently have discussed, generativity becomes an important need in middle adulthood for most individuals, and workplace relationships are one important way to fulfill it. Somewhat less studied is the impact of mentorship on organizations, where strong mentors may contribute to a productive climate. Finally, the role of the mentor as a trustee of the profession and preserver of its standards of conduct has been almost completely ignored. Yet any healthy society needs continuity in its fundamental institutions: in schools and churches, hospitals and courtrooms, in the car repair shop and the manufacturers' factories.

This book has attempted to lay the foundation for a more complete study of mentoring, one taking into account what benefits accrue to the apprentice, the mentor, the organization, and the broader profession—thereby indirectly benefiting society as a whole. Although the focus was on only a handful of science labs, we hope that the investigation has illuminated a set of issues relevant to mentoring processes more generally. When good work is embodied by individuals with whom a novice interacts, it can have profound formative impact. As Albert Einstein argued, "It is not enough to teach a man [*sic*] a specialty. . . . It is essential that the student acquire an understanding of and a lively feeling for values. He must acquire a vivid sense of the beautiful and the morally good. . . . These precious things are conveyed to the younger generation through personal contact with those who teach, not—or at least not in the main—through textbooks. It is this that primarily constitutes and preserves our culture" (1954, pp. 66–67).

Further, good work and good mentoring are intimately connected, in that mentoring is an important way that professionals can contribute to the perpetuation of their vision of good work. The commitment is to the survival of a fundamental stance toward one's profession. One of Lewontin's former students recalled his mentor's speech on the occasion of his Festschrift:

Then he gave this speech, which is the thing he wanted us to remember. And it was so interesting, because the speech was all about how we were supposed to treat our students. He didn't say anything about how grateful he was for having been associated with us, or that he had a good time, or any scientific message. He left us telling us that you don't put your name on your students' papers, you know. You have to behave ethically. And you have to teach that to your students. And if I've given anything to you that you've found useful, you have to pass that on to your students. And that was all he talked about. And we really couldn't figure out why. Why he was doing this. But now I see that I think that's the legacy he wants to leave. Not the legacy of his scientific accomplishments, but a legacy of a proper ethos and behavior in the field that will lead to good science if it's practiced properly. It's the same stuff that we had been told the whole time.

Thus, good mentoring is not just about advancing a protégé's career. It also involves passing on the practice of good work, including the capacity to be a good mentor when one's own turn comes.

Appendix A

DATA COLLECTION, CODING, AND ANALYSES

Collecting the Data

Participants were recruited through a letter of invitation that described the study and requested a two- to three-hour meeting; they were offered no monetary compensation. The letter was followed up with a telephone call in which any questions were answered and an interview was scheduled with those who agreed to participate. The rate of participation was high (88 percent). The reason given for most refusals was being too busy to accommodate the significant time commitment.

The protocol was to collect the data in a single face-to-face, audiotaped session conducted by one or two interviewers. Each author of *Good Work* (2001), Howard Gardner, Mihaly Csikszentmihalyi, and William Damon, interviewed one of the Generation 1 scientists. Other GoodWork Project investigators, including this book's coauthors, interviewed the thirty-three other participants. In a handful of cases, circumstances required modifying this procedure: part or all of an interview was conducted by telephone, or the interview was conducted over more than one session.

For each participant, supplementary materials were collected prior to the interview. They included information about basic biographical background, scientific research and major accomplishments, and relationships to the expected mentor, students, and other significant figures. Following each session, a brief interview summary was written by the interviewer(s), and the audiotaped interview was transcribed.

Two versions of the interview protocol were designed and pilot-tested: one for the G1 scientists and one for the G2 and G3 scientists. The G2/G3 protocol, which was used for thirty-three of the thirty-six participants, is presented in Appendix B. The G1 protocol was similar, but it focused on the training of younger practitioners more than the participant's own apprenticeship experiences.

Coding Procedures

Coding of the interview transcripts occurred in two passes. In the first pass, transcripts were parsed into broad categories, or metacodes. These metacodes corresponded to sections of the interview protocol: memes, mechanisms or pathways for transferring memes, the lab environment, and relationships between mentor and student. This first coding pass served to chunk the data, making the second, finer-grained coding pass more efficient.

For the second pass, interview content was coded into emerging patterns or themes within each meta-level category (for example, "research skills and knowledge" within the memes metacode). The investigators discussed these themes and possible content categories based on them, and developed a coding system and a codebook that defined each code in detail and provided examples.

We next conducted tests of coder dependability. Three investigators independently applied the coding system to a transcript portion and then discussed the coding of each passage, noting agreements and disagreements. In the case of disagreements, we built consensus and, if necessary, modified the coding system and codebook to improve subsequent agreement. Six iterations of this process were undertaken to refine the coding system and establish coder dependability. Each investigator then coded several transcripts. Overlooked themes and organizational strategies were noted and shared. Final adjustments to the coding system were made based on these coding exercises before proceeding with coding.

The final coding system contained seventeen categories or codes for memes and qualities (for example, intrinsic motivations for doing science, extrinsic motivations for doing science, practices for navigating the social field, mental ability and cognitive traits), fourteen for mechanisms (for example, direct collaboration, feedback), ten for the laboratory environment (for example, lab demographics, physical layout, competition among labmates, regular lab meetings), and fourteen for relationships and interactions (for example, being an active presence in the lab, interactions extending beyond the lab).

The thirty-six transcripts were distributed evenly among investigators by interviewee generation, lineage, and other factors to avoid systematic coder bias. In addition, to prevent drift during the coding period, three transcripts were coded by all three investigators as periodic tests of coder dependability. Each test was followed by analysis and discussion of agreements and divergences in coding decisions. Each investigator testified to gaining increasing confidence in coder dependability from test to test. We then constructed a database of coded transcripts using NUD*IST 4.0 software for qualitative data analysis.

Development of a Global Code Sheet

In addition to coding the text of each transcript, a global code sheet (GCS) was developed to provide summary assessments for the transcript as a whole. We refined the GCS items and established coder dependability much as we had for the coding scheme. That is, we each read and completed GCSs for test transcripts, followed by consensus-building discussions of coding decisions and further modification of the GCS. The GCS was finalized only after all of the investigators were satisfied with coder dependability.

On the GCS (see Appendix C), the coder first listed all of the significant professional influences mentioned by the interviewee, identifying the expected mentor, and then rated the relative importance accorded to each professional influence. Item 1 indicates the person whom the interviewee considered most responsible for his or her choice of genetics as a profession. Item 2 indicates which memes on a checklist of thirty-one "G1 memes" were inherited by the interviewee. To create the list of G1 memes, the investigators agreed on approximately ten memes that most characterized each lineage head (G1) based on his interview transcript. A G1 meme was coded as inherited if the interviewee stated explicitly or strongly suggested that the meme was transmitted by or inherited from the expected mentor. Items 3 through 5 rate the quality of the relationship with the expected mentor and with another strong professional influence (if any), and the degree to which the interviewee had multiple formative influences. Item 6 identifies the interviewee's own memes, based on the transcript as a whole. For most participants, the coder identified six to twelve memes. The coder indicated whether a meme was described as absorbed from the expected mentor, absorbed from another professional influence, taught by the interviewee to the next generation, or some combination of these. Items 7 through 10 rate the formality of the relationship with the expected mentor, the amount of time spent with him or her, and the relative quality and importance of the lab environment.

Analytical Approach

For each lineage case study (Chapters Two through Four), we examined the qualitative interview data for a single lineage. In Chapter Five, we supplemented these qualitative portrayals with quantitative analyses of possessed and inherited memes by lineage and by generation. In order to triangulate, we used items 2 and 6 from the GCS to identify memes that had been inherited. The use of item 2 ensured that each respondent's mention of inheriting memes possessed by the lineage heads was counted as such.

The use of item 6 ensured that the most salient memes in each respondent's self-description were counted as inherited if the participant stated so. The thirty-one G1 memes from item 2 and the participant memes from item 6 were then combined to yield a set of twenty-five types of memes (see Table 5.1). Each of the thirty-one G1 memes was assigned to one of the twenty-five new categories, and each of the respondents' own memes was consensus-coded as belonging to one of the twenty-five new categories. A respondent was coded as possessing a particular meme type if one of the corresponding G1 memes was indicated in item 2, a meme belonging to that category was noted in item 6, or both. A respondent was coded as inheriting a particular meme type from his or her expected mentor if one of the corresponding G1 memes was indicated in item 2, a meme belonging to that category was cited in item 6 and coded as inherited from the expected mentor, or both. Finally, a respondent was coded as teaching a particular meme type if a meme belonging to that category was cited in item 6 and coded as being taught to students by the respondent.

Chapter Five reports on several statistical analyses and tests. We first compared the number of participants inheriting specific memes by lineage, using chi-square tests to determine if differences among the lineages were significant (see Tables 5.2 and 5.3). Next we examined the percentage of participants possessing and inheriting memes by lineage and by generation (see Tables 5.4 and 5.5), based on frequency counts by lineage and generation.

Chapters Six and Seven report on means of transmitting memes and relationship qualities, respectively, drawing on the full corpus of interviews to formulate conclusions about these topics for the sample as a whole. NUD*IST reports were generated on these topics. The mechanisms of transmission and relationship qualities most frequently mentioned were analyzed, and the patterns that emerged were reported.

We applied a set of coding categories to all passages that concerned either an interviewee's own means of influence on students or the mechanisms used by the interviewee's mentors. The fourteen mechanism categories were (1) published works, (2) classroom instruction, (3) scolding and prescribing, (4) sermonizing, (5) stories and sayings, (6) Socratic questioning, (7) feedback, (8) informal conversations and exchanges, (9) other verbal exchanges, (10) collaboration, (11) other references to learning by doing, (12) lab structure, (13) modeling/observation, and (14) use of extrinsic incentives. Chapter Six discusses the mechanisms that the lineage heads favored according to both the G1s and their former students.

The fourteen categories for dimensions of mentoring relationships were (1) formal versus informal; (2) extent of relationship beyond formal training; (3) supportiveness, subcoded to include characteristics such as giving encouragement, freedom, and respect; (4) providing resources; (5) setting up challenges; (6) being an active presence in the lab; (7) commonalities; (8) intimacy; (9) providing authorship credit; (10) extent the relationship was paternalistic; (11) nature of nonwork relationship, if any; (12) extent of mentee's admiration; (13) level of mentor's guidance; and (14) extent the mentor individualized treatment of the student. For each relationship category, both positive and negative examples were coded. We discuss these data in Chapter Seven. Chapters Six and Seven also draw on analyses of GCS items. We report correlations between the strength of influence (that is, the transmission of memes) and the quality of the lab environment (item 10 on the GCS) or the quality of the mentoring relationship (item 3 on the GCS) in Chapters Six and Seven, respectively. Chapter Seven compares data about strong and weaker relationships as defined by a cutoff point on item 3 of the GCS.

Appendix B

SCIENCE APPRENTICESHIP STUDY–G2 AND G3 INTERVIEW QUESTIONS

A. INTRODUCTION

1. *Briefly only:* What initially attracted you to science? To your subfield?

   a. How did you come to pursue a career in genetics?

2. In what areas of your life do you invest the most energy/attention?

   a. *If unclear:* Are there areas where you feel you don't invest enough?

   b. When do you feel most energized, engaged? What do you most enjoy in life?

B. VALUED GOALS, BELIEFS, AND PRACTICES

3. *Briefly only:* Can you summarize the kinds of things you are trying to accomplish in your work right now?

   Probe for larger picture if Respondent (R) focuses on day-to-day goals, and vice versa.

   a. Why are these important or interesting to you?

4. Are there some specific practices or principles that characterize your approach to science that you consider important (for example, distinctive ways of interacting with colleagues, standards of quality, precepts/maxims)?

   Probe for things unique to R, if s/he focuses only on universal scientific practices.

   a. What are some of the important considerations for you, when choosing a question to investigate?

If unclear: Is any of them *most* important?

b.   What qualities characterize the work that you've been most proud of?

If needed: What qualities characterize work that you respect/ don't respect?

5. What is your ideal image of the kind of scientist you want to be?

6. Are there any moral and ethical values that inform your work?

   a.   What beliefs are these values based on (for example, religious, humanistic)?

   b.   Are these values the same as or different from those of colleagues in your field?

   c.   *If in conflict:* What effect does this have, if any, on pursuit of your goals?

C. FORMATIVE EXPERIENCES

7. In your lifetime, who most helped shape your approach to being a scientist?

   Probe for influence on R's values, especially on *key values identified in Section B*.

   If unclear: How did these individuals influence your approach to work?

   a.   How has your family background influenced your approach to work?

   b.   What about peers, colleagues, or friends?

   c.   What about "antimentors"?

   If time permits:

   a.   What about someone you didn't know personally, a book you read?

   b.   Are there aspects of your approach to work that seem original/that you can't ascribe to outside influences?

D. APPRENTICESHIP (POSITIVE AND NEGATIVE ASPECTS)

8. *Unless clear:* Who was the single greatest influence during your years of formal training as a geneticist?

   If needed: Who made the greatest contribution to the kind of geneticist you've become?

- Elicit information about the expected mentor (for example, the graduate advisor) in questions 9 to 18 unless s/he isn't mentioned as a formative influence. If unmentioned, probe why.

- Use C1, C2, and C3 to learn about *other* important influences during R's apprenticeship years, especially anyone named in question 8.

C1. What were the most important things you learned from [mentor]? *[See question 11 for probes and follow-up questions.]*

C2. For someone who doesn't know [mentor] at all, what were some of the ways that s/he taught or interacted with you and with other students? *[See question 12 for probes and follow-up questions.]*

C3. How was the influence of [expected mentor] similar to or different from [mentor]'s influence?

We'd like to explore [expected mentor]'s influence in more detail.

9. Broad outlines of the relationship:

   Briefly only: How and when did you meet?

   How did you come to want to learn with ___?

   G3s: What was ___ 's position/standing within the field, when you began?

   How much time did you spend together?

10. Was there a certain culture or atmosphere that character-ized ____ 's lab (for example, intensity, competition, humor, exchange of ideas, socializing, common interests and concerns, shared goals, ways of thinking, beliefs)?

   a. *Unless clear:* What did you find valuable about that? What was difficult?

   b. What was ____'s role in creating this atmosphere?

   c. How does your own lab compare?

11. What were the most important things you learned from ____?

   When possible: Probe for modes of transmission here.

   a. Did you learn:

   - Work practices, values and ideals, an approach to genetics?

   - The field and how to navigate it?

   - Goals and priorities in work and outside it?

   - Things outside genetics (for example, balancing life and work; political/social issues; interface of domain and society)?

   b. What was the *single most important* thing you learned from ____?

   c. Do you still invoke things you were taught?

   If needed: What things did you learn or experience in ____'s lab that you would not have gotten in someone else's lab?

12. For someone who doesn't know ____ at all, what were some of the ways that ____ taught or interacted with you and with other students?

   Probe: How would you describe ____'s particular teaching style? Any unique ways of getting something across (for example, humor, stories)?

   a. What did you learn from ____ just through observation?

   - To what extent did s/he teach or train by example?

    b. Were there any things you made it a point to emulate/ *not* emulate?

    c. Were there any particular sayings s/he used that have stuck with you?

If needed: Do you have a favorite story about ___ that conveys what s/he was like?

13. What were ___'s distinctive qualities (positive and negative)?

If relationship has continued: Ask about ___'s personal qualities during the apprenticeship.

    a. How broad or inclusive was his/her interest in the world?

    b. What did ___ believe in most deeply? Seek to accomplish?

       • Did s/he have particular ethical commitments that stand out? (probe nature of evidence)

    c. *For any salient qualities:* What impact did this have on you?

14. How would you characterize your relationship with ___?

    a. Was it personal or mostly professional? Hierarchical/equal?

       • What kinds of things did you talk about?

    b. What did you have in common? Philosophically or ideologically?

    c. Were there aspects that could have been better?

       • Any tensions or differences that you encountered?

       • Any problems with his/her style of leadership (especially autonomy versus control)?

       • Any times when ___ wasn't there for you? What did you do then?

15. How did ___ provide support/affirmation?

If unclear: Were there ways s/he showed confidence in you?

    a. What potentials, talents, and abilities did ___ see in you?

    b. What do you think ___ saw as his/her primary responsibility to students?

16. How did ___ set challenges for you?

If unclear: Did you ask for new challenges/responsibilities, or did ___ recommend them?

   a.   What degree of freedom for creativity did ___ allow?

   •   For example, could ___ tolerate your disagreeing with his/her ideas? Did you feel any pressure to stay in his/her lab or in his/her field?

17. Current contact:

   a.   To what extent are you still in touch with others from the lab?

   b.   Do you still keep in touch with ___?

   If yes: Do you still consult him/her?
   If no: Why not? [probe how relationship ended]

18. How do you define "mentor"?

   a.   Would you characterize ___ as a mentor?

If multiple important mentors were named (for example, in question 8):

   •   How have you combined these distinct influences?

E. OBSTACLES, PRESSURES, AND REWARDS

19. How have your commitments and values changed since your apprenticeship? Why? What led to those changes?

   a.   *Positive pressures:* Have your initial values/approach to work been affected by opportunities, changes in genetics, the kind of work that is rewarded/encouraged?

   b.   *Negative pressures:* Any difficulties or pressures that have challenged, or led you to rethink, your initial values/approach to work?

Probe for times when it was difficult to pursue *values identified in section B.*

20. *If negative pressures:* How did you go about dealing with these pressures?

    a. Who or what supported you in dealing with them?

    b. How did you come to deal with them in this way?

    c. Were you ever in a situation that challenged your basic [scientific] commitments or goals? What did you do?

21. Are there things [R's mentor] believed in doing that haven't made sense in your experience, or that you've had to adapt because conditions in genetics changed?

    Probe how the changes have made ___'s lessons less relevant.

22. Are there specific qualities that have contributed to your achievements (qualities = personal attributes; for example, determination, persistence)?

F. TRAINING THE NEXT GENERATION

23. How would you characterize the practice of apprenticeship in genetics?

24. During your career, to what extent have you worked with students?

    a. How much interaction do you have with them?

    b. How important is it for you to work with young people?

        Note. If R has not had students, skip ahead to questions 28 and 29 and ask R to speculate.

25. What qualities characterize the students you prefer to work with?

    a. How do students typically wind up working with you?

26. What do you see as your responsibilities to these students?

    a. What do you expect of them?

27. How would you characterize your relationships with students (for example, personal/professional, formal/informal, equal/hierarchic)?

28. What are the most important things that you hope to convey to students?

    Anything else?

    - Practices, guiding principles, values, and ethics
    - Goals and priorities
    - Ways of navigating the field
    - Things outside of work itself (for example, work/nonwork balance; political and social life; interface of domain and society)

    a. *If needed:* Why do these things, in particular, matter to you?
       If not addressed, probe:

    b. What kind of work do you reward/encourage? Discourage?

    c. Are there any opportunities, or pitfalls and pressures, that you try to prepare your students for? How?

       - Are they different from the opportunities and constraints that you faced? Why?

29. You identified several things that you hope to convey to students. How do you go about encouraging these things? Any other ways?

    a. How would you characterize your teaching style?

       - Explaining, using stories/sayings/bromides
       - Personal example
       - Collaborating
       - Exhorting, encouraging, critiquing

       If not addressed, probe:

    b. How do you provide support for the development of your students' talents?

- Can you describe a time when a student was struggling with a problem or ethical dilemma and you helped them?

c. How do you provide challenges?

30. Do you keep in touch after they leave?

a. To what extent do they continue to consult you for advice?

G. CLOSING

31. Over the course of your career, has there been an overarching purpose or goal that gives meaning to what you do that is essential to making your work worthwhile? What is it?

a. What experiences or influences were most important in forming this goal?

32. Are any public/social issues of special concern to you?

a. *If concerned:* Who or what inspired this concern?

33. Are there ways that you try to contribute to society or the communities to which you belong?

Probe for both contributions through work and contributions outside work.

If yes: Why is this important to you?

If no: Probe for reasons.

34. We are coming to the end of our interview. Is there anything you would like to add?

a. Check notes for things left out.

b. May I follow up with you in the future?

Appendix C

GLOBAL CODE SHEET

Significant Professional Influences	EM?*	Importance?
1. _____	_____	1 2 3 4 5
2. _____	_____	1 2 3 4 5
3. _____	_____	1 2 3 4 5
4. _____	_____	1 2 3 4 5
5. _____	_____	1 2 3 4 5
6. _____	_____	1 2 3 4 5

*EM: expected mentor (for example, graduate advisor).

1. Person most responsible for Respondent's (R's) choice of genetics as profession (check all that apply):

_____ Parent/family was most responsible.

_____ High school influence was most responsible.

_____ College professor was most responsible.

_____ Expected mentor was most responsible.
　　　_____ Graduate _____ Postgraduate

_____ Other graduate influence was most responsible.

_____ Other postgraduate influence was most responsible.

2. G1 memes (check R's memes that were transmitted by expected mentor, as suggested or explicitly stated in transcript):

_____ Collaboration/ cooperation

_____ Honesty, integrity, and ethics in research

_____ Political consciousness

_____ Moralist (judgmental, moralistic)

_____ Intellectual freedom and guidance

_____ Credit based on contribution (authorship)

_____ Science is the art of the solvable

_____ Flow (enjoyment, concentration, curiosity)

_____ Neatness

_____ Love of nature

_____ Broad interests (nonscientific)

_____ High intellectualism/ elitism

_____ Avoiding scientific overspecialization

_____ Independence, resolve, robust ego

_____ Providing an intellectually exciting ambiance/ infrastructure

_____ Dogged, determined (as opposed to brilliant)

_____ Marxist/socialist politics

_____ Aesthetic values (visualization, patterns, order)

_____ Serious/intense avocation

_____ Self-directed research goals

_____ Humanitarianism/social responsibility

_____ Industrious (hard work, persistence, preparation)

_____ Physician-scientist

_____ Weekly lab meetings

_____ Educating the public about science

_____ No weekly lab meetings

_____ Choosing good colleagues

_____ Treat people equally (fairness)

_____ Empiricism

_____ Methodologist/ epistemologist

_____ Anticareerism

3. Overall *quality* of relationship with expected mentor:

   Negative   1   2   3   4   5   Positive

           (Uncertain)

4. Overall *quality* of relationship with other professional influence:

   Negative   1   2   3   4   5   Positive

           (Uncertain)

   N/A (no other professional influence)

5. Multiple influences: (Circle one) Yes   No

   Salience of having multiple influences (interactions among them):

   Weak   1   2   3   4   5   Strong

           (Uncertain)

6.   R's own memes:

Codes: Insert superscript "b" = came from expected mentor; "c" = came from other professional influence; "f" = transmits to next generation.

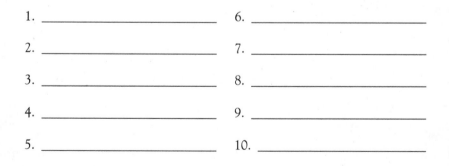

1. _____   6. _____

2. _____   7. _____

3. _____   8. _____

4. _____   9. _____

5. _____   10. _____

7.   Relationship with expected mentor was mostly:

   Formal   1   2   3   4   5   Informal

           (Uncertain)

8. Amount of time spent with expected mentor:

   A little   1   2   3   4   5   A lot

         (Uncertain)

9. Lab atmosphere and culture was:

   Unimportant   1   2   3   4   5   Important

         (Uncertain)

10. Overall quality of lab atmosphere and culture:

   Negative   1   2   3   4   5   Positive

         (Uncertain)

References

Albom, M. (1997). *Tuesdays with Morrie: An old man, a young man, and life's greatest lesson*. New York: Doubleday.

Alexander, C. N., & Langer, E. J. (Eds.). (1990). *Higher stages of human development: Perspectives on adult growth*. New York: Oxford University Press.

Allen, T. D., & Eby, L. T. (Eds.). (2007). *Blackwell handbook of mentoring*. Oxford: Blackwell.

Baltes, P. B. (1987). Theoretical propositions of life span developmental psychology: On the dynamics between growth and decline. *Developmental Psychology, 23*, 611–626.

Bandura, A. (1985). *Social foundations of thought and action: A social cognitive theory*. Upper Saddle River, NJ: Prentice Hall.

Barker, K. (2002). *At the helm: A laboratory navigator*. Cold Spring Harbor, NY: Cold Spring Harbor Laboratory Press.

Baumrind, D. (1989). Rearing competent children. In W. Damon (Ed.), *Child development today and tomorrow* (pp. 349–378). San Francisco: Jossey-Bass.

Blasi, A. (2005). Moral character: A psychological approach. In D. K. Lapsley & F. C. Power (Eds.), *Character psychology and character education* (pp. 67–100). Notre Dame, IN: University of Notre Dame Press.

Bonetta, L. B. (Ed.). (2004). *Making the right moves: A practical guide to scientific management for postdocs and new faculty*. Research Triangle Park, NC, and Chevy Chase, MD: Wellcome Fund and Howard Hughes Medical Institute.

Bourdieu, P. (1985). The forms of social capital. In J. G. Richardson (Ed.), *Handbook of theory and research for the sociology of education* (pp. 241–258). Westport, CT: Greenwood Press.

Brandstadter, J. (2006). Action perspectives on human development. In R. M. Lerner (Ed.), *Handbook of child psychology* (Vol. 1, pp. 516–568). Hoboken, NJ: Wiley.

Cameron, S. W., & Blackburn, R. T. (1981). Sponsorship and academic career success. *Journal of Higher Education, 52*, 369–377.

Campbell, D. T. (1976). Evolutionary epistemology. In P. A. Schlipp (Ed.), *The library of living philosophers* (pp. 413–463). La Salle, IL: Open Court.

Carnegie Institution for Science. (2006). *Carnegie's Joseph G. Gall wins 2006 Lasker Award*. Retrieved October 26, 2008, from www.ciw.edu/news/carnegie_s_joseph_g_gall_wins_2006_lasker_award.

Carson, R., & Pratt, C. (1965). *The sense of wonder*. New York: HarperCollins.

Clark, R. A., Harden, S. L., & Johnson, W. B. (2000). Mentor relationships in clinical psychology doctoral training. *Teaching of Psychology, 27,* 262–268.

Cohen, J., & Taubes, G. (1995). The culture of credit. *Science, 268,* 1706.

Colby, A., & Damon, W. (1992). *Some do care*. New York: Free Press.

Cole, J. R. (1979). *Fair science*. New York: Free Press.

Collins, R. (1998). *The sociology of philosophies*. Cambridge, MA: Harvard University Press.

Coyne, J., & Jones, S. (1995). 1994 Sewall Wright Award. *American Naturalist, 146,* U2–U8.

Cronan-Hillix, T., Gensheime, L. K., Cronan-Hillix, W. A., & Davidson, W. S. (1986). Students' views of mentors in psychology graduate training. *Teaching of Psychology, 13,* 123–127.

Csikszentmihalyi, M. (1988). Society, culture, and person: A systems view of creativity. In R. J. Sternberg (Ed.), *The nature of creativity* (pp. 325–339). Cambridge: Cambridge University Press.

Csikszentmihalyi, M. (1990). *Flow: The psychology of optimal experience*. New York: HarperCollins.

Csikszentmihalyi, M. (1996). *Creativity: Flow and the psychology of discovery and invention*. New York: HarperCollins.

Csikszentmihalyi, M. (1999). Implications of a systems perspective for the study of creativity. In R. J. Sternberg (Ed.), *Handbook of creativity* (pp. 297–312). Cambridge: Cambridge University Press.

Csikszentmihalyi, M., & Massimini, F. (1985). On the psychological selection of bio-cultural information. *New Ideas in Psychology, 3,* 115–138.

Cuomo, M. (2002). *Who mentored you? The person who changed my life*. New York: Barnes & Noble.

Daloz, L. A. (1999). *Mentor: Guiding the journey of adult learners*. San Francisco: Jossey-Bass.

Davis, M. (2002). *Profession, code, and ethics*. Burlington, VT: Ashgate.

Dawkins, R. (1976). *The selfish gene*. New York: Oxford University Press.

Dewey, J. (1916). *Democracy and education*. New York: Macmillan.

Dreifus, C. (2008, April 29). What we know about the genome today is not enough for all the miracles many expect from this field. *New York Times,* p. F2.

Dutton, J., & Ragins, B. (Eds.). (2007). *Exploring positive relationships at work: Building a theoretical and research foundation*. Mahwah, NJ: Erlbaum.

Einstein, A. (1954). *Ideas and opinions*. New York: Crown.

Endow, S. A., & Gerbi, S. A. (2003). Joseph G. Gall. *Journal of Cell Science, 116*, 3849–3850.

Erikson, E. (1980). *Identity and the life cycle*. New York: Norton. (Original work published 1959)

Evertson, C. M., Emmer, E. T., & Worsham, M. E. (2003). *Classroom management for elementary teachers*. Needham, MA: Allyn & Bacon.

Evertson, C. M., & Weinstein, C. S. (2006). Classroom management as a field of inquiry. In C. M. Evertson & C. S. Weinstein (Eds.), *Handbook of classroom management* (pp. 3–17). Mahwah, NJ: Erlbaum.

Fischman, W., & Gardner, H. (2005, Spring/Summer). Inspiring good work. *Greater Good, 10*–13.

Fischman, W., Solomon, B., Greenspan, D., & Gardner, H. (2004). *Making good: How young people cope with moral dilemmas at work*. Cambridge, MA: Harvard University Press.

Fredrickson, B. L. (2001). The role of positive emotions in positive psychology: The broaden-and-build theory of positive emotions. *American Psychologist, 56*, 218–226.

Gamble, J. (2001). Modeling the invisible: The pedagogy of craft apprenticeship. *Studies in Continuing Education, 23*, 185–200.

Gardner, H. (2007). Irresponsible work. In H. Gardner (Ed.), *Responsibility at work* (pp. 262–282). San Francisco: Jossey-Bass.

Gardner, H., Csikszentmihalyi, M., & Damon, W. (2001). *Good work: When excellence and ethics meet*. New York: Basic Books.

Golde, C. M., & Dore, T. M. (2004). The survey of doctoral education and career preparation: The importance of disciplinary contexts. In D. H. Wulff, A. E. Austin, & Associates, *Paths to the professoriate: Strategies for enriching the preparation of future faculty* (pp. 19–45). San Francisco: Jossey-Bass.

Gould, S. J., & Lewontin, R. C. (1979). The spandrels of San Marco and the Panglossian paradigm: A critique of the adaptationist programme. *Proceedings of the Royal Society of London Series B, Biological Science (1934–1990), 205*, 581–598.

Haidt, J. (2003). Elevation and the positive psychology of morality. In C. L. M. Keyes & J. Haidt (Eds.), *Flourishing: Positive psychology and the life well-lived* (pp. 275–289). Washington, DC: American Psychological Association.

Hall, S. S. (1998, November 29). Lethal chemistry at Harvard. *New York Times*, p. 120.

Hardcastle, B. (1988). Spiritual connections: Protégés' reflections. *Theory into Practice, 27*, 201–208.

Heath, C. (1996). Do people prefer to pass along good or bad news? Valence and relevance as predictors of transmission propensity. *Organizational Behavior and Human Decision Processes, 68*, 79–94.

Higgins, M. C., & Kram, K. E. (2001). Reconceptualizing mentoring at work: A developmental network perspective. *Academy of Management Review, 26*, 264–288.

Hochschild, A. R. (1997). *The time bind: When work becomes home and home becomes work.* New York: Holt.

Hooker, C., Nakamura, J., & Csikszentmihalyi, M. (2003). The group as mentor: Social capital and the systems model of creativity, a case study in space science. In P. Paulus & B. Nijstad (Eds.), *Group creativity* (pp. 225–244). New York: Oxford University Press.

Inghilleri, P. (1999). *From subjective experience to cultural change.* Cambridge: Cambridge University Press.

Johnson, W. B., & Zlotnik, S. (2005). The frequency of advising and mentoring as salient work roles in academic job advertisements. *Mentoring and Tutoring, 13*, 95–107.

Kanigel, R. (1986). *Apprentice to genius: The making of a scientific dynasty.* New York: Macmillan.

Kealy, W. A., & Mullen, C. A. (1996). *Re-thinking mentoring relationships.* Paper presented at the annual meeting of the American Educational Research Association, New York.

Kegan, R. (1982). *The evolving self.* Cambridge, MA: Harvard University Press.

Keinänen, M., & Gardner, H. (2004). Vertical and horizontal mentoring for creativity. In R. J. Sternberg, E. L. Grigorenko, & J. L. Singer (Eds.), *Creativity: From potential to realization* (pp. 169–193). Washington, DC: American Psychological Association.

Kennedy, D. (1997). *Academic duty.* Cambridge, MA: Harvard University Press.

Keyes, C. L. M., & Haidt, J. (2002). *Flourishing: Positive psychology and the life well-lived.* Washington, DC: American Psychological Association.

Kluckhohn, C., & Murray, H. A. (1953). *Personality in nature, society, and culture.* New York: Knopf.

Kram, K. E. (1985). *Mentoring at work.* Glenview, IL: Scott Foresman.

Kram, K. E., & Isabella, L. A. (1985). Mentoring alternatives: The role of peer relationships in career development. *Academy of Management Journal, 28*, 110–132.

Lapsley, D. K. (2005). Moral stage theory. In M. Killen & J. Smetana (Eds.), *Handbook of moral development* (pp. 37–66). Mahwah, NJ: Erlbaum.

Lapsley, D. K., & Narvaez, D. (2006). Character education. In W. Damon & R. Lerner (Eds.), *Handbook of child psychology* (6th ed., pp. 248–296). Hoboken, NJ: Wiley.

Lave, J., & Wenger, E. (1991). *Situated learning: Legitimate peripheral participation.* Cambridge: Cambridge University Press.

Levins, R., & Lewontin, R. C. (1985). *The dialectical biologist*. Cambridge, MA: Harvard University Press.

Levinson, D. J. (1978). *Seasons of a man's life*. New York: Knopf.

Lewontin, R. C. (1974). *The genetic basis of evolutionary change*. New York: Columbia University Press.

Lewontin, R. C. (1991). *Biology as ideology: The doctrine of DNA*. New York: HarperCollins.

Lewontin, R. C. (2000a). *It ain't necessarily so: The dream of the human genome and other illusions*. New York: Granta Books.

Lewontin R. C. (2000b). *The triple helix: Gene, organism, and environment*. Cambridge, MA: Harvard University Press.

Lewontin, R. C., Rose, S., & Kamin, L. J. (1984). *Not in our genes: Biology, ideology and human nature*. New York: Random House.

Lovitts, B. E. (2001). *Leaving the ivory tower: The causes and consequences of departure from doctoral study*. Lanham, MD: Rowman & Littlefield.

Magnusson, D., & Stattin, H. (2006). The person in context. In R. M. Lerner (Ed.), *Handbook of child psychology* (Vol. 1, pp. 400–464). Hoboken, NJ: Wiley.

Massimini, F., & Delle Fave, A. (2000). Individual development in a bio-cultural perspective. *American Psychologist, 55*, 24–33.

Merton, R. (1973). The normative structure of science. In N. Storer (Ed.), *The sociology of science: Theoretical and empirical investigations* (pp. 267–278). Chicago: University of Chicago Press.

Nakamura, J. (2007). Practicing responsibility. In H. Gardner (Ed.), *Responsibility at work* (pp. 285–310). San Francisco: Jossey-Bass.

Nakamura, J., & Csikszentmihalyi, M. (2005). Engagement in a profession: The case of undergraduate teaching. *Daedalus: Journal of the American Academy of Arts and Sciences, 134*, 60–67.

National Academy of Sciences. (1997). *Adviser, teacher, role model, friend: On being a mentor to students in science and engineering*. Washington, DC: National Academy Press.

Neugarten, B. (1969). Continuities and discontinuities of psychological issues into adult life. *Human Development, 12*, 121–130.

Ortolani, A. (1998). *Mentoring graduate students at U.C. Davis: Results of the 1998 mentoring study. Professors for the Future Project*. Davis, CA: University of California.

Pais, A. (1991). *Niels Bohr's times: In physics, philosophy, and policy*. New York: Oxford University Press.

Palmer, P. J. (1998). *The courage to teach: Exploring the inner landscape of a teacher's life*. San Francisco: Jossey-Bass.

Pardue, M. L. (1998). Joseph Gall—Pioneering nuclear biology. *Trends in Cell Biology, 8*, 208–209.

Peterson, C. (2006). A *primer in positive psychology*. New York: Oxford University Press.

Peterson, C., & Seligman, M. E. P. (2004). *Character strengths and virtues: A handbook and classification*. New York: Oxford University Press and Washington, DC: American Psychological Association.

Pfund, C., Pribbenow, C. M., Branchaw, J., Lauffer, S. M., & Handelsman, J. (2006). The merits of training mentors. *Science, 311,* 473–474.

Piliavin, J. A. (2003). Doing well by doing good: Benefits for the benefactor. In C. L. M. Keyes & J. Haidt (Eds.), *Flourishing: Positive psychology and the life well-lived* (pp. 227–248). Washington, DC: American Psychological Association.

Pledge, H. T. (1966). *Science since 1500: A short history of mathematics, physics, chemistry, biology*. London: Her Majesty's Stationery Office.

Polanyi, M. (1958). *Personal knowledge: Towards a post-critical philosophy*. London: Routledge/Kegan Paul.

Ragins, B. R., & Kram, K. E. (Eds.). (2007). *The handbook of mentoring at work: Theory, research, and practice*. Thousand Oaks, CA: Sage.

Rathunde, K. (1996). Family context and talented adolescents' optimal experience in school-related activities. *Journal of Research on Adolescence, 6,* 605–628.

Reskin, B. F. (1979). Academic sponsorship and scientists' careers. *Sociology of Education, 52,* 129–146.

Rest, J., & Narvaez, D. (1994). *Moral development in the professions: Psychology and applied ethics*. Mahwah, NJ: Erlbaum.

Rhodes, J. E. (2002). *Stand by me: The risks and rewards of mentoring today's youth*. Cambridge, MA: Harvard University Press.

Riordan, M. (1998, October 4). The nuclear family. *New York Times,* p. 24.

Roazen, P. (1975). *Freud and his followers*. New York: Knopf.

Rogoff, B. (1990). *Apprenticeship in thinking: Cognitive development in social context*. New York: Oxford University Press.

Ryan, R. M., Deci, E. L., & Grolnick, W. S. (1995). Autonomy, relatedness, and the self: Their relation to development and psychopathology. In D. Cicchetti & D. J. Cohen (Eds.), *Developmental psychopathology* (Vol. 1, pp. 618–655). Hoboken, NJ: Wiley.

Sawyer, R. K. (2003). *Group creativity*. Mahwah, NJ: Erlbaum.

Schlosser, L. Z., Knox, S., Moskovitz, A. R., & Hill, C. E. (2003). A qualitative examination of graduate advising relationships: The advisee perspective. *Journal of Counseling Psychology, 50,* 178–188.

Schneider, A. (1998, October 23). Harvard faces the aftermath of a graduate student's suicide. *Chronicle of Higher Education,* p. A12.

Segerstrale, U. (2001). *Defenders of the truth: The sociobiology debate*. New York: Oxford University Press.

Seligman, M. E. P. (2002). *Authentic happiness: Using the new positive psychology to realize your potential for lasting fulfillment*. New York: Free Press.

Seligman, M. E. P. (2006, August). *Centering on mentoring*. Paper presented at the annual meeting of the American Psychological Association, New Orleans, LA.

Seligman, M. E. P., & Csikszentmihalyi, M. (2000). Positive psychology: An introduction. *American Psychologist, 55,* 5–14.

Shernoff, D. (2001). *The individual-maker: A master teacher and his transformational curriculum*. Palm Desert, CA: William & Sons.

Simonton, D. K. (1999). *Origins of genius: Darwinian perspectives on creativity*. New York: Oxford University Press.

Smith, E. P., & Davidson, W. S. (1992). Mentoring and the development of African American graduate students. *Journal of College Student Development, 33,* 531–539.

Smith, R. E., & Smoll, F. L. (1990). Self-esteem and children's reactions to youth sport coaching behaviors: A field study of self-enhancement processes. *Developmental Psychology, 26,* 987–993.

Snyder, C. R., & Lopez, S. (Eds.). (2001). *Handbook of positive psychology*. New York: Oxford University Press.

Solomon, J. (2007). A balancing act: How physicians and teachers manage time pressures and responsibility. In H. Gardner (Ed.), *Responsibility at work* (pp. 107–132). San Francisco: Jossey-Bass.

Stover, R. V. (1989). *Making it and breaking it: The fate of public interest commitment during law school*. Chicago: University of Illinois Press.

Taylor, E. F. (1972). The anatomy of collaboration. In J. R. Klauder (Ed.), *Magic without magic: John Archibald Wheeler* (pp. 475–485). New York: Freeman.

Tenenbaum, H. R., Crosby, F. J., & Gliner, M. D. (2001). Mentoring relationships in graduate school. *Journal of Vocational Behavior, 59,* 326–341.

Tenner, E. (2004, August 13). The pitfalls of academic mentorships. *Chronicle of Higher Education,* p. B7.

Vaillant, G. E. (1977). *Adaptation to life*. New York: Little, Brown.

Vogel, F., & Motulsky, A. G. (1979). *Human genetics: Problems and approaches*. New York: Springer-Verlag.

Vygotsky, L. (1978). *Mind in society: The development of higher psychological processes*. Cambridge, MA: Harvard University Press.

Walker, L. J., & Henning, K. H. (2004). Differing conceptions of moral exemplars: Just, brave, and caring. *Journal of Personality and Social Psychology, 86,* 629–647.

Watson, J. D. (1968). *The double helix: A personal account of the discovery of the structure of DNA*. New York: Atheneum.

Watson, J. D., & Crick, F. H. C. (1953). A structure for deoxyribose nucleic acid. *Nature, 171,* 737.

Wentzel, K. R. (2002). Are effective teachers like good parents? Teaching styles and student adjustment in early adolescence. *Child Development, 73,* 287–301.

Wilson, E. O. (1985). *Sociobiology*. Cambridge, MA: Belknap Press.

Wilson, E. O. (1994). *Naturalist*. Washington, DC: Island Press.

Zhao, C.-M., Golde, C. M., & McCormick, A. C. (2005). *More than a signature*. Paper presented at the annual meeting of the American Educational Research Association, Montreal, Canada.

Zuckerman, H. (1977). *Scientific elite: Nobel laureates in the United States*. New York: Free Press.

Zuckerman, H. (1978). Theory, choice, and problem choice in science. In J. Gaston (Ed.), *The sociology of science* (pp. 65–95). San Francisco: Jossey-Bass.

Index